Distributed Real-Time Systems

Distributed Real-Time Systems

Monitoring, Visualization, Debugging, and Analysis

JEFFREY J. P. TSAI

YAODONG BI

STEVE J. H. YANG

ROSS A. W. SMITH

A Wiley-Interscience Publication
JOHN WILEY & SONS, INC.
New York • Chichester • Brisbane • Toronto • Singapore

Library of Congress Cataloging-in-Publication Data
Distributed real-time systems : monitoring, visualization, debugging,
    and analysis / Jeffrey J.P. Tsai . . . [et al.].
        p.   cm.
    ''A Wiley-Interscience publication.''
    Includes bibliographical references and index.
    ISBN 0-471-16007-5 (cloth)
    1. Electronic data processing—Distributed processing. 2. Real
    -time data processing. I. Tsai, Jeffrey J.-P.
    QA76.9.D5D587   1996
    005.2—dc20   96-15274

Printed in the United States of America

10 9 8 7 6 5 4 3 2 1

To our families,

Thanks for all your encouragement and support.

Contents

List of Tables

List of Figures

xiii

Preface

Distributed real-time systems (DRTSs) are becoming ever more important to our everyday lives. Given current advances in personal computers and workstations, many computer systems no longer fit the traditional mainframe or single computer model. In addition, as computers become cheaper, smaller, and more powerful, they are increasingly being used in more real-time applications. Before reliable, high-performance DRTSs can be produced, we need to be able to verify the timing and functionality of the system and to find performance bottlenecks.

In a distributed real-time system the correctness of the system depends not only on its logical behavior but also on the time at which the results are produced. Because of its nondeterministic character, the system may not exhibit the same execution behavior upon repeated execution of the program. Furthermore, in a distributed real-time system the rate of the process execution is determined not only by internal criteria, such as the execution speed of the underlying processor, but also by the timing constraints imposed by real-world processes. Proper operation of the whole system, which consists of the real-time target processes and the real-world processes, depends on the capability of the target processes to comply with certain timing constraints.

In the past few years methods have been developed for the analysis of distributed and/or parallel systems. Generally, these methods can be classified as static or dynamic analysis methods. The static analysis methods analyze the program source codes or the abstractions derived from them to detect anomalies of the concurrent programs. However, static analysis is not adequate to deal with the violation of timing constraints inherent in distributed real-time systems. Monitoring techniques must be used to monitor and collect run-time information so that the execution behavior of distributed real-time systems can be investigated. The collected run-time information can be used to understand and detect errors in a distributed real-time system as well as to improve its performance.

In this book we discuss a methodology for verifying and debugging distributed real-time systems. The verification and debugging process consists of three steps: monitoring the system and collecting the relevant data, filtering and visualizing the collected data, and finally, analyzing the data. The book includes introductory material that will be helpful to graduate students and computer engineers in understanding distributed systems and how they can be analyzed. To clarify and illustrate the concepts, the book has many examples. Frequently we have thoroughly worked out the examples so that the reader will be able to understand and use the concepts presented more effectively. The book also describes research efforts in a variety of areas that should be helpful for researchers interested in more detailed information on the topics presented. The range is from practical to theoretical. We discuss issues ranging from the coding of an event to static modeling and analysis techniques that have more theoretical interest.

The book is divided into two parts. The first part develops the main concepts, and the second part provides examples of implementation and additional theoretical issues. The book is organized as follows:

Chapter 1 introduces basic concepts necessary to understand DRTSs. It discusses different architectures and algorithms used to implement DRTSs. It describes the mechanisms needed for DRTSs, such as communication, synchronization, and switching, and includes examples of DRTSs, such as the distributed telephone switching system and a fault-tolerant distributed system. The chapter concludes with a model of DRTSs that is used throughout the book.

Chapter 2 introduces basic issues related to monitoring and covers the different types of monitoring and the levels of detail that can be monitored. Included is a survey of different monitoring approaches. This information is expanded in the following chapters, which more fully describe the different types of monitoring: hardware, software, and hybrid (hardware and software). Each of the chapters includes the steps required to implement monitoring and presents examples.

After describing the basic software monitoring issues, Chapter 3 describes different approaches to software monitoring that have been proposed or implemented. Also examined is perturbation analysis which can be used in software monitoring.

Chapter 4 shows how to monitor a single processor and gives examples of hardware monitors. Examples of hardware monitors for multiprocessors are considered. Finally, the monitoring of distributed systems is discussed.

Chapter 5 focuses on hybrid monitors for single-processor systems and then for multiprocessor systems, and provides examples of each type. In particular, the chapter gives examples of a memory-mapped monitor and of a coprocessor used to monitor a system, and it ends with a discussion of monitoring distributed systems.

In Chapter 6 we describe approaches that can be used to debug DRTSs. A variety of static analyses are presented as well as dynamic analyses (debugging) with and without monitoring. Also discussed are debugging approaches that have been proposed.

Chapter 7 develops issues of static analysis presented in Chapter 6. It shows how to model processes and how to specify them. Such analysis techniques as timed Petri nets, temporal logic, timed state transition systems, timed process algebra, and synchronous programming languages are presented. A variety of literature is discussed for each technique.

The second part of the book considers how the analytic ideas of the first part can be implemented. It is less concerned with introducing a framework for examining DRTSs than with presenting detailed examples of implementation techniques.

Chapter 8 presents an example of a noninterference hardware monitor, with a discussion of the design and implementation in both hardware and software. For example, details on constructing graphs to represent parent-child relationships are given in order to illustrate concepts introduced in the first part of the book.

Chapter 9 is concerned with timing errors. It examines the causes of timing errors based on the different states of a process and offers a method for determining such causes. The chapter also examines how to represent timing relationships graphically by a process interaction graph. Then it shows how to use this framework to analyze timing errors. Included in the discussion are detailed examples of the algorithms under discussion.

Chapter 10 describes how one can debug a DRTS graphically. The first portion of the chapter describes the graphs that are needed to debug a DRTS and provides algorithms for each of the graphs. The graphs display process interactions, timing constraints, subsets of larger graphs, parent-child relationships, message passing, and semaphore allocation. Finally, an algorithm that uses all these graphs to debug a system is presented.

Chapter 11 expands the description of Petri nets introduced in Chapter 7. Its main focus is on timing constraint Petri nets (TCPNs), which are a modification of time and timed Petri nets. The relationship of TCPNs to other types of Petri nets is explained, and the chapter shows how TCPNs can be used to perform schedulability analysis and run-time analysis based on data collected from monitoring. Finally a synthesis using TCPNs is presented.

Acknowledgment

The work reported here was supported in part by National Science Foundation under Grants CCR-8809381 and CCR-9106540 and from the IEEE and the Engineering Foundation Society under Grant RI-A-88-11. We also wish to thank Jeff K. Y. Fang of Utek, Inc. and Horng-Yuan Chen of AT&T Bell Laboratories for their contribution to the early work of our research project. Yee-Tsong Juan of the University of Illinois at Chicago has helped us to prepare the diagrams and the index.

We would like to thank George J. Telecki for his interest in our project and assistance in preparing the book. Kimi Sugeno and her staff have done an excellent job on the production of the book. The help from Rose Leo Kish, Karen Ball, Edith Covington and other staff at Wiley is greatly appreciated.

Finally, we would like to thank our families for their support throughout this project, Jean, Edward, and Christina, Li and Meida, Yaling, Christopher, and Albert, and Lois.

Jeffrey J. P. Tsai

Yaodong Bi

Steve J. H. Yang

Ross A. W. Smith

Part I

BASIC CONCEPTS

Chapter 1

Distributed Real-Time Systems

Distributed real-time systems (DRTSs for short) are becoming more important to our everyday life. Examples include command and control systems, flight control systems, space shuttle landing control systems, aircraft avionics control systems, robotics, patient monitoring systems, and nuclear power plant control systems [369]. With increasing computing power, it will be possible to have larger and more complex DRTSs. However, the development of DRTSs is difficult and takes more time than the development of a distributed system that does not have real-time constraints or a single processor real-time system. The development is more difficult partly because DRTSs are inherently more complex than the systems mentioned, and partly because the software for support and development has not kept pace. When supporting software lags hardware developments, systems can become error prone, since in software development a significant portion of the entire effort is devoted to the testing and debugging phase of the software life cycle [436]. Statistical evidence indicates that testing and debugging represents approximately 50% of the cost of developing a new system. In real-time software systems the percentage can be as high as 70% because some of the bugs are "immune" to conventional debugging aids [343]. Thus improvements in the usability and reliability of DRTSs depend on improvements in the supporting software and development tools.

This book provides an overview of various systematic approaches to monitoring, debugging, and analyzing DRTSs. These monitoring, debugging, and analysis techniques are used in distributed systems, real-time systems, as well as distributed and real-time systems. Distributed systems are characterized by interprocess communication, and real-time systems are characterized by *timing constraints*; thus timing factors need to be taken into account when applying most of the distributed debugging techniques to DRTSs. We will begin by discussing the characteristics of distributed systems, real-time systems, and DRTSs in this chapter.

3

1.1   Real-Time Systems

A real-time system is characterized by the need for timing constraints. Typically real-time systems consist of controlling subsystems (the computer controllers) and controlled subsystems (the physical environment). The interactions between the two subsystems are described by three operations: sampling, processing, and responding. The computer subsystems continuously sample data from the physical environment. Sampled data is processed immediately by the computer subsystems, and a proper response is sent to the physical environment. All three operations must be performed within specified times; these are the *timing constraints*. For example, it is imperative that the controlling subsystem of a multiple-leg robot respond to the continuous changes of the robot's physical environment in a timely manner (neither too early nor too late), or the robot may fall down.

Real-time systems can be classified as *hard real-time systems* or *soft real-time systems* depending on the consequences of timing constraint violations. Hard real-time systems must meet their timing constraints to avoid disastrous consequences. Typical hard real-time systems involve human lives, such as flight control systems, chemical process control systems, and patient-monitoring systems, or time-critical environments such as robot-control systems and telephone switching systems. An error-recovery routine is usually triggered by a missed deadline so that the disastrous consequences can be avoided. The consequences of not meeting timing constraints in soft real-time systems are not as disastrous as hard real-time systems. Soft real-time systems are still considered functionally correct if timing constraints are not seriously violated. Examples of soft real-time systems are remote data acquisition systems, airline ticket reservation systems, and automatic teller machines. In contrast, interactive systems do not have deadlines, but they must be capable of responding quickly.

The notion of time is important to real-time systems. There are four aspects of time [58]:

1. Clock access.

2. Process delaying.

3. Time-out handling.

4. Deadline specification and scheduling.

Obviously a system that is concerned with time must have access to a clock so that it knows the current time, or at least can measure the passage of time. Time can be specified by an absolute time or an elapsed or execution time relative to the start of an activity. Although all nodes in a distributed system may have access to a clock, it is difficult to synchronize the clocks. Synchronization is important because if two processes are working with timing constraints but have separate clocks, the worst-case timings must be adjusted to account for slower clocks and clock skew. The second ability needed for a real-time system is the ability to delay a process, which is useful because a process can queue on a future event instead of using a busy wait. Time-outs are used to detect the nonoccurrence of an event. The system can set a timer when it begins to wait for an event. If the event does not arrive when the timer finishes counting, the system assumes that the event will not occur. Essentially a time-out limits the length of time a process will wait for an event. Finally, in addition to being logically correct, real-time programs must satisfy timing constraints imposed by the physical environment. These are referred to as the *deadline specifications*. A deadline refers to constraints such as the minimum and maximum execution time. Deadline scheduling refers to the satisfying of timing constraints by scheduling processes to meet deadlines.

1.2 Periodic Processes and Aperiodic Processes

Real-time processes can be classified as periodic processes or aperiodic processes. *Periodic processes* are executed at regular intervals and their behavior is known beforehand. For example, periodic processes may sample data or execute a loop every N time units. Periodic processes are characterized by their start time, worst-case execution time, laxity, and deadline (here laxity refers to the latest time for a process's execution to meet its deadline). A process with all of these characteristics that executes only once is still considered periodic. In contrast, *aperiodic processes* are initiated by asynchronous (unpredictable) external events. Thus besides the characteristics noted for periodic processes, aperiodic processes are characterized by their arrival time. Aperiodic processes can be described using a stimuli-response model. How the stimuli is handled can be specified in advance by the responding procedure. However, the arrival time of the stimuli is unknown before execution. In general, the use of aperiodic processes distinguishes hard real-time systems from other systems.

Except for the arrival time of an aperiodic process, which cannot be predicted, we can model an aperiodic process as a periodic process because the types of stimuli and the corresponding procedures used to respond to the stimuli are known *a priori*. With this information we can create a dedicated periodic process that will look for the arrival of stimuli periodically. For example, a CPU checks for interrupts before the execution of every instruction. If there are interrupt requests from other devices (stimuli), then an interrupt handling routine will be executed to service the interrupt. In this case the arrival time of the interrupt cannot be predicted, but the types of interrupts are known and can be checked for periodically. In addition the responding procedures are all predefined. For processes with bursty events a different model may be needed.

1.3   Distributed Systems

A distributed system has many processes running on different processors working toward specific functional requirements. The distributed processes are coordinated by interprocess communication and synchronization. Potential benefits of distributed processing are increased performance by executing processes in parallel, increased availability because a process is more likely to have a resource available if multiple copies are available, increased reliability because the system can be designed to recover from failures, increased adaptability because parts can be added or removed easily, and expensive resources can be shared. Not all of these benefits are realized in a typical system, but it is clear that distributed computing offers the potential for significant benefits.

Distributed systems can take a variety of forms. For example, a computer can have distributed hardware, control, and data [344]. The hardware can range from a single CPU to multiple computers. The control can range from a single control unit to multiple control units cooperating with messages. The data can range from a single copy located at a central point to a distributed database with no central file or directory. A fully distributed system refers to a system where all three components are distributed. Within this taxonomy, many options exist. Examples include SIMD machines, which have multiple hardware units and centralized control, and MIMD machines, which have multiple hardware units and decentralized control. The processors may be dispersed geographically or located at one site or in one machine. Each node can have one processor or many processors. Distributed systems can also be classified as homogeneous or heterogeneous. As shown in Fig. 1.1, the nodes in homogeneous distributed systems have the same architecture and supporting software. In contrast, as shown in Fig. 1.2, heterogeneous systems have different architectures and/or supporting software. Distributed systems can also be classified as centralized or decentralized. *Centralized* distributed systems have master-slave or server-client relationships between their distinct computing nodes, and *decentralized* distributed systems have autonomous computing nodes. Thus a wide variety of distributed systems exist, and different techniques for debugging are appropriate for different architectures, although several techniques for debugging are appropriate for a wide range of distributed systems.

1.4   Architectural Issues

Knowledge of the hardware can aid analysis and is important to understanding monitoring choices. The monitor's job is to collect data, but if the data is inaccessible or difficult to capture, then the monitor's task becomes more difficult. Knowledge of the architecture of the DRTS helps one understand how messages are transmitted and the processes required, among other issues. We will also clarify some terms such as multiprocessor, interleaving,

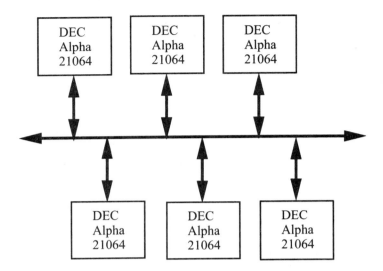

Fig. 1.1 Homogeneous architecture.

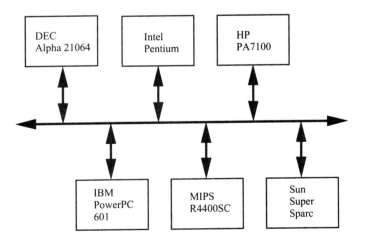

Fig. 1.2 Heterogeneous architecture.

multitasking, and parallelism.

A machine with multiple processors can be classified as multiprocessor if it has shared memory or as a multicomputer or distributed system if it has distributed memory. The former tends to be tightly coupled and the latter tends to be loosely coupled. The term coupling refers to the speed and bandwidth of the communication. Multiprocessors have a set of cooperating processors that are interconnected as a single computer, whereas multicomputers have a set of cooperating computers that are connected over a communication network. Every computer on the multicomputer has its own processors (uniprocessor or multiprocessor), memory, and resources. Multicomputers communicate with message passing, and multiprocessors communicate with shared memory.

A common approach to distributed processing uses a network to connect a group of workstations together. Every workstation can work alone as well as communicate with other workstations over the network. Applications running on a local workstation can use resources on a remote workstation. Ideally the access of resources would be transparent to the user. However, the programmer may be forced to specify the resource's location and which portion of the application will use that resource. In other words, users may need to partition their applications into many subapplications and to keep track of the resources available at various workstations. Obviously distributed operating systems can be very useful to the programmer and also help to achieve maximum parallelism. Two important distributed operating systems are Mach of CMU [1, 28, 45, 49, 323, 337] and Amoeba of Vrije University, Amsterdam [276, 384, 383, 190, 106].

A computer achieves parallelism with internal parallelism and external parallelism. *Internal parallelism* refers to the execution of instructions in parallel using hardware techniques such as pipelining and multiple function units. *External parallelism* refers to the execution of independent processes in parallel on different processors by using software techniques such as dependency analysis. The performance of internal parallelism can be measured by the time required to execute a program by the processor (*CPU time*). Many techniques used to improve hardware performance can complicate the monitoring and debugging process. For example, an on-chip cache will make memory coherency issues more complicated. Pipelining makes exceptions more difficult to handle because more than one instruction is being executed simultaneously. Superscaling adds a level of parallelism to the code that makes the code more difficult to debug. Optimizing compilers that move code to exploit these features and others, such as delayed branches, can make it more difficult to construct debugging tools and to reconstruct the program's behavior.

Concurrent processing on a single processor can be achieved by interleaving whereby multiple processes are interleaved on a single processor to give the illusion of parallelism, though only one process is executing at a time. Interleaving improves the system performance by eliminating busy waiting;

whenever a process must wait, it is preempted by a process ready for execution (context-switching). This is different from multitasking where every task shares a single CPU and can only use resources in the centralized computer. Traditional operating systems such as VM/CMS or UNIX are capable of handling multiple tasks at the same time. Scheduling techniques such as round robin scheduling will assign each task time slices to use the CPU. This type of time-sharing computation is transparent to the user, so that the machine seems dedicated her, even though she is sharing the CPU and its resources. This is why time-sharing machines are often called *virtual machines*.

Multiprocessing increases a system's *throughput*, which is the total number of tasks completed within a unit of time, and often decreases a single task's *response time*, which is time interval between the submission and completion of a task. There are two forms of multiprocessing: One partitions a process into numerous independent subprocesses and executes them simultaneously on different processors; the other executes an entire process on a processor without partitioning it. The former can decrease the response time for a process, whereas the latter only increases the system throughput.

1.4.1 Distributed Processing Algorithms

The main algorithms that must be considered in distributed computing are algorithms to handle election and mutual exclusion, detection and resolution of deadlock, termination detection [71, 81, 83, 109, 135, 198, 205, 286, 331, 353, 354, 356, 419], and the Byzantine agreement problem [326]. The problem of election and mutual exclusion is related to the competition for resources. With *mutual exclusion*, all processes have access to a resource, although priorities may differ. Thus the problem is to equitably give processes the privilege to access a resource. With mutual exclusion, while one process is accessing the resource, no other process may access it. The most appropriate algorithm to use depends on the network used. For example, in a ring, a token can be used to allocate resources. On other networks, time stamping may be introduced to ensure equitable allocation. With a time stamp, priority can be given to messages which have been outstanding for the longest amount of time. In contrast to mutual exclusion, with *election*, one process permanently has privilege to the resource. This is referred to as the client-server relationship. The server acts as a centralized coordinator for the other processes. The danger of this method of allocating resources is that if the server fails, the resource is no longer accessible. Election algorithms are used to elect a new server from the remaining processes.

Deadlock refers to the mutual blocking of processes. One can either attempt to prevent deadlock or detect deadlock when it occurs. To be able to prevent deadlock, the resources needed by the processes must be known in advance. This is not possible with dynamic databases and in other situations. If the resource allocation is represented graphically, then detecting deadlocks is the same as finding a cycle in the graph. A detection algorithm would be straightforward, except it is difficult to obtain a global picture of the state of the system.

At first glance, *termination* may not seem to be difficult. However, a process may be inactive for quite a while, receive stimuli, and then set off a series of activities that activates a number of long inactive processes. Like deadlock the problem is that a global state is not available. There are a variety of algorithms that detect termination.

The *Byzantine agreement* refers to the problem of gaining consensus in the presence of uncertainties. If a node is unreliable, then the information transmitted by it cannot be assumed to be reliable. The solutions depend partly on the assumptions made. The more unpredictable the faulty node's behavior, the more complex is the algorithm required.

1.5   Communication and Synchronization Primitives

Communication and synchronization allow distributed nodes to be coordinated [360]. Synchronization is used to coordinate to processes with respect to time [18, 61, 115, 148, 201, 319, 320, 322, 350], for example, by sequencing events or granting a process exclusive access to a resource. Communication refers to the exchange of information between processes and does not imply synchronization [11, 17, 29, 43, 57, 131, 286, 324, 347, 361]. As will be shown, synchronization and communication are closely related. In debugging distributed system software, the ability to monitor the messages and synchronization is crucial to understanding the behavior of the program.

The most basic communication operations are send and receive. Generally, to receive a message, the process must be explicitly looking for a message. The simplest receive operation blocks. That is, if the message was not available when the receive command was executed, the program waits until the message arrives. Blocking provides a synchronization mechanism. Blocking can cause problems if the message does not arrive. Thus there are other receive operations. With a conditional receive, if no message is available, then nothing happens and the next operation is executed. With a time-out receive, if a message does not arrive after a certain period of time, then the receive is aborted.

The send operation can be asynchronous or synchronous. With the asynchronous send operation, the sender simply sends the message and does not wait for a reply. With a synchronous send, the sender waits for an acknowledgment. Obviously the synchronous send provides synchronization as well as communication. Since the synchronous send is blocking, if the receiver is delayed, the sender is delayed. Worse, if the receiver fails, then the sender will hang. So mechanisms to prevent these situations are necessary.

A bidirectional transaction may also be used. A simple example is to send a message with parameters. Then a reply is sent with return parameters. Bidirectional transactions are frequently used in client-server communications.

An exception is another type of transaction. Exceptions enable the reliability features of a distributed system to be implemented. Although lower-level transmission errors can often be masked, many cannot be masked. Exceptions provide an asynchronous method of handling events that cannot be masked. A synchronized method of handling errors is to send a code to indicate a successful transaction, and another if something went wrong. Then the process can take appropriate action. Both error-handling methods are needed.

1.6 Processor Interconnection

Processors must be physically connected by interconnection networks in order to communicate. The time required to send even a short message is much longer than the time required for a simple computation because of the overhead required to transmit a message. Thus processes must divide the tasks in such a way to minimize communication and maximize computation. In addition the organization of the processors (the topology) and the communication protocols are important factors in the communication time of a DRTS message. The topology determines the number of nodes a message needs to pass through to reach its destination. Topologies with greater connectivity have shorter paths, but they are much more expensive. The communication protocol affects the reliability of the message passing, the bandwidth, and the latency. These performance metrics are defined as follows: *Reliability* refers to the successful transmission of data in the proper order. *Latency* is the time from the beginning of the transmission to the end of the reception of the transmission. *Bandwidth* is the number of transmissions completed per unit time.

1.7 Network Topologies

The two main categories of interconnection networks are a single connection system, such as a bus or ring, and a multiple connection path system, such as a multiple bus, star, or mesh.

The network topology influences the cost of adding another node, the ability to modify the topology, the reliability, the complexity of the protocols needed, the throughput, and delays, and the ability to broadcast data [360, 429]. In broad terms, networks can be classified as either broadcast or store-and-forward. With a broadcast network all nodes are connected by a common connection. This is most appropriate for a local area network (LAN), which is typically used by a single organization at a single site. With a store-and-forward topology a message or packet is received by a node, placed into a buffer, and forwarded to an adjacent node, if the message is not addressed to that node. Store-and-forward networks are used with a wide area networks (WAN). In WANs, the nodes are geographically dispersed. Fig. 1.3 shows

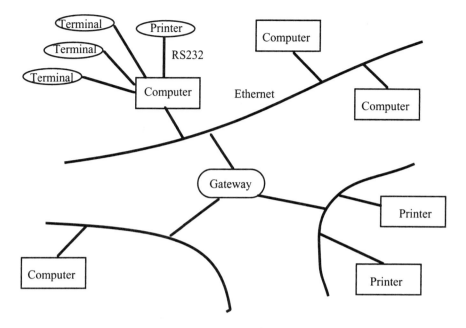

Fig. 1.3 Networks.

a typical network. An additional type of network is the terminal network. *Terminal networks* use an RS232 to connect a variety of terminals and printers to a central computer. In this centralized point-to-point starlike network, the central computer communicates with each terminal over slow but cheap dedicated wires. The RS232 provides a transmission rate of up to 19 K bps and a range of up to 0.1 km.

We will now discuss different topologies used to interconnect computers.

1.7.1   Buses

As shown in Fig. 1.4, buses are simple. All data is transferred over a single path to which all nodes have access. A limitation of buses is their lack of scalability when many nodes are required. That is, large numbers of nodes cannot be easily added. Local area networks frequently use an Ethernet network (a kind of bus) to connect a variety of nodes to form a heterogeneous system. To add a new node to the network, it is simply connected to the bus and given an identification number. The number of nodes on an Ethernet is limited to 1024. The carrier-sense multiple access with collision detection (CSMA/CD) protocol is used with Ethernet. Multiple access refers to the bus, which allows all nodes to access the transmission medium. Since there is no central arbiter to decide who is the bus master, every node must listen to the bus before sending or receiving messages. To receive a message, a

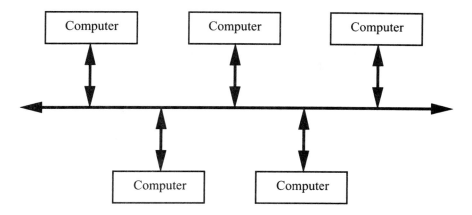

Fig. 1.4 Bus topology.

node looks for a message with its address. To send a message, the sending node first listens to the bus to make sure there is no message on the bus. When the bus is idle, the node can attempt to send a message. If another node has been waiting to send a message and attempts to send a message as well, then a collision results. The nodes transmitting can detect these collisions by listening to the bus. When a collision is detected, they send a jamming sequence so that all nodes know that a collision occurred. The nodes involved in the collision then stop, wait for a random period of time, and then attempt to resend the message. As a consequence the performance of the Ethernet is degraded when the number of collisions increases. The Ethernet provides a transmission rate of up to 10,000 K bps and a range of up to 1 km. Several Ethernet networks can be connected with a gateway. These independent networks can send and receive message simultaneously. Nodes in one Ethernet can send a message to nodes on a different Ethernet bus over the gateway. The gateway keeps a routing table. When a node in one Ethernet bus tries to send a message to a node on another Ethernet, the gateway looks up the destination address in the routing table in order to route the message over the appropriate Ethernet to the destination node.

1.7.2 Stars

Centralized communication is used with the star network, as shown in Fig. 1.5. The central node is the bottleneck in this network. If the central node crashes, the whole network crashes. The routing is simple and the delays are small, but the central node can limit the throughput.

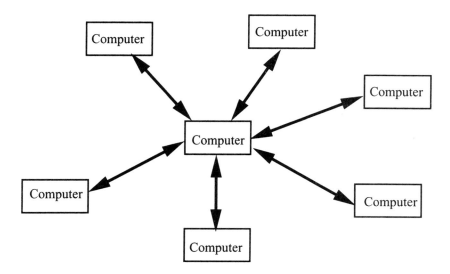

Fig. 1.5 Star topology.

1.7.3   Rings

In a ring there is no central arbiter (Fig. 1.6), the node that has the token has the right to send messages. The token is passed from node to node until a node that needs to transmit a message is encountered. The links are unidirectional. The disappearance of a token causes the whole network to crash, so steps must be taken for token management. Communication software is simple, since routing is simple. The delays are dependent on both the number of nodes in the ring and the number of bits buffered by each node, typically 1 to 16 bits. The message length can be variable. Other advantages of the token ring is that there is no starvation and no deadlock; every node has its turn to posses the token, and only one node at a time is permitted to do so. Priority-based access can be established. A disadvantage of the ring is the token management. Unless time-outs are used, it is impossible to detect if a token is lost because the amount of time a node can use the token is unbounded. Another disadvantage of the ring is that if a single node fails, the entire ring fails. To detect a node failure, the node receiving a token should acknowledge its receipt. If a node does not receive an acknowledgment after a certain amount of time, then a failure can be assumed. To make the ring more reliable, the network must be able to route messages around failed nodes. This increases the hardware and software complexity.

Rings can also use slotted rings. With a slotted ring, a monitor node sets a fixed number of bits for the ring. For example if there are N bits in the ring at any time and messages are of length m, then N/m slots for messages are available. The advantage of this technique is that more than one message

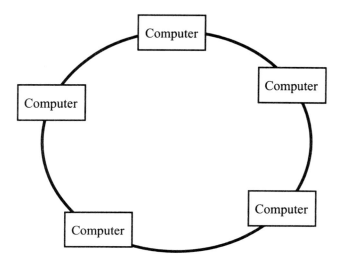

Fig. 1.6 Ring topology.

can be transmitted simultaneously. The disadvantage is the work required by the monitor. Note that a bus can use a token for control, but it cannot use a slotted ring.

1.7.4 Meshes

As shown in Fig. 1.7, a mesh has links between some but not all nodes. If the number of links for each node is at least two, then alternative routes are available for messages. The network delay is dependent on the number of nodes a message must pass through and the traffic on the network.

1.7.5 Trees

As shown in Fig. 1.8, a tree is an extension of the star. It may be used in a terminal network, where the root is the main computer and the leaves are the terminals. It is also used in process control.

1.8 Switching Techniques

Switching techniques determine how messages are transmitted across networks. In debugging a network switching techniques are important to understand when determining how a message became lost, how the messages were ordered, or how to improve the network's message-passing performance. There are three main types of switching techniques: circuit switching, message switching, and packet switching.

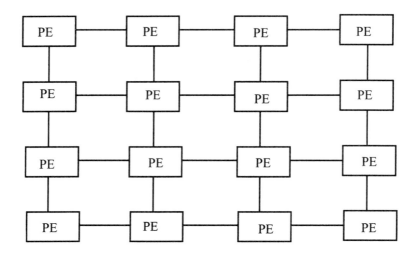

Fig. 1.7 Regular mesh topology (PE stands for processing element).

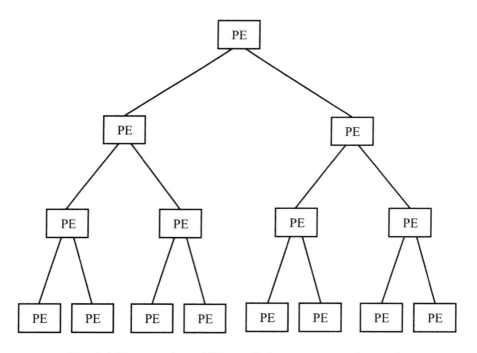

Fig. 1.8 Tree topology (PE stands for processing element).

With circuit switching a dedicated communication path is established on the network. Once the path is established, data is transferred. When the path is no longer needed, it is released. The advantage of circuit switching is that messages can be transmitted quickly after the path is established. The disadvantage is that it is expensive to establish the path and if the path is not being utilized, then bandwidth is wasted. Circuit switching is appropriate when the path will be heavily used and needed for a longer period of time.

With message switching a message is sent from node to node. When a node receives a message that is not addressed to it, it forwards it to another node. Compared to circuit switching, line utilization is higher because no lines are held idle. Also messages can be broadcast easily using this method, and communication paths are not as easily blocked. The disadvantage is that messages take longer, so message switching is inappropriate for interactive applications.

Packet switching is similar to message switching, except that messages have a smaller maximum size because most messages are broken up into packets of a fixed size. Like pipelining instructions, the packets can be pipelined so that more than one node can transmit a portion of the same message at the same time. Packet switching is responsive enough that it can be used for interactive communication. Packets can be transmitted as datagrams. Each datagram has its own destination address and is treated independently. Datagrams for a particular message may arrive at their destination in a different order than they were sent, so postprocessing the message is necessary. Datagrams can be transmitted in parallel along different paths, so a message can be transmitted very quickly. Packets can also be transmitted using a virtual circuit approach. This technique is similar to the circuit switching technique. The virtual circuit is a logical path established between the sender and receiver. This is not a dedicated path, that is, portions of the path can shared. Packets are transmitted with a virtual circuit identifier.

1.9 Distributed Real-Time Systems

Having examined distributed systems and real-time systems, we will now look at the features of distributed real-time systems (DRTSs). The terms *distributed real-time systems* and *real-time distributed systems* are considered interchangeable in this text. Using distributed computing to exploit the inherent concurrency of real-time systems leads to distributed real-time systems. For example, a real-time system that can meet all deadlines with five processes in a single processor may not be able to handle two extra aperiodic processes, so distributed processing may be a solution. In this example we can let one processor handle the two aperiodic processes while the other processor handles the five periodic processes. A real-time distributed system is a distributed system whose correctness depends on meeting timing constraints as well as logical requirements. For example, an application may be distributed, as in the case of an airline ticket reservation system. From these descriptions it should be clear that the terms *distributed real-time* and *real-time distributed* can be used interchangeably because they both are characterized by distributed computing with timing constraints.

As mentioned earlier, distributed computing may be introduced to improve a real-time system's response time and/or reliability. By decomposing a large real-time application into a set of processes, the decomposed processes can operate concurrently using interprocess communication and synchronization. Thus the response time can be improved with parallel processing. Reliability can be increased with distributed systems. This is important because real-time systems are expected to operate continuously with extremely high reliability even with the presence of a faulty processor. Fault tolerance can be achieved by detecting a faulty processor, saving and restoring the computational tasks of the faulty processor, and then distributing the recovered tasks to the remaining processors so that the DRTS can continue to operate, although with a degradation of computing power. However, better performance and increased reliability come at a cost; despite the speed gains due to parallel operation, the response time of DRTSs is not guaranteed to improve, and the system reliability is not necessarily high because of the increased complexity of task partitioning and task allocation, as well as the resource constraints among processes and the overhead caused by the nondeterministic interprocess communication delays. This raises the issues of how to reduce the complexity caused by extra task partitioning and interprocess communication, and how to debug timing errors caused by process distribution. We will focus on these matters in this book.

1.10   Characteristics of DRTSs

What follow are some characteristics of distributed real-time systems that distinguish them from nondistributed non-real-time systems [413].

1. *Continuous operation.* Most distributed real-time controlling systems must operate continuously in order to maintain close interaction with their controlled environments.

2. *Stringent timing constraints.* The correctness of the execution of a DRTS is determined not only by the speed of the underlying processors but also by the timing constraints imposed by the execution environments.

3. *Asynchronous process interaction.* DRTSs are designed to interact with physical environments, and their processors are usually geographically dispersed. Asynchronous processes, including internal DRTSs processes and external physical processes, communicate with each other by exchanging messages. The sequence of events in asynchronous processes are very difficult to predict, and often the assumptions made in design phase are violated during run-time.

4. *Unpredictable communication delays and race conditions.* Due to the unpredictable traffic on the communication network and the distance between two communication nodes, the delays caused by the interprocessor communication are unpredictable and nonnegligible. In addition a race condition can occur when two processes share the same resource. Thus the synchronized event sequence specified in the design phase may change during run-time because of unpredictable communication delays.

5. *Nondeterministic and nonrepeatable.* Because of the unpredictable communication delays and race conditions among processors and processes, the execution behavior of DRTSs is not deterministic. Re-execution of the same program running with the same input will not necessarily produce the same result.

6. *Global clock reference and global state.* Each processor may have its own clock running separately from the clocks of other processors. It is very difficult to determine the precise global time that is mandatory for determining accurate global states and debugging erroneous timing behavior.

7. *Multiple threads of process interaction.* In contrast with a sequential program having a single control flow, DRTSs have multiple threads of control. Such control flows are loosely or tightly coupled depending on their communication protocols (message passing or shared memory). In addition the multiple threads of interaction among processes are difficult to display for debugging; presenting text as done with sequential software is not helpful. Therefore program visualization using modern computer graphics techniques is essential for data presentation.

In sum, real-time systems differ from non-real-time systems by their timing constraints. The most essential issue regarding debugging real-time systems is to find timing constraint violations (or timing errors in general). Interprocess communication and synchronization are a major source of timing constraint violations. Therefore debugging timing constraint violations caused by interprocess communication and synchronization is the unique feature that distinguishes the debugging of DRTSs.

1.11 Review of Architectures of DRTSs

Having examined the principles of DRTSs, let us look at a number of DRTS architectures that have been proposed or developed.

The number five electronic switching system, 5ESS [107], is a distributed telephone-switching system developed at Bell Laboratories. Fig. 1.9 shows the 5ESS architecture. Its control network consists of a *central processor* and a collection of *module processors*. The central processor is associated with systemwide functions, while each module process is logically as well as physically associated with a switching module and a set of peripherals. The task load of the system is statically distributed among the module processors, which are identical both in hardware and software. As shown in Fig. 1.9,

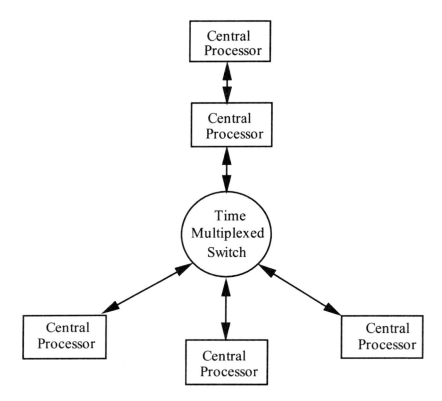

Fig. 1.9 The number five electronic switching system (5ESS). (Reprinted, by permission, from [107]. ©1982 IEEE.)

the processors are connected as a star network with a message switch. Each processor can communicate with the other processors via a "fixed" communication path through the message switch.

The software of 5ESS consists of an operating system kernel and a set of application processes that are identified by a name that is unique across the distributed control network. The kernel provides the facilities for dynamic process creation and destruction. The primary method of interprocess communication is message passing. To send a message, a process needs only a message buffer and the "name" of the destination process. After preparing the message, the process invokes an operating system primitive to transmit the message. The operating system will transmit the message (e.g., intraprocessor memory transfer versus data-link transfer) for the process. Each message has a header attached that includes the name of the receiving process, the name of the sending process, the message type, and the message length. The processes can be classified as *general processes* and *interrupt processes*. For the general processes, the process scheduling is not preemptive. Once scheduled,

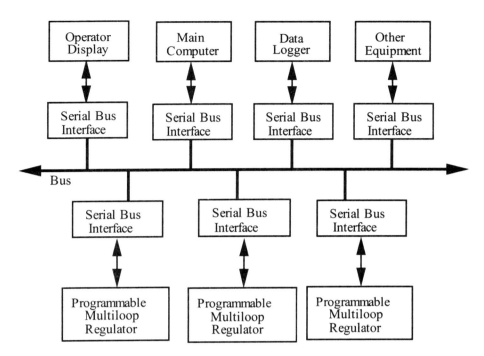

Fig. 1.10 Hardware architecture of REBUS. (Reprinted, by permission, from [22]. ©1982 IEEE.)

a process is allowed to run continuously until it voluntarily gives up control. The interrupt processes respond to prioritized hardware interrupts. They have strict response time requirements and are allowed to preempt other processes.

REBUS [22] is a fault-tolerant distributed system designed for real-time control applications. The hardware architecture of REBUS is shown in Fig. 1.10. The system consists of operator displays, a main computer, a data logger, programmable multiloop regulators, and additional equipment. The system is connected via a serial bus through serial bus interface boards. The bus is duplicated for fault-tolerant purposes. The programmable multiloop regulator consists of eight process interface modules that provide an interface with the environment, and one multiloop processing unit that supervises the process interface modules. REBUS provides reliable facilities for interprocessor communication.

MARS [200] (maintainable real-time system) is a distributed fault-tolerant system for real-time applications for fault tolerance and maintainability in both hardware and software. The hardware architecture consists of a set of components that communicate by the exchange of state and event messages. All components have access to a global time, which is realized by a fault-tolerant clock synchronization algorithm. The basic communication service in MARS is unreliable and uses unacknowledged datagrams. The messages are classified as event messages that report the occurrence of events and state messages that report the attribute value of objects. An event message is discarded if it is not accessed within its validity period. The validity time is also applied to state messages. A prototype MARS has been implemented in which the components are connected by an Ethernet network.

Schoeffler [340] proposes a hardware architecture for industrial process control. He asserts that all functions of a control system are usually associated with one or more physical modules. Modules associated with one or more functions are usually grouped together into physical structures called *nodes*, which are joined in a plantwide communication system linked by coaxial cable or fiber optics. A node may consist of a set of modules, or computers connected by a node bus. Fig. 1.11 shows the architecture of such a system. The supervisory computer system can be a general-purpose computer for higher-level applications. The communication interface and plantwide communication network are duplicated for fault-tolerant purposes. He also describes three major types of communication systems that can be used for the plantwide communication networks, rings, broadcast networks, and cluster systems. For the software system he only mentions that a real-time, general-purpose operating system can be installed in the supervisory computers. The dynamic control system used depends on the application.

SIFT (Software-implemented fault tolerance) [425, 426, 252] is a multiprocessor computer designed for flight control systems. The SIFT system consists of a set of identical computer units physically isolated from each other to avoid fault propagation. The computers are star-connected through broadcast-mode interprocessor communication interfaces. The architecture of the system is shown in Fig. 1.12. Each computer unit contains a processor, a memory unit, a broadcast interface, and an I/O interface unit. The memory unit of a computer unit cannot be accessed by other computer units. The I/O interface unit provides an interface between the processor and various aircraft sensors and actuators. The processors communicate with each other through the broadcast interface. Because of the characteristics of flight control, the scheduling strategy of SIFT for tasks is a periodic method with multiple priority levels. Each priority level corresponds to an interaction rate within a time frame. The time frame corresponding to the highest priority level is divided into a number of subframes. The highest priority level tasks run in specific subframes so that their results are available to other tasks in the next subframes.

1.12   A Model of Real-Time Distributed Systems

In our research we choose an architecture for our model of a distributed real-time system that could simulate the architecture of most current real-time

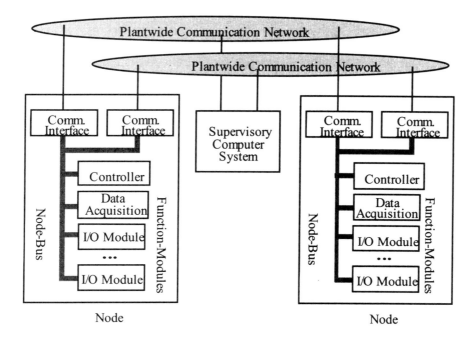

Fig. 1.11 Hardware architecture for industrial process control.

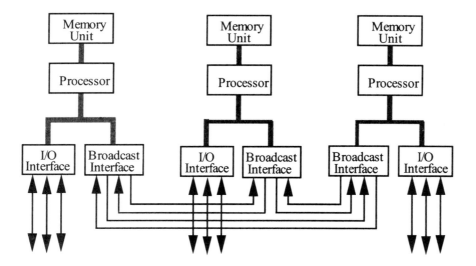

Fig. 1.12 Hardware architecture of SIFT. (Reprinted, by permission, from [252]. ©1982 IEEE.)

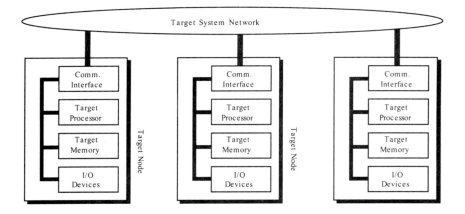

Fig. 1.13 Hardware overview of the target system.

distributed systems. We choose a model similar to the architecture of 5ESS. In our model we view a real-time distributed computing system as a collection of computers that are communicating and cooperating to reach a common goal. The computers, called nodes, are connected with a communication network. They can be geographically dispersed. Each computer has its own memory, I/O devices, and a communication device. Fig. 1.13 shows the hardware architecture of a real-time distributed system. In our model we do not make any assumption about the topology of the communication network.

The software consists of a set of application processes and an operating system. The application processes are distributed throughout the nodes. The operating system of the target system consists of a set of *kernels*, one on each processor. Each kernel runs as the client program on a node. Stankovic [369] points out that today's real-time systems continue to use *priority-driven* scheduling processes with timing constraints. The priority of a process reflects the timing constraints and critical values. In our model the kernels provide a mechanism for preemptive process scheduling and interprocess communication. Processes invoke kernel primitives by submitting *kernel calls*, which are privileged instructions. Fig. 1.14 shows the software architecture of the real-time distributed system.

The application processes are identified by integers known as process identifiers. Each process is assigned a priority by users or by the operating system statically or dynamically. A process in the system can be in one of three states {*running, ready, waiting*} at any time during its lifetime. Changes in a process state are based on its current state and the current state of the system. A process has an initial state when it is created, and it can have one of three ending states corresponding to different terminating conditions: *normal, killed,* and *abnormal*. In the *normal* state the process has finished its job and terminated. In the *killed* state the process has been killed by

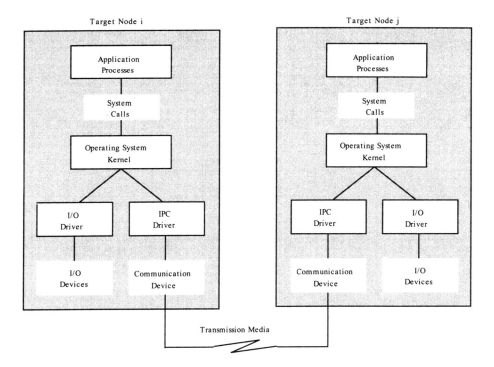

Fig. 1.14 Software overview of the target system.

its parent process. In the *abnormal* state the process has been killed by the operating system because of an error in the process.

Processes in the system can communicate with each other synchronously and asynchronously. For synchronous communication, the sender and receiver must be synchronized. The sending process sends a message to the receiving process, then waits for an acknowledgment that the message has been received by the receiving process. A message exchange without acknowledgment is considered as asynchronous communication. In this case the sending process does not wait for an acknowledgment from the receiving process, and the receiving process does not issue an acknowledgment.

Processes on the same node can also communicate via shared memory. The semaphore mechanism is employed to synchronize the processes accessing the shared memory. All semaphores in the system are initialized to 1. That is, only one process can enter the critical section of a semaphore S. When a process is in the critical section, all other processes that want to enter the critical section have to wait in the waiting list of S. When the process in the critical section executes a V operation, the process with a highest priority in the list will be restarted by the wake-up operation, which changes the state of the process from "waiting" to "ready" and puts the process into the system ready queue. If more than one process has the same highest priority, the process is chosen in a first-in-first-out (FIFO) order. The CPU may or may not be switched from the running process to the newly "ready" process, depending upon the priority of the newly "ready" process.

The semaphore has the following structure:

```
TYPE semaphore= RECORD;
      value: INTEGER;
      L: list of processes;
END;
```

The semaphore operations P and V, on a semaphore, S, are defined as

```
P(S): S.value:= S.value-1;
      IF S.value<0
      THEN BEGIN
            add this process to S.L;
            block;
      END;
V(S): S.value:= S.value+1;
      IF S.value <= 0
      THEN BEGIN
            remove process P with highest priority from S.L;
            wakeup(P);
      END;
```

In the target system, process migration is not allowed. That is, once a process is created on a node, it will stay in the node until terminating. A process can be created on a node different from the node of the creating process. To create a process on the specified node, the creating process makes the request to its local kernel using a system call. The local kernel then sends the request to the kernel of the specified node. The kernel on the node assigns the process an identification number and allocates resources to the newly created process.

1.13 Summary

DRTSs are becoming more important to our everyday lives. With increasing computing power, we will have larger and more complex DRTSs. However, so far the development of DRTSs has taken longer time than the development of a regular distributed system or a single processor real-time system. Mostly this can be attributed to the fact that DRTSs are inherently more complex than these systems, but also the software for support and development of DRTSs has not kept pace. To improve the usability and reliability of DRTSs, the supporting software and development tools need to be greatly improved.

The characteristics of distributed systems, real-time systems, and DRTSs were another topic introduced in this chapter. A real-time system is characterized by the need for timing constraints. Real-time systems can be classified as hard real-time systems or soft real-time systems depending on the consequences of timing constraint violations. Hard real-time systems must meet their timing constraints to avoid disastrous consequences. Soft real-time systems are still considered functionally correct if timing constraints are not seriously violated. A distributed system has many processes running on different processors working toward specific functional requirements. The distributed processes are coordinated by interprocess communication and synchronization. Distributed systems can take a variety of forms. The hardware can range from a single CPU to multiple computers. The control can range from a single control unit to multiple control units cooperating with messages. The data can range from a single copy located at a central point to a distributed database with no central file or directory. Distributed systems can also be classified as homogeneous or heterogeneous. Distributed systems can also be classified as centralized or decentralized.

DRTSs are distributed systems with timing constraints. DRTSs can be characterized by continuous operation, stringent timing constraints, asynchronous process interaction, unpredictable communication delays and race conditions, nondeterministic and nonrepeatable execution, global clock reference and global state, and multiple threads of process interaction. In sum, real-time systems differ from non-real-time systems because of the timing constraints. Therefore when debugging real-time systems, it is important to find timing constraint violations (or timing errors in general). Interprocess communication and synchronization are a major source of timing constraint violations. Debugging timing constraint violations caused by interprocess communication and synchronization is the unique feature that distinguishes the debugging of DRTSs.

Exercises

1. List the three operations that describe the interaction between a real-time system's controlling and controlled systems.

2. What is the difference between a hard real-time system and a soft real-time system?

3. List the four aspects of time that are important to a real-time system.

4. What is the difference between an aperiodic process and a periodic process?

5. How are distributed processes coordinated?

6. Why is termination detection a nontrivial operation for distributed systems?

7. What is the difference between asynchronous and synchronous communication? What are the advantages of each?

8. Which of the three switching techniques described in Section 1.8 (a) are more reliable, (b) result in higher throughput, (c) have the smallest latency?

9. Why is the execution behavior of a DRTS considered nonrepeatable? In what ways is it repeatable, and what conditions are necessary to make it repeatable?

10. What is a semaphore and when is it used?

Chapter 2

Monitoring Systems

2.1 Monitoring Real-Time Systems

In monitoring a system, we collect run-time information on the target system that cannot be obtained by merely studying the program text. The collected information can be used for program testing and debugging, dynamic system safety checking, dynamic task scheduling, performance analysis, and program optimization. Monitoring is accomplished in two operations: *triggering* and *recording*. Triggering is the detection of predefined events during program execution that triggers recording of the data pertinent to the events. Triggering can be accomplished by inserting extra instructions into the monitored system to cause data capture or by passively monitoring the target processor's signal lines such as the data, address, and control buses. Recording is the collection and storage of the data pertinent to the events. The recorded data provides a trace of events that can be used to describe computer operations and execution behavior.

The triggering and recording mechanisms for monitoring can be implemented in hardware, software, or both (resulting in a hybrid monitor). Software techniques use interrupts or embedded code for triggering. Data collection is carried out by software, and the collected data is often stored in the working memory of the monitored system. Hardware techniques passively snoop the system buses of the target system to detect a set of predefined signals, and triggering occurs on specific combinations of signals. Data recording is carried out by hardware, with the recorded data stored in a separate memory independent of the monitored system. Hybrid techniques insert code that triggers the monitoring into the target system. Data recording is carried out by hardware, while the collected data is saved in a separate memory independent of the monitored system.

The open issues in monitoring real-time systems and a sample system are presented in [308]. Plattner points out monitoring interference is frequently not acceptable when debugging a real-time system because the monitored

29

system may not exhibit the same timing behavior as it would when it is not being monitored. Moreover conditions defined at the design level may be violated when monitoring is introduced. The author presents a real-time monitor consisting of a separate hardware monitoring device executing software-monitoring processes. The hardware monitor detects any state changes in the target process through bus snooping and then saves the detected data in a phantom memory in the monitoring system. The software-monitoring processes executing on the separate monitoring device then interpret the low-level data stored inside the phantom memory and reconstruct the low-level data into high-level symbolic representations. The hardware event detection and software interpretation of the event must be completed before the next state change occurs in the target system. The amount that the monitor perturbs the target system, referred to as *monitor perturbation*, is found by analyzing the processing power of the target processor and monitoring processor, the target program being monitored, the code information generated by the target system compiler, and the amount of monitoring data.

As mentioned, inserting code can affect the system's performance by changing the ordering and timing of events. The ordering of events refers to the sequence of events and the timing of events refers to the time when an event occurs. The ordering of events can be classified as a *partial ordering* or a *total ordering*. A partial ordering is a *local* sequence of events occurring within a processor. The timing of the local events is referenced to a processor's local clock. Since the clocks of different processors are not synchronized, the times recorded in one processor cannot be compared to the times recorded in another processor. In contrast, the total ordering is a *global* sequence of all events occurring in a system. In this case the timing of all events are referenced to a single global clock or to synchronized clocks [207]. Therefore an event with an earlier time reading definitely occurred before an event with a later time reading.

The exact impact of monitoring on the system may be difficult to measure because a distributed real-time monitoring system is itself a distributed system with real-time constraints. Thus a goal of distributed real-time monitoring is to minimize the monitoring impact on the target system. If the impact is not minimized, then the ordering and timing of events can be changed. This is not an issue for a single processor with sequential processing because intraprocess events have a total ordering. Therefore interference only affects the event timing of a sequential processor. But in multiprocessor or distributed environments, delaying one of the processors may slow down or stop the execution of a process, thereby causing it to miss a deadline or alter the event ordering with respect to events on remote processors. For example, suppose that process 1 should write to a memory location before process 2 reads from that memory location. If, due to the monitoring overhead on process 1, the execution of the write instruction was delayed (a change in event timing) so that the read instruction of process 2 now is executed ahead of the write instruction (a change in event ordering), then the wrong data will be read.

Two approaches are used to reduce the effect of this interference caused by monitoring: A monitoring hardware device is used to reduce the interference [245, 246]. Then a perturbation analysis is used to predict the effect of monitoring, and changes are made to reduce the interference [246, 235, 237, 239, 236, 240]. Because hardware monitoring does not use any resources of the target system, there is no interference to the execution of the target system. Perturbation analysis examines event ordering and timing in an attempt to find ways to reduce the effects of monitoring interference by adjusting the event ordering and event timing [240, 119]. The event ordering is found by reconstructing the total ordering of the interprocess events based on the knowledge gained from the system kernel and the cross-compiler. The event timing is found by measuring the event delay due to the execution of instrumentation.

Before we introduce the classification of monitoring approaches, some terms will be described while providing an overview of the monitoring process. *Target programs* are the programs to be monitored. *Target systems* consist of the target programs, target operating system, target compiler, and target hardware. The system behavior of the target program, including the program behavior and operating system information, is described as a series of *events*. These events are the visible changes of the system's behavior, such as process creation, process termination, sending a message, or receiving a message. The events monitored are called the *events of interest*. *Instrumentation code* is used to record the events of interest. This code is used to generate event information during the target system's execution. *Instrumented programs* refer to target programs that have had instrumentation code added. When the instrumented code is executed, event traces are produced. They are logs of the events generated.

A *monitoring system* is a system used to monitor a target program's execution. A monitoring system usually consists of *instrumentation software*, a *monitoring control module*, and *monitoring hardware*. The monitoring activities are *event specification* (inserting instrumentation code into target programs), *event detection* (identifying the event occurrence generated by the execution of the instrumentation code), and *event processing* (time stamping and storing the collected event occurrence). The *instrumentation software* generates the instrumentation code needed to collect the events of interest during monitoring. This *instrumentation code* may also be inserted manually. The *monitoring software* detects the events generated during the execution of the instrumented programs. A software module called a *monitoring control module* is used to control the *event detection* and *event processing* of the hardware monitor. *Monitoring hardware* is the hardware used for event detection and processing. *Monitoring intrusion* refers to any attempt to record system execution by using the computing resource of the monitored target system. If monitoring does not affect the timing and ordering of events—that is, the execution of a target system is not affected by the existence of monitoring activities—it is referred as *nonintrusive monitoring.*

2.2   Monitoring at Different Levels of Detail

In testing and debugging a distributed real-time system, different levels of abstraction of the execution information provide different levels of details. Higher-level information refers to events such as interprocess communication and synchronization. In contrast, lower-level information refers to events such as the step-by-step execution trace of a process. The execution data collected at the process level includes the process state transitions, communication and synchronization interactions among the software processes, and the interactions between the software processes and the external process. The execution data collected at the function level includes the interactions among the functions or procedures that compose processes. The user can isolate faults within processes using the process-level execution data and then isolate faults within functions using the function-level execution data. In this section, events of interest at process level and function level are identified.

2.2.1   Process-Level Monitoring

To monitor program execution at the process level, we consider a process as a black box which can be in one of the three states: running, ready, or waiting. A process changes its state depending on its current state and the current events in the system. These events include interactions among the processes and the interactions between the software processes and the environment. We distinguish events that directly affect the program execution at the process level from those events that affect the execution at lower levels. Assigning a value to a variable, arithmetic operations, and procedure calls, for instance, are events that will not cause immediate state changes of the running process. Interprocess communication and synchronization are events that may change a process's running status and affect its execution behavior. Table 2.1 shows the process-level events with the key values that we want to monitor in our target system model at the process level.

There are two reasons for monitoring and debugging at the process level. The first reason is that processes are the minimum program unit that can exhibit nondeterministic behavior. For an individual sequential process that contains no nondeterministic mechanisms (e.g., guarded commands [101]), successive executions with the same input should present the same behavior and produce the same result. That is, an individual sequential process has a deterministic execution behavior [212]. Thus, if one can isolate faults to an individual process, it is possible to use the conventional cyclic debugging method for the successive fault isolation at lower levels of abstraction.

Process interactions are subject to synchronization problems, such as race conditions and illegal access of shared variables [434, 435]. Furthermore sys-

Event	Key Values
Process Creation	Parent Process Identification Create Call Time Node Identification
	Child Process Identification Creating Process Time Node Identification
Process Termination	Parent Process Identification Resuming Time Node Identification
	Child Process Identification Terminating Time Node Identification
Process Synchronization	Process Identification Operation (P/V) Semaphore Identification Value of the Semaphore Time Node Identification
I/O Operation	Process Identification Operation (I/O) I/O Port Identification Message (I/O Buffer) Time Node Identification
Interprocess Communication	Sending Process Identification Message Node Identification Send-Call Time Receiving-Acknowledgment Time
	Receiving Process Identification Message Node Identification Receive-Call Time Receiving-Message Time
Wait Child Process	Parent Process Identification Child Process Identification Time Node Identification
External Interrupt	Interrupted Process Identification I/O Port Identification Message (I/O Buffer) Time Node Identification
Process State Change	Process Identification New State Transition Time Node Identification

Table 2.1 Process-level events and their key values.

tem safety constraints of real-time systems are specified based on the interactions between the software processes and the system environment. The
second reason for monitoring at the process level is that we can reconstruct
the execution behavior for interprocess communication and synchronization
and the interaction between the software processes and the environment using
the collected process-level events. Thus we can localize faults to individual
processes.

From the system's point of view, a process changes states and its execution behavior based on its current state and the current events in the system.
Since the operation sequence internal to a process is determinate, only events
external to a process (external events or process-level events) will affect the
process execution behavior. For example, if a process is synchronized with
other processes with a semaphore mechanism, that is, with P and V operations applied to a shared semaphore, and there is no other interaction among
processes, then the execution behavior can precisely be characterized by the
P/V operation sequence [67].

An event in a distributed real-time system may be modeled as several
subevents. For example, in a single processor system a process exits immediately after its parent process executes the "create" process system call. But
in a distributed real-time system, when it is created on a different node from
its parent, a process does not exit until the kernel of the destination node
executes the "create" command. Because of communication delays, the time
when the parent process executes the "create" call and the time when the
kernel of the destination node creates the new process can be significantly
different. Thus a process creation event may be treated as a "create call"
subevent where the parent process executes the "create" system call and as
a "create action" subevent where the kernel on the destination node creates
the new process. The division of an event into subevents also occurs with
process termination and interprocess communication.

It is important to realize that Table 2.1 only lists the process-level events
of interest for the assumed target system model described in Section 1.12.
For a different target system architecture, the events of interest and their
key values may change. For example, for a tightly coupled multiprocessor
system, the create call time and create process time for a process creation
event may be the same. That is, a process creation event does not need to
be divided into subevents because there is no communication delay. Likewise
the division of process termination events and interprocess communication
events into subevents may also be removed.

2.2.2   Function-Level Monitoring

The collected process-level information can be used to analyze the behavior
among processes. But for repairing faults, the process level may be too abstract. Thus monitoring the system at a more detailed abstraction level,

Event	Key Values
Function Call	Calling Function Identification Called Function Identification Passed-in Parameters Time
Function Return	Calling Function Identification Called Function Identification Returned Parameters Time

Table 2.2 Function-level events and their key values.

function-level abstraction, is needed. After a set of faulty processes is identified, we monitor those processes at the function level in order to identify faulty functions. Thus we first monitor the target system at the process level and localize faults to individual processes. Then we monitor these processes at the function level and localize faults to individual functions.

The goal of monitoring program execution at the function level is to localize faulty functions (or procedures) within a process. At this level of abstraction, functions are the basic units of the program model. Each function is viewed as a black box that interacts with others by calling them or being called by them with a set of parameters as arguments. So the events of interest are function calls and returns. The key values for these events are the parameters passed between functions. Table 2.2 shows the function-level events and corresponding values monitored.

2.3 Spectrum of Monitoring Approaches

As mentioned earlier, monitoring can be done with software, hardware, or a combination of hardware and software. A hybrid monitor refers to a monitor that uses a combination of hardware and software. The principle difference between hardware and software monitoring is that the hardware approach separates the monitoring task from the target system's work load, whereas the software approach adds to the target system's work load. In this section we examine these two approaches more closely.

2.3.1 Software Monitoring

With software monitoring, the monitoring system consists solely of instrumentation code inserted into the target system using instrumentation software [54, 78, 104, 105, 122, 145, 183, 211, 214, 253, 260, 257, 258, 256, 259, 390, 389, 388, 387, 341, 363]. Triggering is accomplished by executing the inserted code, and data pertaining to events of interest is recorded and stored in the memory of the target system. Thus the instrumentation code uses the computing power of the monitored target system. As a result instrumented programs have an execution speed penalty.

The advantages of the software approach are that it is flexible and that no additional hardware is required. Unfortunately, because the monitoring system is part of the target system, software monitoring uses the target system's processor and memory space, so the target system's performance and possibly its behavior will be affected. Without the use of a hardware monitor, the dilemma of finding a balance between perturbation and recording sufficient information always exists. Limiting instrumentation provides inadequate measurement detail, but excessive instrumentation will perturb the measured system to an unacceptable degree. Fortunately there are techniques for reducing the perturbation while retaining sufficient information. In addition to the method mentioned earlier by Malony, Reed, and Wijshoff [240], perturbation can be reduced by altering the instrumentation mechanism, by modifying the monitored target programs or the underlying operating systems. The instrumented event trace can also be adjusted to reduce the effect of perturbation. In general, the problem facing the software monitoring approach is how to control and predict the levels of intrusion (perturbation) and how to automate software instrumentation [119].

Execution behavior can be monitored at the system level and the program level. At the system level, activities and data structures visible to the kernel are monitored. At the program level, activities and data structures visible to the user processes are monitored. Those visible to the kernel include process state transitions, external interrupts, system calls, processor identifications, and data structures like process control blocks (PCBs). Those visible to the user processes include function/procedure calls and returns, and variable value changes. Some of the activities and data structures, such as system calls, are visible to both the kernel and the user processes, and others are visible only to the kernel, like process state transitions and PCBs. Finally, others are visible only to the user processes, like function/procedure calls and returns and variable value changes. To monitor at the system level, the kernel can be instrumented for the events of interest, while the user programs can be instrumented to monitor at the program level. In the following, we briefly overview various systems that monitor at these two levels.

Chodrow, Jahanian, and Donner [78] propose a run-time monitor for specifying and monitoring properties of real-time systems. They model the computation of a real-time system as a sequence of events. The timing properties can be expressed as the relationship between events. The timing constraints are divided into embedded constraints and monitored constraints. The user processes are instrumented to generate the events of interest and also to verify the embedded timing constraints. A specific process, called the *monitor*, collects the event occurrences generated by the user processes and verifies the monitored timing constraints. This monitoring system is extended by Raju et al. [316] to distributed real-time systems. Each node of the target system has a monitor that collects event information generated by the user processes and verifies both embedded and monitored timing constraints.

Joyce et al. [183] propose a distributed monitoring system to detect and collect information on the concurrent execution of interacting processes. Event detection is done inside the target processes. To allow interprocess events to be easily detected, programmers have to modify the monitored processes by loading them with a version of an interprocess communication protocol to incorporate the monitoring activity into the execution of the program. To make the software monitoring approach applicable to DRTSs, the perturbation must be predictable and controllable. Dodd and Ravishankar [183] propose a software-support monitoring system (HMON) for real-time systems (HARTS). HMON is able to provide consistent monitoring and deterministic replay by predicting the overhead caused by monitoring.

Miller, Macrander, and Sechrest [260] propose a measurement tool to monitor and analyze the execution performance of a distributed program running in Berkeley UNIX 4.2BSD. A monitor and a measurement tool are constructed by changing the kernel-level structures of Berkeley UNIX, and some daemon processes are added to allow the monitoring activity to take place across machine boundaries. A low-level routine residing in the kernel, called a *meter*, detects events and collects the data pertaining to the events. The event data is extracted from the data structure of the operating system. Implementing the meter inside the kernel can prevent context switching and thus reduce the degree of perturbation. Tokuda, Kotera, and Mercer [390] propose a real-time monitor featuring the visualization of the internal behavior of a distributed real-time operating system, ARTS, at different levels of abstraction. To predict and reduce the monitoring interference, the monitor is designed as a permanent part of the target system so that target program's scheduler must consider the overhead of monitoring.

2.3.2   Hardware Monitoring

With hardware monitoring, the monitoring system uses hardware to monitor the target system [23, 50, 66, 226, 230, 308, 397]. A hardware device is connected to the buses of the target system to passively detect the events of interest and/or collect the data pertaining to the events. The target system is not instrumented, and the monitoring system does not share any of the resources of the target system. Thus the advantage of hardware monitoring is that the monitoring system does not interfere with the execution of the target system. The disadvantages of hardware monitoring are its cost and the dependency on a specific target processor. For hard real-time systems the advantage of stringent timing and safety constraints overrides the disadvantages.

Since the target system is only monitored at the signal level on the buses, the monitoring system must be able to interpret the signals in order to detect the events of interest and record the data pertaining to the events. This can be done in hardware, software, or a combination of the two. With hardware, the events of interest are specified in signal patterns that can be matched to signals on the buses of the target system. The hardware detection device is designed in such a way that it detects the events and collects only the data pertaining to the events. With software, the hardware has little detection capability but records all the signals on the buses, and a program processes the recorded signals to find the events and event-related data of interest.

The hardware approach requires minimum storage for event data, since only the data needed is recorded. The software approach must store all the signals, including unimportant ones, before processing the data. However, the design of hardware for the hardware detection approach is much more complex than the design of the hardware for the software approach. A compromise between the hardware and software approaches is to use both to detect events and collect the data. The events may be transformed to signal patterns that can be easily detected, and the signals are collected in such a way that the data pertaining to the events can be derived from them [397]. This reduces the complexity of hardware design and the amount of storage needed to save the collected data.

In general, hardware monitoring is used to monitor the run-time behavior of either hardware devices or software modules. Hardware devices are generally monitored to examine issues such as cache accesses, cache misses, memory access times, total CPU times, total execution times, I/O requests, I/O grants, and I/O busy times. Software modules are generally monitored to debug the modules or to examine issues such as the bottlenecks of a program, the deadlocks, or the degree of parallelism. Although it may seem that these two uses of monitoring are different, Brantley, McAuliffe, and Ngo [50] have pointed out that the results of hardware performance measurement can be used for software performance analysis and debugging. For example, bottlenecks may be caused by frequent references to the same memory location.

To monitor single processor systems, only one event detection device is needed because there is only one set of address, data, and control buses that links the target processor with the target memory and I/O devices. To monitor multiprocessor systems, detection devices may be used for each local memory bus and the shared memory and I/O. The data collected can be stored in a common storage device. To monitor distributed systems, each node of the target system needs to be monitored. In order to construct the state of the whole system (i.e., the global state), there must be a common time reference to record the times at which events occur on the nodes, and the data collected from each node must be transferred to a central location. Thus a separate and independent network is needed for transferring data and the synchronization of clocks, for the network of the target system not to be perturbed. In the following discussion we briefly introduce proposed or implemented hardware-monitoring systems. The details of hardware monitoring will be given in later chapters.

Plattner proposes a hardware-monitoring system for single-processor real-time systems [308]. In this system a hardware device called a *bus listener* is attached to the buses of the target processor. A memory called a *phantom memory* is used to mirror the contents of the memory of the target system in real time. This mirroring is realized by using the bus listener to detect all the transactions between the target processor and the target memory and then executing the detected transactions against the phantom memory. It is assumed that the memory of the target system contains all the information about the current state of the target system. Thus the phantom memory for the information to be collected can be accessed. Since the only interaction with the target system is the bus listener which passively detects the transactions on the target buses, the execution of the target system is not perturbed.

Tsai, Fang, and Chen [396] propose a hardware-monitoring system for distributed real-time systems. Each node of the target system is a single-processor computer with its own memory and I/O devices. To monitor each node of the target system, a monitoring node is connected to the address, data, and control buses of the monitored node. A qualification control unit is used to detect preset conditions and trigger the corresponding actions—start or stop the recording process, which latches and saves the signals on the buses of the target system. The user presets conditions so that the signals pertaining to the events of interest are recorded when the event occurs. The collected data is interpreted by a program that derives data for the events of interest. Issues such as global time reference, specific to monitoring distributed real-time systems, were not elaborated in the proposal.

Brantley, McAuliffe, and Ngo [50] describe a unique hardware-monitoring approach for the Research Parallel Processor Prototype (RP3) for performance analysis of hardware devices. Instead of using a hardware device to passively monitor the signals on the buses of the target system, each component of the target system that may generate the events of interest is instrumented in hardware to send signals to the monitor via designated hardware communication lines. The monitor consists of sets of status registers and counters. The status register controls the type and frequency of events collected. The counter accumulates the number of events specified in the status register in order to compute the frequency of events.

Liu and Parthasarathi [226] propose a hardware-monitoring system for multiprocessor systems in which a set of processors shares a common memory and I/O devices. The monitoring system is connected to system buses of the target processor to probe the signals. An event filter compares the specified patterns with the signal pattern on the buses and sends the comparison result to a counter unit. The counters in the counter unit count the number of occurrences of the events and measure in terms of clock cycles the intervals during which a specified pattern was matched and the intervals during which no pattern was matched. The contents of the counters are saved.

Lazzerini, Prete, and Lopriore [230] propose a programmable debugging aid (PDA) for performance evaluation, debugging, and testing multiple microprocessors. A PDA can be connected to the system buses that links the computing elements to the shared memory and I/O devices or to a local bus of a computing element. A PDA can monitor a segment of the target memory through the monitored buses. The user can specify the events to be monitored for each monitored memory location, such as memory reads and writes. The user can also specify the actions to be taken if an event associated with the memory location is detected, such as to save the signals on the monitored buses.

In sum, hardware monitoring uses hardware to passively monitor the activities of the target system. The advantage of hardware monitoring is that the amount of interference of the execution of the target system is none or minimal, since no target software is instrumented and no target hardware resources are used. The disadvantages are its cost and the lack of portability. This is because the monitoring is carried out at the electronic signal level and the hardware is target system dependent, or at least processor dependent. For hard real-time systems with stringent timing and safety constraints, the advantages override the disadvantages.

2.3.3 Hybrid Monitoring

Hybrid monitoring uses both software and hardware to perform monitoring activities [152, 149, 329, 263, 262, 142, 186, 185, 235, 245, 246]. In hybrid monitoring, triggering is accomplished by instrumenting the target systems to trigger recording which is accomplished in hardware. In other words, software specifies the events to be detected in the monitored target programs, and hardware identifies and processes the events. Perturbation to the monitored system is greatly reduced by using hardware to store the collected data into a separate storage. Execution perturbation is minimal if a single instruction causes the monitoring hardware to record all necessary data. A careful design of support hardware can greatly reduce perturbation at a modest cost.

Current hybrid monitoring techniques use two different triggering approaches. One technique uses a set of predefined addresses to trigger event recording. The monitoring unit is mapped into memory addresses, with each address representing an event. In other words, when a predefined address is detected on the system address bus, the monitoring device will record this address and the data on the system data bus. This approach is called *memory-mapped monitoring*. The other approach uses the coprocessor instructions to trigger event recording. The recording unit acts as a coprocessor that executes the monitoring instructions. To trigger an event of interest, a coprocessor instruction is sent by the target processor to the monitoring unit. This is called *coprocessor monitoring*.

In either of the two approaches, the hardware part of a monitoring system can be designed as a permanent part of the target system during the design phase of the target system development, or it can be an individual device or coprocessor integrated into the target system during the testing and debugging phase. As suggested by Mink et al. in [262], manufacturers could provide a monitor as an option. The instrumentation code could be embedded in the target system permanently or only during the testing or debugging phase. Keeping instrumentation code results in an execution time penalty while removing instrumentation code could result in different execution behavior. Instrumenting code in order to monitor at all levels is also very expensive in term of execution time.

To be ready to test and debug systems at all levels without suffering a behavior change, instrumentation code should be kept in the system permanently. The performance penalty can be compensated for by using faster hardware. Furthermore only instrumentation for the process-level information needs to be inserted permanently, and we still can test and debug systems at all levels without behavior changes. This is explained as follows: Since the nondeterministic behavior only arises at the process level, we keep the instrumentation code for the process-level events in the target system. Thus we can always debug the system at the process level. After we localize faults to individual processes based on the information collected at the process level, we can then instrument each faulty process for any lower-level information and execute it with the input collected at the process level. After the process has been debugged, we can remove the lower-level instrumentation. Since a sequential process is deterministic, removing the inserted code should not change its logical behavior. For event timing we can instrument the sequential process to count the number of cycles of loops and record the path of execution; then we can determine the timing by computing the execution time of all the machine instructions that were executed. After all the processes are debugged at lower levels, we execute the whole system and test and debug it at the process level.

Haban and Wybranietz's DTM system [152, 149] uses a hybrid approach to monitor a program's execution. Significant events are marked with software instrumentation, then detected, processed, and displayed with a hardware device. Events are classified as standard events associated with the operating system and optional events associated with the target programs. Each distributed target node has a monitor for event detection and collection. The collected event data with intraprocess relationships is locally processed, whereas event data pertaining to interprocess relationships is sent to the central monitor for global processing. The central monitor is also responsible for clock synchronization. It does this by computing the clock difference with respect to each local timer using the following equation, $D = (D_1 - D_2)/2$. D_1 is the difference between the local node's message-receiving time stamp and the central node's message-sending time stamp, and D_2 is the difference of the central node's acknowledge-receiving time stamp and the local node's acknowledge-sending time stamp.

Reilly [329] proposes a monitoring system developed by DEC for extracting information from a parallel processor in order to debug, find the hardware bottlenecks, and determine the software performance. The monitored programs are first instrumented by the programmer; then the monitoring hardware recognizes the event signals generated during the execution of the monitored programs.

Mink et al. [262] propose a hybrid monitor for measuring the performance of MIMD multiprocessor systems. By combining pattern-matching triggering (hardware sampling) with embedded-code triggering (software triggering), a hybrid technique is created that adds levels of hardware support to some familiar software tools. With the availability of off-chip VLSI processors, the hardware support of a performance measurement system is realized by configuring the VLSI chip set used to measure the architectural (hardware) performance and the target program (software) performance of a MIMD multiprocessor system.

Gorlick [142] proposes similar to a flight recorder a monitoring coprocessor in order to off-load the execution of monitoring instructions from the target processor. He uses the monitoring coprocessor along with a compiler to produce monitoring information for use in testing and debugging real-time systems. Monitoring code is inserted manually by users for the recording of kernel-level data such as the state of process dispatching, or automatically by a compiler for the recording of language-level data such as the sequence of a procedure call. The instrumented target program with monitoring code is compiled to object code which is composed of nonmonitoring instructions and monitoring instructions. During execution the recording of monitoring data is triggered by an event occurrence on the target processor; then the monitoring coprocessor takes over the recording while the target processor proceeds to other tasks. Since the monitoring activity is separated from the target processor, this approach can reduce monitoring perturbation to less than 1% of the total execution time.

In sum, with a hybrid system the target system is only responsible for generating the events of interest by executing the instrumented programs. After that the monitoring hardware identifies and processes the events of interest. Hybrid monitoring not only reduces the complexity of hardware-only monitoring but also minimizes the perturbation of software monitoring. However, even this minimal amount of interference caused by software instrumentation may still be unacceptable for hard real-time software environments. In addition the hybrid approach suffers the same architecture adaptability limitations as the hardware approach. Thus the goal of a hybrid approach is to provide hardware assistance which minimizes interference yet maximizes flexibility.

2.4   Monitoring DRTSs

The major concern of monitoring is to keep the overhead low and record as much information as possible. In general, there are four tasks that we face in developing such monitoring systems:

1. *Allow transparent monitoring.* Monitoring requires software and/or hardware support. However, the majority of target programs are not designed for monitoring. In addition users of monitoring systems may not have the necessary program instrumentation background, and more human involvement causes more errors. If programmers need to insert their own instrumentation code, errors might be introduced by the instrumentation code. To reduce programmer errors, transparent monitoring that does not require programmer involvement is preferred. In addition a high-level user interface is needed for the programmer to specify what to monitor rather than how to monitor. Programmers should be able to specify only the events of interest, with the monitoring system automatically inserting the code necessary to monitor these events. The interface also should provide multiple levels of monitoring so that the programmers can control the levels of detail.

2. *Minimize and predict monitoring overhead.* Due to the overhead of instrumentation, the monitored target system may exhibit different behavior because of the existence of monitoring. This altered behavior may lead to system errors such as changing the ordering of events, which results in the violation of the precedence constraints and causes deadlock or starvation, and changing the timing of events, which results in increased execution time and causes the system to miss deadlines. Therefore the overhead caused by instrumentation must be predictable and not change the ordering and timing of events. This can be done by considering monitoring activities as processes that are scheduled with other target processes and then performing analysis to evaluate the intrusiveness of the extra monitoring activities. This leads to the research of perturbation, which is a mathematical approach to predict the degree of interference of the monitored target system. In addition the software parts and hardware parts in hybrid monitoring should be classified clearly. This classification can reduce perturbation analysis to only the software portion, and it also helps determine which part of software monitoring will be more effective if implemented in hardware.

3. *Improve memory speed and space limitation.* For nonintrusive monitoring, data has to be detected and saved at the execution rate of the target processor. This requires high-speed monitor memory. In addition continuous monitoring results in a large data log which may consume the entire memory space. There are two approaches to solve this problem:

One is to flush the memory contents to secondary memory devices once the memory is full, then filter the collected data and extract the data of interest. The other approach is to restrict the data collection during monitoring; only events of interest will be recorded. Obviously a memory hierarchy for fast and economic use of memory is needed.

4. *Minimize the machine dependency of monitoring hardware.* Most systems are not designed to be monitored. To be most efficient, monitoring systems should be considered during target system design. These extra costs will be paid off with the reduction of the cost in testing and debugging. Therefore the development of architecture, compiler, and operating systems should take into account monitoring issues, making the monitoring system embedded into the target systems. However, this approach will make the monitoring extremely machine-dependent. To reduce such dependence as well as the cost, monitoring hardware should be standardized and built like a coprocessor for the target processor, which would make installing the monitoring system as simple as installing other peripheral devices to the target system. However, standardization cannot solve all of the debugging problems because increased densities of integrated circuits makes interconnection buses no longer accessible. For example, by building a processor and memory into a single chip, the memory addresses (both physical and virtual) become unavailable. The problem of inaccessible on-chip buses can be solved by fabricating a monitor inside the chip, but this increases the cost of the target processor.

2.5   Summary

Monitoring a system means collecting run-time information on a target system. Monitoring is accomplished in two operations: triggering and recording. *Triggering* is the detection of predefined events during program execution that activates recording of the data pertinent to the events. *Recording* is the collection and storage of the data pertinent to the events. The triggering and recording mechanisms for monitoring can be implemented in hardware, software, or both (resulting in a hybrid monitor). Software techniques use interrupts or embedded code for triggering. Data collection is carried out by software, and the collected data is often stored in the working memory of the monitored system. Hardware techniques passively snoop the system buses of the target system to detect a set of predefined signals, and triggering occurs on specific combinations of signals. Data recording is carried out by hardware, with the recorded data stored in a separate memory independent of the monitored system. Hybrid techniques insert code that triggers the monitoring into the target system. Data recording is carried out by hardware, while the collected data is saved in a separate memory independent of the monitored system.

A major challenge in monitoring distributed real-time systems is how to minimize the interference with the execution of the monitored systems caused by monitoring. As pointed by Plattner, monitoring interference is not acceptable when debugging a real-time system because the monitored system may not exhibit the same timing behavior as it would when it is not being monitored. Two approaches can be used to reduce the effect of this interference caused by monitoring: A monitoring hardware device can be used to reduce the interference, and perturbation analysis can be used to predict the effect of monitoring and then changes can be made to reduce the interference. Because hardware monitoring does not use any resources of the target system, there is no interference to the target system. Perturbation analysis examines event ordering and timing in an attempt to find ways to reduce the effects of monitoring interference by adjusting the event ordering and event timing.

In testing and debugging a distributed real-time system, different levels of abstraction of the execution information provide different levels of details. In this chapter we identified the events of interest at process level and function level. The events of interest at the process level are the process state transitions, communication and synchronization interactions among the software processes, and the interactions between the software processes and the external process. The events of interest at the function level are the interactions among the functions or procedures that compose processes. The user can isolate faults within processes using the process-level execution data and then can isolate faults within functions using the function-level execution data.

Monitoring can be done with software, hardware, or a combination of hardware and software. A hybrid monitor refers to a monitor that uses a combination of hardware and software. With software monitoring, the monitoring system consists solely of instrumentation code inserted into the target system using instrumentation software. The advantage of the software approach is that it is flexible and no additional hardware is required. The disadvantage is that since the monitoring system is a part of the target systems, software monitoring uses the target system's processor and memory space, thus affecting the target system's performance and possibly its behavior. With hardware monitoring, the monitoring system uses hardware to monitor the target system. A hardware device is connected to the buses of the target system to passively detect the events of interest and/or collect the data pertaining to the events. The advantage of hardware monitoring is that the monitoring system does not interfere with the execution of the target system. The disadvantages of hardware monitoring are its cost and the dependency on a specific target processor. Hybrid monitoring uses both software and hardware to perform monitoring activities. In hybrid monitoring, triggering is accomplished in software by instrumenting the target systems to trigger recording. Perturbation to the monitored system is greatly reduced by using hardware to store the collected data into a separate storage. Execution perturbation is minimal if a single instruction causes the monitoring hardware to record all necessary data.

Exercises

1. What does instrumentation mean?

2. What software problems cannot be detected at the process level?

3. Table 2.1 lists the basic process-level events for a system. Describe a situation where knowing the key values of a process' creation would be useful.

4. Table 2.2 list the function-level monitoring events. If a function alters data using a pointer instead of by passing parameters, how can that be detected?

5. Is stack overflow a process-level event or a function-level event?

6. What is program monitoring? How can program monitoring be used?

7. Program monitoring can be classified into three approaches: software monitoring, hardware monitoring, and hybrid monitoring. Describe each of the three in terms of triggering and recording conditions.

8. Describe the procedure used in software monitoring. What are the advantages and disadvantages of this approach?

9. Describe the procedure used in hardware monitoring. What are the advantages and disadvantages of this approach?

10. Describe the procedure used in hybrid monitoring. What are the advantages and disadvantages of this approach?

11. Why is it not possible to directly apply conventional monitoring techniques used for distributed systems to distributed real-time systems?

12. What are the open issues regarding monitoring real-time systems addressed by Plattner?

13. What are event ordering and event timing? How will the event ordering/timing be affected when different monitoring approaches are used?

14. Describe two approaches for reducing the interference caused by monitoring.

15. Monitoring can be performed at the process level and the function level, describe the pros and cons of performing monitoring at each level.

16. List the four problems facing the development of monitoring systems.

17. What is transparent monitoring, and why it is difficult to reach?

18. Memory space is a big concern when recording run-time information. How can the amount of memory needed during run-time information collection be reduced?

Chapter 3

Software Monitoring Systems

3.1 Introduction to Software Monitoring

To monitor software, a specified set of events are recorded during program execution in order to gain run-time information. Run-time information cannot be obtained by merely studying the program text. Software monitoring only uses software to monitor the target systems [54, 78, 104, 105, 122, 145, 183, 211, 214, 253, 260, 257, 258, 256, 259, 390, 389, 388, 387, 341, 363]. The advantages of the software approach are that it is flexible and that no additional hardware is required. The monitoring system consists solely of instrumentation code inserted into the target system. The events of interest are detected as well as recorded by using the resources of the target system, and the instrumentation code uses the computing power of the target system. As a result instrumented target systems have a performance penalty.

Execution behavior can be monitored at the system level and the program level. At the system level, information visible to the kernel is monitored. At the program level, information visible to the user processes is monitored. Information visible to the kernel includes process state transitions, external interrupts, system calls, the processor identification, and kernel-maintained data structures like process control blocks (PCBs). Information visible to the user processes includes system calls, function/procedure calls and returns, and variable value changes. Some of the information, such as system calls, is visible to both kernel and user processes, and other information, such as process state transitions, is visible only to the kernel. Finally, some information, such as function calls, is visible only to the user processes. To monitor at the system level, the kernel can be instrumented for the events of interest, while the user programs can be instrumented to monitor at the program level.

To monitor the process-level events listed in Table 2.1, the kernel needs to be instrumented to detect the events and collect event data, since the process state transitions and external interrupts listed in the table are not visible to the user processes. On the other hand, to monitor the function-level events

49

listed in Table 2.2, the user processes need to be instrumented to detect the events and collect event data, since the function calls and returns in the table are not visible to the kernel. Thus, in order to monitor at both levels, both kernel and user processes need to be instrumented. To monitor events arbitrarily specified by the user, the user program should be instrumented even if these events are visible to the kernel. Otherwise, a different kernel would be needed for each target program.

Event detection and data collection can be achieved in the following ways:

1. The target program detects the events and collects the event data (see [78]).

2. The target program detects the events, and the monitor collects the event data (see [316], [183], and [105]).

3. The kernel detects the events, and the monitor collects the event data (see [260, 257, 258, 256, 259], [390, 389, 388, 387]).

The first two methods can be employed to monitor all the program level events and some of the system-level events. The user programs are instrumented for event detection, and the kernel of the target system is not modified for monitoring. The last method can monitor all the system level events. The kernel of the target system is instrumented for event detection and the user programs are not modified. Thus, in the third method, the monitoring is transparent to the user processes. The three methods are not mutually exclusive to each other. Any combination of the three can be employed in the same system. All three methods have their advantages and disadvantages. Implementing both event detection and collection inside the target program is the easiest way to monitor the system. On the other hand, at the kernel level, the monitoring is transparent and perturbation is reduced. Transparency is easily achieved because users do not need to modify their target programs for event detection and collection. Perturbation is reduced because the context switching between the target program and the kernel is avoided. In contrast, event detection at the program level requires system calls, and this causes many context switches because system calls are implemented with exceptions.

With the first two methods, software monitoring generally consists of the following steps:

1. Instrumentation software instruments target programs to create instrumented programs.

2. The instrumented programs are executed on the target system to generate the events of interest.

3. The monitoring software detects and records the events of interest.

With the last method, software monitoring may consist of the following steps:

1. The kernel of the target system is instrumented for event detection, and a monitor is created for data collection.

2. The user programs are executed on the target system, and the kernel detects the events of interest.

3. The monitor collects the data pertaining to the events detected in the second step.

The first step for the last method may only be needed once if the instrumentation code is inserted in the target system permanently. Thus only steps 2 and 3 need to be repeated for different user programs and different executions. For distributed real-time systems, each node of the target system may need a monitor to collect the event data that occurred on that node. Thus multiple monitors may be created in the first step.

Inserting code into the target system causes an execution speed penalty as discussed earlier in this section. Removing the inserted monitoring code after monitoring can definitely restore the target system's performance. However, the target system with the monitoring code removed may present different behavior from the one with the monitoring code inserted. Thus a system that works perfectly with the monitoring code inserted may not work at all when the inserted code is removed. For example, suppose that during the development of a system, monitoring code is inserted into the kernel and that after the development stage, the inserted code for monitoring is removed from the kernel. This will alter the timing of the system, and may alter the behavior of the system. To make the system predictable, the code for monitoring should be kept in the system permanently. The trade-off is that the target system suffers some speed penalty, but the behavior does not change due to the removal of the instrumentation code.

To monitor real-time systems, each event must be recorded with the time at which the event occurred. Since there is no hardware support for monitoring, the monitoring system must rely on the target system's clock(s) to provide time stamps. Thus the instrumentation code must access the target system clock and stamp events with the clock reading. In single-processor or tightly coupled multiprocessor systems, there is only one system clock. So it is guaranteed that an event stamped with an earlier time occurred before events stamped with later times. In other words, events are totally ordered by their time stamps. However, in distributed systems, each node has its own clock which may have a different reading from the clocks on other nodes. There is no guarantee that an event with an earlier time stamp occurred before events with a later time stamp in distributed real-time systems.

The collected data may be used in either an on-line or off-line fashion. In single-processor or tightly coupled multiple processor systems, it makes no difference to the monitoring system which way the collected data is used. The monitoring system collects event data and stores them in either the memory or on the hard disks of the monitored system. It is only important to know whether or not the stored data is accessed in real time. However, in distributed systems, the collected data need to be transferred to other nodes so that the systemwide or global states can be constructed. If the collected data is used in an off-line manner, the monitor on each target node collects data pertaining to the events on that node, and it can send the necessary data to other nodes while the target node and the network are not busy. If the collected data is used in an on-line manner, they have to be transferred in a real-time manner so that the current systemwide state can be constructed in real time. Furthermore, since the monitoring system uses the same network as the target system (HMON is an exception), it is desirable to minimize the amount of data to be passed between nodes to reduce the interference to the network caused by monitoring.

Because the monitoring system is part of the target system, software monitoring uses the target system's processor and memory space, so the target system's performance and possibly its behavior will be affected. Without the use of a hardware monitor, the dilemma of finding a balance between perturbation and recording sufficient knowledge for the execution behavior always exists. Limiting instrumentation may provide inadequate measurement detail, but excessive instrumentation may perturb the measured system to an unacceptable degree. Fortunately there are techniques for reducing the perturbation while retaining sufficient information. In addition to the method mentioned earlier by Malony, Reed, and Wijshoff [240], perturbation can be reduced by altering the instrumentation mechanism and modifying the monitored target programs or the underlying operating systems. Then the instrumented event trace can be adjusted to reduce the effect of perturbation. In general, the problem facing the software monitoring approach is how to control and predict the levels of intrusion (perturbation) and how to automate software instrumentation [119].

In the following sections we will discuss software monitoring at both the system level and the program level. We will introduce systems in which user programs are instrumented for monitoring program-level events, and systems in which the kernel of the target system is instrumented for monitoring system-level events. Then we will describe perturbation analysis for reducing the effect of interference due to monitoring code.

3.2   Monitoring at the Program Level

Monitoring at the program level is used to detect events visible to the user processes and to collect the data pertaining to these events. Events that can be detected at the program level are limited because events such as process state transitions are not visible to the user processes. To monitor at the program level, the user programs are instrumented to detect the events of interest. The event data can be collected by user processes [78] or by the monitor [316, 183, 105]. In this section we will discuss the four monitoring systems proposed in the four references.

We first introduce a monitoring system proposed by Chodrow, Jahanian, and Donner that monitors and verifies timing properties of the target system in real time. In this system the user processes are instrumented to detect user-specified events and record the event data into a repository. The user processes then access the repository for execution history and verify the timing constraints of the target system. This monitoring system is extended to monitoring distributed real-time systems by Raju, Rajkumar, and Jahanian. We then describe the monitoring system proposed by Joyce, Lomow, Slind, and Ungar for a distributed programming environment called Jade. Finally, we describe the monitoring system (HMON) proposed by Dodd and Ravishankar for monitoring the hexagonal architecture for real-time systems (HARTS).

3.2.1   Chodrow, Jahanian, and Donner's Monitor

Chodrow, Jahanian, and Donner [78] propose a run-time monitor for monitoring and verification of real-time systems. A prototype has been implemented on IBM RS/6000 workstations running AIXv.3. In their approach an event is defined as an activity of interest occurring in a system, and the computation of a real-time system as a sequence of events. An occurrence of an event is the point in time at which an instance of the event occurs. The timing constraints of the target system can be expressed as the relationship between these events. The timing constraints are classified as embedded or monitored constraints and are monitored synchronously and asynchronously, respectively. The synchronous monitoring is similar to a breakpoint model; a constraint is embedded into the monitored real-time tasks and examined at a particular point in time during the computation of the tasks. In the case of asynchronous monitoring, a constraint is specified and monitored by a separate monitoring task rather than by the monitored real-time tasks.

Events to be monitored are classified into *label events* and *transition events*. Label events denote the initiation and completion of a sequence of program statements. The programmer can insert a start label right before the statement sequence and a stop label right after the last statement of the sequence. Transition events are used to denote value changes of a watchable variable. An assignment to a watchable variable represents a potential change in a system state. The computation of a program can be modeled as a sequence of label and transition events.

Fig. 3.1 shows the architecture of this monitoring system. Application processes denoted as filled circles are annotated with the events of interest. The left half of the figure represents the architecture for monitoring the embedded constraints, while the right half represents the architecture for monitoring the monitored constraints. For embedded constraints, which can be checked

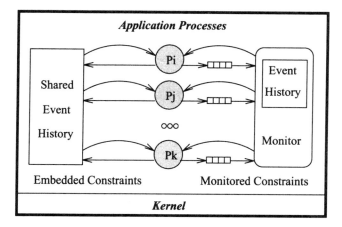

Fig. 3.1 Architecture of Chodrow, Jahanian, and Donner's monitor. (Reprinted, by permission, from [78]. ©1991 IEEE.)

by the application processes during their execution, the application processes record events in the shared event history repository (which is denoted as a rectangle in the figure), and they verify their embedded constraints by retrieving the history. Since all the processes share the event history, they are synchronized for mutually exclusive writes. A programmer can insert an embedded constraint at any appropriate place in the program and can also program the actions to be taken. Thus the checking of constraints and the corresponding programmed actions are part of the application processes.

For monitored constraints, which may need to be enforced continuously, the monitor process (denoted as a round-cornered rectangle in Fig. 3.1) is employed to collect events from the application processes, and it provides asynchronous monitoring of the constraints. A queue is used for the interprocess communication between each application process and the monitor. The monitor saves the received events into its own independent local event history repository. During execution each application process sends events to the monitor and requests to initiate or cancel the monitoring of the monitored constraints. If a constraint is violated, the process is notified by the monitor with a software signal that can activate a programmer specified action.

Both the shared and local event history repositories in the monitor have a finite length. To effectively monitor the target system, the storage is preallocated. All the monitored constraints are specified in a file and are parsed during compilation. After parsing, constraints are associated with events and the maximum number of occurrences of each event type is determined. Thus, at the beginning of the execution of the program, the necessary memory for the event history repositories can be allocated.

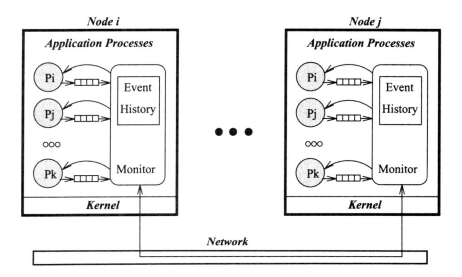

Fig. 3.2 Architecture of Raju, Rajkumar, and Jahanian's monitor.

3.2.2   Raju, Rajkumar, and Jahanian's Monitor

The monitoring architecture described in the previous section was extended to distributed real-time systems by Raju, Rajkumar, and Jahanian [316]. In this architecture each application process is annotated with the events of interest. Each node of the target system has a monitor similar to the one described above. It collects occurrences of events from the application processes on the node it resides. Instead of using application processes to check the embedded constraints, the monitor checks the embedded constraints as well as the monitored constraints. The advantages of employing a separate process to monitor both types of system constraints are twofold. First, the constraints can be treated in a uniform fashion by the programmer. That is, the programmer only needs to insert event labels into appropriate places and provide one routine to handle both types of constraint violations. Second, the specification of constraints can be independent of the program so that the programmer does not need to know how to specify and verify the timing constraints.

Timing constraints in distributed real-time systems can be divided into intramachine constraints and intermachine constraints. Intramachine timing constraints are those that can be verified by using the occurrences of events on a single node, while intermachine timing constraints need the occurrences of events from more than one node to be verified. To verify an intermachine constraint, the occurrences of events related to it need to be sent to the node where the constraint will be verified. They must be sent in a real-time manner so that the constraint is verified and the process responsible for the constraint is notified early enough to take any necessary action. Furthermore since the network of the target system is used for this communication, the size of the messages passed between target nodes must be minimized to reduce interference to the network.

Fig. 3.2 shows the architecture of the extended monitoring system. The user processes denoted as filled circles are annotated with the events of interest. The monitor on each node of the target system records events detected by the user processes into its local event history repository. A user process sends events to a queue that is shared by the process and the monitor. The monitor also receives events from the monitors on other nodes and sends local events to other monitors for intermachine constraints. The monitor on each node verifies the intramachine and intermachine timing constraints assigned to it and notifies the responsible process if a violation is detected.

3.2.3   Joyce, Lomow, Slind, and Ungar's Monitor

Joyce, Lomow, Slind, and Unger [183] propose a distributed monitoring system to detect and collect information on the concurrent execution of interacting processes. This monitoring system instruments the user processes to detect the events of interest and employs monitors to collect the event data. The user can decide whether or not a process is to be monitored by compiling the program with different versions of system library routines. The events monitored in this system are any process operations that may have a direct effect on other processes. The monitoring system is a part of a distributed programming environment called Jade which was developed at the University of Calgary. Before describing the monitoring system, we will introduce the operating system on which it is built.

Jade is a distributed programming environment that provides a message-passing interprocess communication (IPC) facility called Jipc (pronounced "gypsy"). A Jade system consists of a set of processes that communicate with each other using the Jipc message-passing facility. Jipc employs a synchronous IPC protocol. That is, a sending process transmits a message to a receiver and waits for an acknowledgment from the receiver. A receiver can directly reply to the sender of a message or forward the message to another process, which then may reply to the sender. The monitoring system is built upon the Jipc IPC facility. The monitored processes send event data to the monitor using Jipc in the same way application processes communicate with each other using Jipc.

The monitoring system is designed to monitor process events visible from outside of the process. In other words, it monitors any Jipc operations that have a direct effect on other processes. Such an event occurs whenever a process initiates the following operations: entering or leaving the system, creating or killing a process, searching for another process's ID, and message sends, forwards, receives, and replies. Except for state transition events, these events closely match the process-level events listed in Table 2.2.1. Computations internal to a process, such as changing the content of a variable or manipulating an internal data structure, are not treated as events in this system.

The architecture of the monitoring system is shown in Fig. 3.3. Application processes are classified as monitorable and unmonitorable. A process to be monitored is compiled with a version of Jipc that is instrumented for monitoring. While a monitorable process is executed, it sends events to an event collector called a channel. The channel is used to collect event data generated by the machine it resides on. Each machine has only one channel that collects all the events sent by monitorable processes. Monitorable processes are represented as filled circles and unmonitorable processes as empty circles in Fig. 3.3. A channel may send the collected event data to consoles to display different aspects of the execution behavior or forward the data to a controller. A console is a process that collects, interprets, and displays event information and serves as the interface between the user and the monitoring system. A controller is a central processing process. It collects event data from all the channels and then distributes them to consoles for display.

Event detection is embedded in the monitorable version of the Jipc library. A process can be compiled with either the monitorable version of the library or the unmonitorable version. When a process is compiled with the monitorable version, it will detect events of interest and send them to a channel.

Both the monitor and the target system in Jipc employ synchronous message-passing communication. With synchronous communication, after sending a message, a process is blocked until it receives a reply. To be able to monitor the system with synchronous communication, the monitorable version of Jipc is designed so that the event reported to a channel will not occur until a reply is received from the channel. Thus a channel can prevent the application process from generating that event. The channel could forward to the controller the event data and the responsibility of replying. The controller can then delay replying and thereby control the sequence of events. A system can have only one controller. A controller can be started or terminated at any time. But once a controller is started, all the channels must forward the collected event data to the controller, and the controller distributes them to consoles.

As mentioned in the previous paragraph, the controller can postpone replying to a monitorable process and then control the occurrence of events. The controller provides an interface that allows the user to determine when to reply and thus to control the execution of the monitored processes. That is, at a given time there will be a set of pending events waiting for replies from the controller; the user can direct the controller to release a pending event or to continue receiving event information from other monitored processes. Once a pending event is released, the controller distributes the event to consoles, and the blocked process continues. With the controller the user

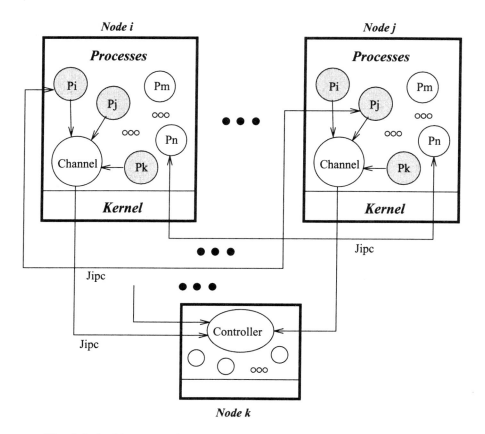

Fig. 3.3 Architecture of Joyce, Lomow, Slind, and Ungar's monitor.

is able to produce any sequence of events that the processes generate.

This controller together with a console can also be used to repeat the execution of a target program. The console records all the events that occur in the program, and the user commands that can affect the program's execution. After the program finishes its execution, the controller can repeat the execution of the program by forcing the program to exercise the same event sequence as recorded by the console. It does this by holding every pending event until it matches the next event in the recorded sequence. At all times the controller knows what event should occur next and ensures that the execution repeats the original history.

Because processes may be suspended, there can be times when the system must manage a large number of pending events. When a process for a pending event is blocked, it cannot generate another event until its current pending event is released. Therefore the maximum number of pending events is equal to the number of processes being monitored.

With the current design of this monitoring system, state transition events cannot be monitored because an application process cannot detect its own state change. To collect those events, the kernel must be instrumented to send state transition events to the channel on that machine. In addition the function-level events cannot be monitored with the current design. To monitor at the function level, the monitored processes must be able to be instrumented to send function calls and returns to the channels.

3.2.4 Dodd and Ravishankar's HMON for HARTS

To make the software monitoring applicable to DRTSs, the perturbation must be predictable and controllable. Dodd and Ravishankar [183] propose a software-support monitoring system (HMON) for monitoring the hexagonal architecture for real-time systems (HARTS) [349]. In HMON the target programs and the kernels are instrumented to detect events of interest, and monitors are employed to collect the event data. Without adding any special hardware, HMON is able to provide consistent monitoring and deterministic replay by predicting the overhead caused by monitoring. HMON assumes that because the monitoring code is part of the target system, it is predictable.

Before we describe the design of HMON, let us consider the HARTS system, since the design of the monitor is closely dependent on the hardware architecture of HARTS. HARTS is an experimental distributed system developed in the Real-Time Computing Laboratory at the University of Michigan. The nodes of the HARTS are connected via a hexagonal mesh interconnection network. Each node is a tightly coupled multiprocessor system and is directly connected to six neighbors. The nodes have up to three application processors, a network processor, an Ethernet processor, and a system controller, as shown in Fig. 3.4. The application processors run the HARTOS distributed operating system which is built on the pSOS uniprocessor real-

Node i

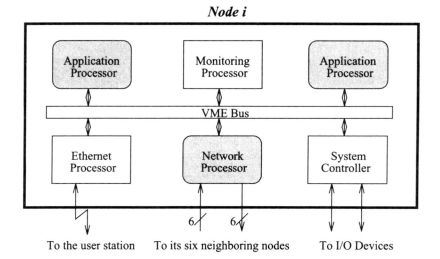

Fig. 3.4 Structure of a HARTS node. (Reprinted, by permission, from P. S. Dodd and C. V. Ravishankar, Monitoring and debugging distributed real-time programs, *Software-Practice and Experience*, 22(10):863-877, October 1992. Copyright ©1992 by John Wiley & Sons, Inc.)

time kernel. Synchronous signals and messages are used by the processes to communicate.

The HMON monitor has a monitor processor (MP) on each node and a workstation external to the HARTS for data logging. The monitor processor is an application processor dedicated to monitoring on each node. In this system the data of interest is first extracted from the application processors and the network processor, then the data is compressed on the monitoring processor, and finally the data is logged on the external workstation. The application processors and the network processor are instrumented to detect events and extract event data. The two application processors and network processor are represented as filled round-cornered squares to emphasize the instrumentation. Data extraction code on each application processor writes event data directly to the monitor processor's memory over the system bus in the node. The monitor processor periodically polls the application processor buffers to retrieve the data. The collected data is sent to an external user workstation for processing. Before sending the data, the monitor processor compresses the data to reduce overhead and transmission time. The monitor processors use the Ethernet controller on each node to send data to the user workstation in order to minimize the interference to the real-time hexagonal mesh network. Fig. 3.5 illustrates the architecture of HMON. Circles representing application processes are filled to emphasize that the processes are instrumented with monitoring code. Round-cornered rectangles are the application pro-

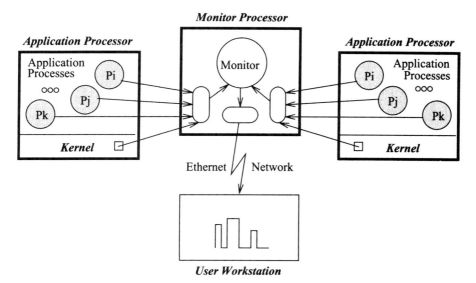

Fig. 3.5 Architecture of HMON. (Reprinted, by permission, from P. S. Dodd and C. V. Ravishankar, Monitoring and debugging distributed real-time programs, *Software-Practice and Experience*, 22(10):863-877, October 1992. Copyright ©1992 by John Wiley & Sons, Inc.)

cessor buffers and a buffer for the Ethernet controller. The user workstation is drawn with thin lines to emphasize that it is not part of HARTS.

The classes of events monitored are pSOS and HARTOS system calls, context switches, interrupts, shared variable references, and application-specific events. The system calls include interprocess communication calls such as sending and receiving messages, process management calls such as creating and killing processes, and time management calls such as setting and reading the clock. To monitor system calls, the existing system call libraries are instrumented with monitoring code. The calling process's ID and the call parameters are collected by the monitoring code. To monitor context switches, a hook provided by the pSOS kernel is used to log the process IDs involved. To monitor application-specific events, a monitoring procedure is provided. The user can insert it into processes as appropriate.

To monitor interrupts, interrupt handlers with monitoring code are used to record where each interrupt occurred in the execution of a process. To reproduce an interrupt at the exact "time" at which the interrupt occurred, an instruction counter counts the number of machine instructions that have been executed before the interrupt handler is invoked. The value of the instruction counter and the value of the program counter together define a unique state in a process execution. To replay an interrupt, the interrupt handler can be invoked at the state defined by the two values. Since commercial processors do not have hardware instruction counters, a software instruction counter is implemented. It counts backward branches, traps, and subroutine calls. The implementation of this software instruction counter can be found in [253].

Since the HARTOS does not support shared variables, two library routines for read and write are provided to coordinate access to shared variables. Monitoring code is inserted into these routines to collect sufficient information so that the read/write operations can be deterministically replayed. Read operations do not need to be replayed in the exact order in which they occurred, as long as each of read is replayed between the appropriate write operations. Thus only write operations need to be logged.

Each shared variable is associated with a set of access counters, one for each process that accesses the variable. Each counter counts the number of accesses (read and write) by the corresponding process. When a read operation is performed, the corresponding counter is incremented. When a write operation is requested, all of the variable's access counter values are recorded in the monitor log before the writing process's access counter is incremented and the write operation is performed. During a replay a process can only read if all preceding write operations have been replayed. This is guaranteed by comparing the value of the access counter with the value recorded in the next logged write event of the monitor log. If the counter is less then the recorded value, then the read proceeds; if they are equal, a pending write must take place before the access counter changes, so the process should wait. During replay a process is prevented from writing until all preceding read and write operations have taken place by comparing the values of counters with the recorded value.

3.3   Monitoring at the System Level

The purpose of monitoring at the system level is to detect events visible to the kernel of the target system and to collect the data pertaining to these events. Events that can be detected at the system level are limited because events such as function calls and returns are not visible to the kernel. To monitor at the system level, the kernel is instrumented to detect the events of interest. In this section we will describe two systems that monitor at the system level. We first introduce the monitoring system proposed by Miller, Macrander, and Sechrest for monitoring and analyzing the execution performance of distributed systems running in Berkeley UNIX. A routine is inserted into the kernel of each node of the target system to detect the events of interest. The process control block of each user process is also modified for monitoring. We then introduce a real-time monitor proposed by Tokuda, Kotera, and Mercer featuring the visualization of the internal behavior of a distributed real-time operating system, ARTS, at different levels of abstraction.

3.3.1 Miller, Macrander, and Sechrest's Monitor

Miller, Macrander, and Sechrest [260] propose a measurement tool to monitor and analyze the execution performance of distributed programs running in Berkeley UNIX 4.2BSD. A model of distributed computation and measurement is used to describe the activities of processes in terms of their internal events (computation) and external events (communication). Based on this model, a monitor and a measurement tool are constructed by changing the kernel-level structures of Berkeley UNIX and adding some daemon processes to allow the monitoring activity to take place across machine boundaries. Events are detected by a meter, which is a low-level software routine residing inside each kernel. The data pertaining to an event is extracted from the data structure of the operating system. Implementing the meter inside the kernel can avoid context switching and thus reduce the degree of perturbation caused by monitoring.

The measurement is carried out in three stages: metering, filtering, and analysis. Metering extracts event data at the process level from the operating system. The extracted data is sent to the filtering stage. Filtering selectively reduces the amount of data. The filtered data is sent to an analyzer which extracts information from the recorded data. Metering is implemented in the kernel by examining the system calls made by the monitored processes and generating event messages that trigger the filter. The messages are sent through the communication path provided for each monitored process.

The measurement system consists of four parts: the meters, the filter processes, a control process, and analysis routines. Each node has a meter in its kernel. The meter detects events and extracts the event data from the operating system's data structures; then the event data is sent to a filter process. The filter process selects and reduces the received event data. The meter detects IPC events by intercepting system calls made by the monitored processes. When an event is detected, the meter extracts the event data from the data structure in the kernel. The meter can send the extracted data immediately to the filter or store them in a buffer and send all of the data in the buffer when the buffer is full. The former has a higher overhead than the latter. However, if the collected data is used for the on-line analysis, then only the former is acceptable because the data may be stored in the buffer for a long time before the buffer is filled.

A monitored process can only be connected to one filter at a time. The owner of the monitored process or the superuser may change a process's filter. A filter process may serve several monitored processes, and it can be located in a machine different from that of the monitored processes. A monitored process is connected to a filter through a socket called a *meter socket* as shown in Fig. 3.6. Sockets are an interprocess communication facility provided by Berkeley UNIX. Meter sockets are only used to transfer event data between monitored processes and their filters. This connection is set up by the control

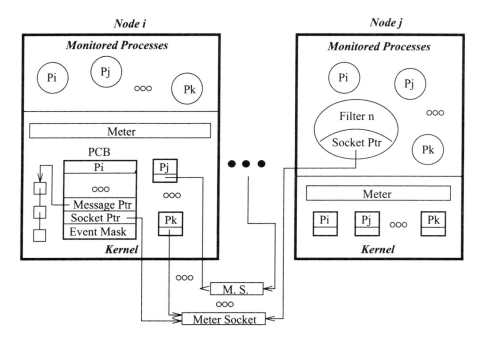

Fig. 3.6 Architecture of Miller, Macrander, and Sechrest's monitor. (Reprinted, by permission, from B. P. Miller, C. Macrander, and S. Sechrest, A distributed programs monitor for Berkeley UNIX, *Software-Practice and Experience*, 16(2):183-200, February 1986. Copyright ©1986 by John Wiley & Sons, Inc.)

process upon the user's request. It is built as a pointer to the socket into the process control block (PCB) that is maintained by the kernel. It is transparent to the monitored process, and the monitored process cannot read from or write to it. This connection is used by the meter to find which filter the event data should be sent to. The other two entries added to the PCB are a pointer to the event data buffer and an event mask. The event mask is used by the meter to determine what events are to be monitored. Both the meter socket and the event mask can be changed by the user and the superuser.

A filter process selects, reduces, and stores the event records received from meters. It uses event record descriptions and selection rules to specify the criteria for data collection and reduction. The event record descriptions specify the event record formats sent by meters. Each event record consists of a header and event data. The header is common to all the event records. It specifies the event type, the size of the event record in bytes, the machine ID that generated the event, the time at which the event was detected, the process ID that caused the event, and the program counter where the event occurred. The event data is unique for each event type. For example, the send event has a socket ID, a message size, and a destination. These descriptions are saved in a file and are used in the communication between meters and filters.

The selection rules are used by a filter to select and edit the event records received from the meters. They can be specified by the user or superuser based on the objective of the monitoring. For example, a selection rule to detect any event sent by machine 5 and time stamped with a time before 100 ms can be specified as

$$machine = 5, \; time < 100$$

A selection rule to detect any send event with a socket value of 4 and a destination of 200 can be specified as

$$socket = 4, \; destname = 200$$

The user can specify which fields will be saved for each event type to reduce the size of the event records.

The filter also uses a history file or log file. The filter writes the filtered event records into its log file. This file is located in a temporary directory. Event records are sent to the filter directly, and the logged records are not seen by the user until the monitoring is finished. The user can retrieve and analyze the logged event records from the log file produced by the filter. This configuration can only be used for off-line analysis because the user cannot observe the execution behavior until the execution is completed. The results can be analyzed in an on-line manner by programming the filter to send the logged event records to an analyzer instead of a file. The analyzer processes the records and displays the analysis results in an on-line manner.

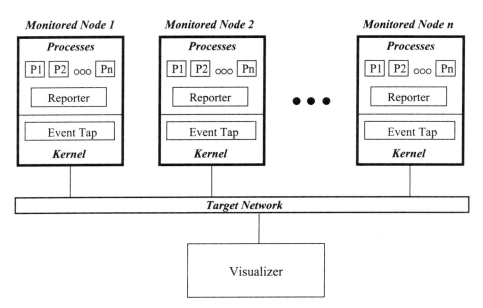

Fig. 3.7 Architecture of Tokuda, Kotera, and Mercer's monitor. (Reprinted, by permission, from H. Tokuda, M. Kotera, and C. W. Mercer, A real-time monitor for a real-time operating system, *Proc. of ACM Workshop on Parallel and Distributed Debugging*, Madison, WI, pp. 68-77, May 1988. ©1988 Association of Computing Machinery, Inc.)

3.3.2   Tokuda, Kotera, and Mercer's Monitor

Tokuda, Kotera, and Mercer [390] propose a real-time monitor featuring the visualization of the internal behavior of a distributed real-time operating system, ARTS, at different levels of abstraction. To predict and reduce the monitoring interference, the monitor is designed as a permanent part of the target system so that target program's scheduler must consider the overhead of monitoring. In this monitor the kernel of the target system detects the events, and the monitor collects the event data.

As shown in Fig. 3.7, the monitor consists of three functional units: the event tap, the reporter, and the visualizer. The event tap is a software module embedded inside the operating system kernel for event detection and event collection. An event is detected when the event causes a state change. For example, a wake-up event causes the process state to change from waiting to ready. Event collection follows event detection so that the detected event and its related timing information can be stored inside the target memory. The reporter sends the event message from the target system to the visualizer which is located on a remote host. The visualizer utilizes the event messages sent by the reporter and displays the events in an execution history diagram.

To avoid behavior changes in the target system after the removal of the monitoring mechanism, the monitoring mechanism is built into the target system in such a way that each periodic monitoring activity is taken into account for the schedulability analysis. The time critical tasks and the monitoring processes are verified together for schedulability. System monitoring activities are built as a permanent part of the target system. If the monitor were removed from the target system after development, the behavior of the target system might change.

The event tap is a software module that enables the kernel to capture the events of interest at the process level. The events monitored include process creating, waking up, blocking, scheduling, freezing, unfreezing, killing with completion, killing with missed deadline, and killing with frame overrun. The event tap is permanently built into the kernel of each target node. The event tap collects these events and related timing information and stores them in the event message buffer inside of the kernel. The event tap is transparent to users.

The reporter is a periodic process built into the target host. It periodically reports events to the visualizer. The reporter invokes a kernel primitive to package the events into an event message and sends the message over the network to the visualizer. Since the reporter process is added into the task set of the target system, the interference by the reporter can be taken account into the schedulability analysis.

The visualizer is located on a remote host. It utilizes the event messages sent by the Reporter and displays the events in an execution history diagram. Since the visualizer needs many system resources in terms of time and memory space, it is separated from the target system to reduce perturbation. Since the visualizer communicates with reporters through target system network, perturbation exists in the target network. During system design this interference should be taken into account.

3.4   Perturbation Analysis

Software instrumentation for monitoring perturbs the execution of the target system. If the instrumentation code is inserted during monitoring and removed after the monitoring is done, we want to discover the "true" execution behavior by predicting and removing the perturbations caused by monitoring. A technique for perturbation analysis is presented by Malony et al. [246, 235, 237, 239, 236, 240]. Perturbation analysis examines event ordering and timing in an attempt to find ways to reduce the effects of monitoring interference by adjusting the event ordering and event timing [240, 119]. They provided two perturbation analysis models. The first model predicts the "true" total execution time of a program from a given collected event trace by removing the effect of instrumentation. The second model adjusts each individual event to its "true" time by removing the effect of the instrumentation before the event occurred.

Both models can be applied to sequential and concurrent programs. The accuracy of the two models depends on the interaction between the instrumentation code and the program code. It was assumed that the execution of instrumentation can be decoupled from the execution of the program and that indirect perturbations such as register dependencies can be neglected. They have shown that with the proper perturbation model and analysis, perturbations to the execution time can be reduced to less than 20% of the total execution time according to their experimental study conducted on an Alliant FX/80 vector multiprocessor operating in sequential, parallel, and vector modes.

3.5   Summary

Software monitoring detects events and collects event data by instrumenting the target system. The monitoring can be performed at the system and program level. At the system level, events and event data visible to the kernel are monitored, while events and event data visible to the user processes are monitored at the program level. Monitoring at the system level can make instrumentation transparent to the user, since the user programs do not need to be instrumented. Monitoring at the program level makes instrumentation easier. At either of the two levels, only certain kinds of events and information can be detected and collected. For example, process state transition events cannot be monitored at the program level because they are not visible to the user processes, and function calls and returns and variable value changes cannot be monitored at the system level because they are not visible to the kernel.

Software monitoring perturbs the execution of the target system because monitoring code is inserted into the target system. Removing the monitoring code may cause different execution behavior from the instrumented code. Thus, if the instrumentation is only used during system development, the system may not be correct after the instrumentation is removed. To avoid this problem, the instrumentation should not be removed. The speed penalty can be compensated for by using faster hardware. This is especially true for hard real-time systems where guaranteeing system correctness is the highest priority.

Fortunately, to avoid behavior changes and still be able to test and debug at all levels of detail, only instrumentation for process-level information needs to be kept permanently; instrumentation for other levels can be removed after the monitoring is completed. This is because the non-deterministic behavior only arises at the process level. A sequential process that contains no nondeterministic constructs such as random select structures will present the same behavior with the same input in different executions. Thus one can use the collected process level information to localize faults to processes, and then for each individual faulty process, one can isolate it from other processes by giving it the same input and monitor the process at any level of detail. The timing of a individual process can be determined by computing the execution time of the instructions that were executed. To find the executed instructions, the process can be instrumented to count the number of cycles of loops and the path of execution.

Monitoring single processor and tightly coupled multiprocessor systems is much simpler than monitoring distributed systems. Since there is no hardware support in software monitoring, the clock(s) of the target system is used to time stamp events. In single processor and tightly coupled multiprocessor systems, there is only one clock and it can be used to time stamp events in a nondecreasing order. That is, it guarantees that an event stamped with an earlier time really happened before the events with a later time. In contrast, in distributed systems, there is one clock on each target node. An event with an earlier time stamp may not have occurred before events with a later time stamp. To deal with this problem, Raju et al. [316] implemented an algorithm to synchronize all the clocks in the system.

In distributed systems, to examine the behavior of the whole system, global states need to constructed. This implies that the collected events from individual nodes have to be sent to a central location in order to build the global states. If the global states are constructed off-line, the monitor on each target node can send the collected data when the network and the node are not busy. If they are constructed on-line, then each node must send the collected data for its local events to a central location in real-time. For example, the monitor proposed by Raju et al. verifies timing constraints at run-time and notifies the responsible process if a constraint is violated. For intermachine timing constraints, the data must be transmitted in real-time; that is, the responsible process can be notified quickly so that it can respond to the violation. Since the data transmission uses the target system's network, the data passed should be minimized to reduce the interference with the network.

Instrumentation code for monitoring can be kept permanently or temporarily in the target system. If it is kept permanently, the overhead due to the execution of the code must be considered during the system design and system scheduling. If it is only inserted temporarily, for instance, during system development, then we need to predict the "true" execution behavior when the system is in operation after the instrumentation code is removed. Malony et al. proposed two perturbation analysis models to remove the direct perturbations caused by the execution of the inserted instrumentation code. The accuracy of the models depends on the interactions between the instrumentation code and the program code. It was assumed that the execution of the instrumentation code does not cause any indirect perturbations such as different register reference and cache reference patterns.

Exercises

1. Write a program that has a semaphore and two processes.

   a. Process A waits until the semaphore is 0; then it updates its counter
   by 1 and sets the semaphore equal to 1. Finally, it returns a RE-
   TURN_OK value. When its counter reaches 5, it returns a RET_DONE
   value and quits.

```
processA() {
        static countA = 0;
        while ( semaphore != 0 ); // NOP wait loop
        semaphore = 1; // set global variable semaphore
        countA++; // increment counter A
        int return_value = RETURN_OK;
        if ( countA == 5 ) return_value = RET_DONE;
        return return_value;
}
```

   b. Process B waits until S is 1; then it updates its counter by 1 and
   sets the semaphore equal to 0. When it reaches 5, it stops.

```
processB() {
        static countB = 0;
        while ( semaphore != 1 ); // NOP wait loop
        semaphore = 0; // set global variable semaphore
        countB++; // increment counter B
        int return_value = RETURN_OK;
        if ( countB == 5 ) return_value = RET_DONE;
        return return_value;
}
```

   To write this program, you will need to write a simple monitor that
   controls the execution of both processes. Here is an example of how the
   monitor could be implemented:

```
monitor() {
        state processA_state = RETURN_OK;
        state processB_state = RETURN_OK;
        while (processA_state == RETURN_OK
                && processB_state == RETURN_OK) {
```

```
                    if (processA_state == RETURN_OK)
                        processA_state = processA();
                    if (processB_state == RETURN_OK)
                        processB_state = processB();

            }
    }
```

c. Write the program above in your favorite language and execute it. Does it complete? If the semaphore begins in an uninitialized state, will the program complete? Change the program so that processB() counts to 6 before returning RET_DONE. Can this program complete?

2. a. Write a simple program to simulate finding the sum of an array on a parallel processor with 4 processors. Each processor is given an identical program but is passed a different processor identification number and a different set of data.

```
// Assume that if the size of the array divided by the number of
// processors has a remainder, that the size of the array will be
// increased by adding zeros so that the there is no remainder.
int local_array_size = array_size / num_processors;


int sum_program( int processor_id, int local_array_size,
        int data[local_array_size] ) {
    int sum = 0;
    for ( int i = 0; i < local_array_size; i++ ) {
        sum += data[i];
    }
    return sum;
}
```

The parallel processor has a front-end which controls each processor.

```
int sum_program_for_front_end() {
    // loop to start the programs
    for ( int i = 0; i < number_of_processors; i++ ) {
        start sum_program( i, local_array_size,
            &data[i*local_array_size] );
    }
    // loop to receive the result from each processor
    int sum = 0;
```

```
for ( int i = 0; i < number_of_processors; i++ ) {
    sum += sum_program( i );
}
}
```

It is assumed that the front_end has a mechanism to receive the return values from the different processors. For our purposes there would be only one loop.

b. Modify the above programs to implement the return mechanism so that the programs can be sent data and later be asked to send the result back.

3. Modify the above programs so that after each program sends its result, a new array is formed and sent to processor 0 which will sum the sums sent by the processors.

4. a. Model a simple parallel processor program that simulates message passing and processing. Each message consists of a command and an array of data. The array is of type int and can be of variable length. In addition the message has an address, which can be given to all processors or a specific processor. All messages are broadcast to all processors, so that processors will look at the address of a message to see if they should read the message.

```
processor_program( int processor_id ) {
    while (1) { // infinite loop
    // look for message
    if ( get_message( &message ) == MESSAGE_RECEIVED )
        // see if message is addressed to you
        if ( message − > processor_id == processor_id ——
            message − > processor_id == ALL )
            // process message if it is addressed to you
            switch ( message->command ) {
            case ADD : add( message − > data );
                break;
            case SUBTRACT : subtract( message->data );
                break;
            }
}
```

A send function is available.

b. Using the above program as a model, write a program to sum an array. Assume that there is no front-end machine. Instead, processor 0 acts as the front end.

5. Write a similar type of simulator; this time assume shared memory. Implement the sum of array program.

6. You now have models of a shared memory machine and a parallel processor. How can you debug programs on these models? What events are of interest in your monitoring?

7. a. In this exercise you will write a small instrumentation program. A certain programming language uses the following functions for interprocess communication:

send(Message message);

receive(Message message);

Write a preprocessing routine for a compiler in the language of your choice that causes the send and receive functions to take the key data, and write it to a file.

Where

```
class Message {
        int sending_process_id;
        int node_id;
        int send_call_time;
        int receive_ack_time;
        int receive_process_id;
        int receive_node_id;
        int receive_call_time;
        int receive_message_time;
        char* message;
}
```

b. Estimate how many clock cycles the above program requires. State your assumptions.

8. Assume that the send/receive commands require 15% of a program's execution time. Assume that adding instrumentation code in the target program to the send/receive commands increases the time required to execute a send or receive by 20%. How much longer will the program require to execute? What additional assumptions are required to answer this question?

9. Compare using the kernel to using the target program to collect data. Assume that both require the same steps to save data. Why would one be better than the other?

Chapter 4

Hardware Monitoring

4.1 Introduction to Hardware Monitoring

Hardware monitoring only uses hardware to monitor the target systems [23, 50, 66, 226, 230, 308, 397]. The primary advantage of hardware monitoring is that the interference with the execution of the target system caused by monitoring is minimized. A hardware monitoring system generally consists of the monitoring hardware and its control module, and it is separate from the target system. The execution of the target programs is monitored directly via the monitoring hardware connected to the system buses without any instrumentation code embedded in the target system. The passive monitoring devices controlled by the monitoring control module will record every signal passing through the buses for later processing. The procedure to implement a hardware monitor is as follows:

1. Connect the hardware monitoring devices to the target systems.

2. Start the monitoring control module software and the target program.

3. Detect and process the events of interest with the monitoring hardware.

The monitoring systems and target systems do not share any computational resources. Consequently the hardware monitoring approach causes no or minimum monitoring intrusion on the execution of the target system and is the most suitable approach for systems with stringent time constraints. The disadvantage of hardware monitoring is its cost and that it is usually machine dependent or at least processor dependent. This is because the monitoring system must be able to interpret the electronic signals on the buses of the system to detect the events of interest and collect the data pertaining to the events. The snooping device and the interpretation are target bus structure and target processor dependent. With a different bus structure or a different processor, the snooping device and the interpretation mechanism need to be modified.

In general, hardware monitoring is used to monitor the run-time behavior of either hardware devices or software modules. Hardware devices are generally monitored to examine issues such as the cache accesses, cache misses, memory access time, total CPU time, total execution time, I/O requests, I/O grants, and I/O busy time. Software modules are generally monitored to debug them or to examine issues such as the bottlenecks of a program, the deadlocks, and the degree of parallelism. Although it may seem that these two uses of monitoring are different, Brantley, McAuliffe, and Ngo [50] have pointed out that the results of hardware performance measurement can be used for software performance analysis and debugging. For example, bottlenecks may be caused by frequent references to the same memory location.

The steps in hardware monitoring are three:

1. Detect the events of interest by snooping the signals on the address, data, and control buses.

2. Match the events by comparing the signals with predefined signals of interest such as *read, write, interrupt,* or *wait* signals or specific memory addresses, or instructions.

3. Collect the event data by saving the signals pertaining to the detected event.

4.2   Monitoring Single-Processor Architectures

In a single-processor system, a processor is connected to memory and I/O devices via a single set of system buses: address, data, and control buses. The system state is determined by interpreting the signals on the system buses of the target processor. Single-processor real-time systems can be monitored by using a hardware device to monitor the transactions between the target processor and the target memory. These transactions may be either saved for postprocessing or used to update a memory that mirrors the contents of the memory of the target system in real time. In the former approach, a program detects the events of interest and collects the data pertaining to the events. In the latter, a monitor process is used to access the data pertaining to the events of interest. The former approach is employed in Tsai, Fang, and Chen's system, and the latter is employed in Plattner's system. In this section we first elaborate on the two approaches with two monitoring architectures for single-processor real-time systems proposed by Plattner and Tsai et al. We then discuss how they can be used to monitor at different levels of abstraction.

4.2.1   Architectures for Hardware Monitoring

We will consider two monitoring systems proposed by Plattner and Tsai et al. In Plattner's system [308] a hardware device is used to listen all the transactions between the target processor and the target memory. A phantom memory is used to mirror the contents of the target memory in real-time. This real-time mirroring is realized by executing the detected transactions against the phantom memory. Information about the state of the target system is collected from the phantom memory. In Tsai, Fang, and Chen's system [396] a monitor is connected to the buses of the target processor to latch all the signals on the buses. A hardware device detects the events of interest and controls the recording process which collects the signals from the target buses. To collect the state of registers in the target processor, which are not directly visible on the buses, a dual processor is employed to mimic the state of the target processor.

Plattner's monitor

Plattner proposed a monitoring system with hardware support for single-processor real-time systems [308]. In this system a hardware device called a *bus listener* monitors all the transactions between the target processor and the other parts of the target system. All of the memory transactions generated by the target processor are recognized by the bus listener. A memory separate from the target system's, called a *phantom memory*, is used to mirror the current contents of the target memory in real time. This mirroring is realized by executing the memory transactions detected by the bus listener against the phantom memory. A monitoring process can be employed to access all the information from this phantom memory.

Fig. 4.1 depicts the architecture of this monitoring system. Here we highlight one software and four hardware components of the system. The hardware components are the bus listener, a FIFO queue, a breakpoint register, and the phantom memory. The software component is the monitor process. The bus listener is attached to the system bus of the target system to passively listen to all the transactions between the target processor and the target memory. The transactions are fed into the FIFO queue.

The output of the FIFO queue is used to manipulate the phantom memory to mirror the target memory in real time. The phantom memory is a dual port memory with the same word size and memory range as the target memory. It is accessed by both the bus listener and the monitor process. The monitor process can read the contents of the phantom memory at any time and interpret the data available in the phantom memory and the data in the FIFO queue in order to construct the state of the target system. When the monitor process needs to access the phantom memory exclusively, it can prevent the bus listener from modifying the phantom memory by locking the output of the FIFO queue. When the FIFO is locked, the detected transactions are saved in the FIFO queue.

The breakpoint register is connected to the output of the FIFO to report any memory transactions referencing any memory locations that were

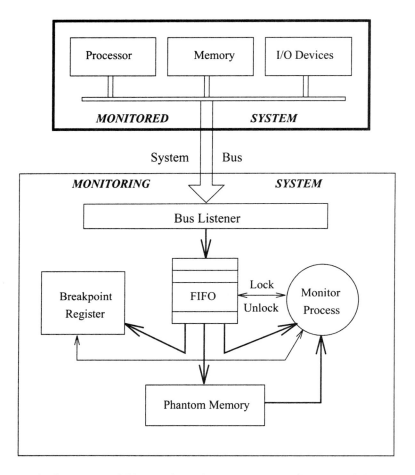

Fig. 4.1 Architecture of Plattner's real-time monitor. (Reprinted, by permission, from [308]. ©1984 IEEE.)

previously specified. For each memory location there is a bit in the register. Thus multiple breakpoints can be implemented. The breakpoint register makes possible event-driven processing of the information kept in the phantom memory. For example, one can set a breakpoint at the address of the fork service routine for process creation. Thus, when a fork call is invoked, the monitor process is informed by the breakpoint register of the process creation event.

It is obvious that this implementation of monitoring does not interfere with the execution of the target system, since it does not use any resources of the target system. The only interaction with the target system is the bus listener which passively listens to the transactions generated by the target processor. Here it is assumed that the phantom memory and the target memory are properly initialized. The monitoring process only accesses the phantom memory and the output of the FIFO queue, and the breakpoint register only monitors for predefined addresses from the output of the FIFO queue. So no intrusion to the execution of the target system exists.

The drawback with this system is, of course, the memory cost. For a real-time system with N bytes of memory, this system needs $N/8$ bytes of memory for the breakpoint register and N bytes of dual port memory for the phantom memory. Also a FIFO buffer is needed. In fact the memory cost for the monitor is higher than the target system. Thus this system is limited to target systems with small memories or target systems that need dual memory for reliability.

Tsai, Fang, and Chen's Monitor

Tsai, Fang, and Chen [396] propose a hardware monitoring system that consists of a set of monitoring nodes. Each monitoring node detects and collects user-defined events from the target program's execution by monitoring the data, address, and control buses of the target processor. The architecture of this monitoring system is shown in Fig. 4.2. The system consists of an interface module and a development module. The interface module interfaces with the target system. Its main function is to latch the internal states of the target system based on the user-specified conditions. The development module is the host computer for the interface module. It contains all the supporting software for the initialization of the interface module and postprocessing activities.

Fig. 4.3 shows the architecture of the interface module. It consists of five units: the interface control unit (ICU), the dual processor unit (DPU), the dual processor memory (DPM), the qualification control unit (QCU), and the high-speed buffer unit (HSBU). The monitoring system is connected to the target system via the ICU. The DPU contains a dual processor identical to the target processor, and the DPM is used for the synchronization of the dual processor with the target processor.

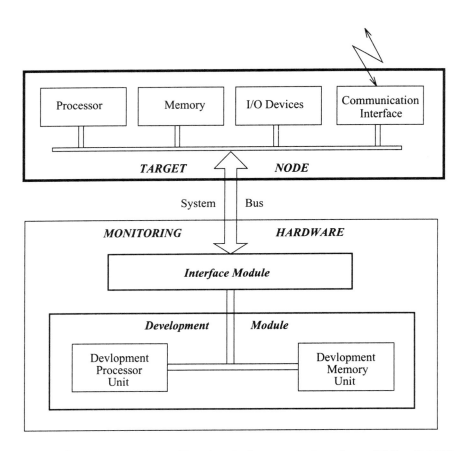

Fig. 4.2 System overview. (Reprinted, by permission, from [396]. ©1990 IEEE.)

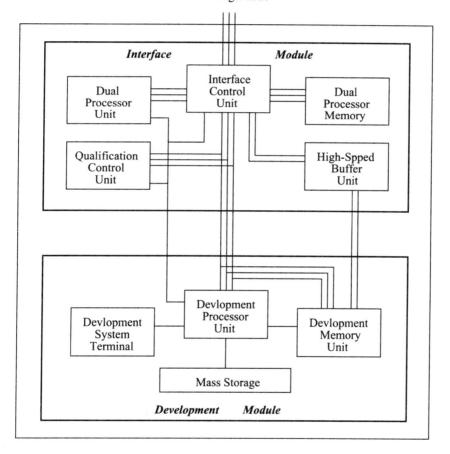

Fig. 4.3 Interface module and development module. (Reprinted, by permission, from [396]. ©1990 IEEE.)

The DPU imitates the target processor after it has been initialized and synchronized until the recording of the execution history is started. It is initialized and synchronized by sending a low-priority interrupt to the target processor. When this interrupt is serviced, the contents of all the registers in the target processor are copied into the dual processor. Then the dual processor starts mimicking the execution of the target system, and the monitoring system is ready to monitor the execution of the target system and collect runtime information. This low-priority interrupt is the only interference with the target system.

The synchronization continues until a starting trigger condition is matched in the QCU. Then the trigger condition is matched, and the QCU sends control signals to the HSBU and DPU. As soon as the control signal is received, the dual processor isolates itself from the target system to freeze and save the internal state of the target processor in the dual processor memory, and simultaneously the HSBU starts recording the data from the buses of the target system. The recording activity continues until a preset stopping trigger condition is matched in the QCU.

As shown in Fig. 4.3, the development module consists of the development processor unit and the development memory unit. It is the central processing unit of the monitoring system and functions as a host machine. The design of the development module is independent of any target processor. This is achieved by separating the target-dependent functions into the interface module. The development module provides an interactive interface to the user and is responsible for all the testing and debugging activities, namely monitoring system initialization, data collection control, and postprocessing the collected data. The development memory unit consists of the development processor memory and the memory configuration unit. Through the HSBU the signals on the target buses are latched into the memory configuration unit.

4.2.2 Monitoring at Different Levels of Abstraction

We have described the two monitoring architectures proposed by Plattner, Tsai, Fang, and Chen. Now we will see how to monitor single-processor systems using these two architectures. With Plattner's system, the phantom memory can be used to collect the data pertaining the events of interest. The breakpoint register can be used as a detector for these events. With Tsai, Fang, and Chen's system, a set of starting and stopping trigger conditions are preset, which start and stop the signal-latching process from the target buses when a starting condition or a stopping condition is met, respectively. The starting and stopping conditions are chosen in such a way that the data pertaining to the events of interest is included in the collected signal blocks. Data for higher-level software constructs can be obtained from these blocks. We will now examine how these systems monitor target systems.

Using Plattner's Monitor

In Plattner's monitoring system the phantom memory mirrors the target memory in real time, and the breakpoint register can be used to report the occurrence of an event to the monitoring process. To monitor the process-level events listed in Table 2.1 using this system, we use the breakpoint register to detect the occurrences of the events and the monitor process to collect and record from the phantom memory the data pertaining to the detected event(s). This is achieved as follows: Assume that all the system service routines such as forks permanently reside in memory at a fixed location. When a system call is invoked, the service routine will start from a fixed address and terminate at one of the fixed exiting locations. We can set breakpoints at these exit locations.

When a system call is completed, one of the exit locations will be accessed. Thus the breakpoint register will notify the monitor process, then the monitor process can determine the type of the system call by examining the transaction that caused the interrupt. Once the monitor process knows the type of the system call, it can find the memory locations for the event data in the phantom memory. We cannot set breakpoints at the beginning address of the service routine, since at that time the data pertaining to the event may not be available. For instance, at the beginning of the service routine for the fork call, the process identification of the new process has not been determined by the service routine, so the process ID, which is necessary for process creation event, is not available.

Monitoring interrupts can be implemented in a similar manner. We set breakpoints at the termination points of the interrupt handlers. Once the monitor process is notified of an interrupt at these locations, it can search the phantom memory for the data pertaining to the interrupt. Here we also assume that the interrupt handlers are located at fixed locations. If any of the system call service routines or interrupt handlers are loaded into the memory dynamically, the monitor process has to determine the location of the service routine or the handler by studying the memory transactions. Based on that information, the monitor process sets the breakpoint register accordingly.

We can use the same strategy to monitor at the function level. As will be discussed in later chapters, most block-structured programming languages pass parameters between the calling function and the called function using a stack. For function calling, once passed, parameters are pushed onto the stack, a machine-level instruction, *call*, is executed, and control is transferred to the called function. For function returning, after the returned parameters are pushed in the stack, another machine-level instruction, *return*, is executed, which transfers control back to the calling function. Thus the monitor process can determine the address of all the call and return instructions of the process to be monitored when the process is loaded into memory. Then the monitor process can set breakpoints at these addresses and, by examining the last memory transaction, determine whether a call or a return was executed. Since the number of parameters to be passed or returned in function calls and returns can be determined statically (i.e., before the process is executed), the monitor process can easily find the relative address for each parameter from the current stack pointer and how many parameters need to be collected.

Using Tsai, Fang, and Chen's Monitor

In Tsai, Fang, and Chen's monitoring system, the qualification control unit (QCU) can detect events, and the recording process can be started or stopped when an event is detected. Thus, to monitor the process-level events listed in Table 2.1, two sets of trigger conditions are preset into the QCU. The conditions are the starting trigger conditions that start the recording process and stopping trigger conditions that stop the recording process. The trigger conditions are specified so that the recording process is started when a sequence of one or more events occurs and stopped when the key values of the event(s) are collected.

To identify the triggering conditions that need to be specified, let us first take a look at how an operating system works. An operating system can be modeled as an interrupt-driven process. When an interrupt occurs, the hardware transfers control to the operating system, which then determines what kind of interrupt has occurred and handles the interrupt by calling the corresponding service routine. A user process can request system services by calling system calls with a parameter specifying what is requested. The system calls are implemented as a privileged instruction that causes a software interrupt, and the operating system will find the service routine for the requested system call. We have five starting trigger conditions:

IF ((system call interrupt) AND (process related activities))
    OR ((system call interrupt) AND (I/O request))
    OR (I/O completion interrupt)
    OR (system clock interrupt)
    OR (program error interrupt)
THEN trigger the recording process.

No matter what type of interrupts are caused by the events, the operating system will return control to an application process after the service for the interrupt is finished. This is done by the operating system executing a privileged instruction that changes the system mode to user mode. So the stopping condition for all the events is

IF (instruction changes the system mode to user mode)
THEN stop the recording process.

With these two sets of trigger conditions, when a process-level event occurs, the starting trigger conditions will invoke the recording process to latch all the signals on the target buses. The signal latching and recording continue until all the key values of the event are collected, or the system mode changes.

4.3 Monitoring Multiprocessor Architectures

In this section we will introduce monitoring systems for multiprocessor real-time systems. We consider tightly coupled multiprocessor systems that contain several processors that share a global memory and have common I/O devices via the system bus. Each processor may have local buses for its own memory and I/O devices. Each processor and its local memory and I/O devices comprise a computing element of the system. We first describe the architecture of some monitoring systems for multiprocessor systems, and then we discuss how to use these systems to monitor at different levels of abstraction.

4.3.1 Architectures for Hardware Monitoring

Three monitoring systems are introduced in this section. In Brantley, McAuliffe, and Ngo's monitoring system [50], each component of a computing element that may generate the events of interest is instrumented in hardware to send electronic event signals to a performance monitor via special communication lines when an event occurs. The performance monitor, which is a hardware device, counts these signals. The performance monitor can be accessed through the local bus of the monitored computing element. Liu and Parthasarathi's monitoring system [226] uses a hardware probe to connect the monitoring system to the system bus of the target system. The monitor counts the number of occurrences of specified single patterns. Only the contents of the counters are saved for analysis. Lazzerini, Prete, and Lopriore [230] designed a monitoring system that can be attached to both the system bus or a local bus of the target system for different purposes. It monitors the accesses to a segment of the memory that is reached through the monitored bus. The monitoring system can put the target processor(s) into a hold state.

Brantley, McAuliffe, and Ngo's Monitor

Brantley, McAuliffe, and Ngo [50] describe monitoring hardware for the Research Parallel Processor Prototype (RP3) developed at the IBM T.J. Watson Research Center. The monitor is mainly used for performance analysis of hardware devices, such as processor-cache interactions, and hardware/software bottlenecks. In their approach, each device in the target system detects its own events and reports their occurrences through special I/O pins to a performance monitor that counts these event signals. The performance monitor consists of a set of status registers and counters. The status register controls the type and the frequency of events to be collected. The counter accumulates the number of events specified in the status register in order to compute the frequency of events. The performance monitor can be controlled by user programs or the operating system (e.g., by starting, stopping, and reading the counters) in the target system. It can also be controlled by a transparent mode in which the user programs are unaware of the monitoring activities. Since the performance monitor is accessed through the processor bus, perturbation may occur when the I/O system reads the contents of the performance monitor.

Liu and Parthasarathi's Monitor

Liu and Parthasarathi [226] propose monitoring hardware for the Testbed for Distributed Processing, or Ted. The Ted consists of Intel iSBC 8086 single-board computers organized in clusters. Each cluster consists of several single-board computers that are connected with a Multibus and share a common memory. Clusters are connected through an Ethernet network. In their approach a hardware device is attached via a probe to the Multibus of the cluster to be monitored. The probe detects events from the Multibus. To reduce the amount of data to be saved, the signals collected by the probe are filtered so that only specified events or signals are recorded. The monitor keeps track of the elapsed time between two events in terms of the number of clock cycles. The collected data is saved in a buffer. Liu and Parthasarathi suggest using an Ethernet controller to monitor intercluster traffic.

Fig. 4.4 shows the architecture of this monitoring approach. The monitoring system is attached to the Multibus of the target cluster. It consists of an event filter, a counter unit, a buffer unit, and a control unit. The event filter selects only specified events or signals from the Multibus. The counter unit counts the elapsed time between two detected events in terms of clock cycles. The buffer unit is used to store the collected data. The control unit coordinates all the actions of the other components. It can also receive commands from external sources and initiate actions for the monitor.

The event filter consists of a bus register, a mask register, a pattern register, a bitwise OR logic, and a comparator. The pattern register contains the specified bit pattern that represents the event(s) to be monitored. The bit pattern consists of the address, data, and memory and I/O read/write of the buses of the target system. For example, for a target processor with 20-bit address lines, 16-bit data lines, and 4-bit I/O and memory read/write lines, the pattern register needs 40 bits. The signals on the Multibus are latched in the bus register. The mask register is used to specify don't-care bits in the pattern and it is ORed with the bus register. The comparator compares the result of the bitwise OR logic with the specified pattern and sends the comparison result to the counter unit.

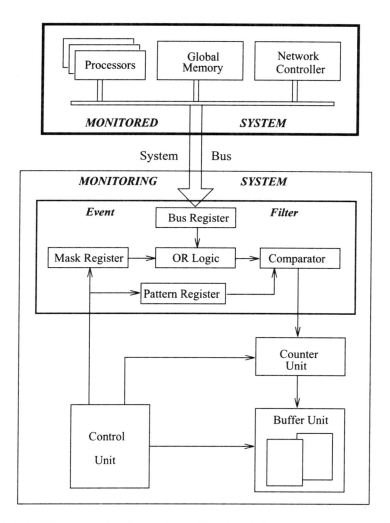

Fig. 4.4 Architecture of Ted monitor. (Reprinted, by permission, from [226]. ©1989 IEEE.)

The result of the comparison is high if the pattern is matched, and low otherwise. The result is high for as many cycles as the pattern is matched. Now we want to count the number of clock cycles during which the result is continually high and count the cycles during which the result is continually low. Two counters are used to count the matched time and unmatched time. When the comparison result is in the same state (high or low), one counter counts the number of clock cycles elapsed. When the state changes, the second counter is started and the value of the first counter is sent to the buffer unit. The first counter is then cleared for the next state change. Thus the elapsed time between two events can be collected.

The buffer unit is used to temporarily store the collected data of the two counters. A double-buffering scheme is employed for this unit so that the buffer can be read and written at the same time. This buffer can be accessed by an external processing unit or a single-board computer of the target node. The external processing unit may process the data and display information to the operator or the programmer for system tuning or debugging. In either case a data path separate from the target system is used so that the interference with the execution of the target system can be minimized.

Lazzerini, Prete, and Lopriore's Monitor

Lazzerini, Prete, and Lopriore [230] propose a programmable debugging aid (PDA) for performance evaluation and testing and debugging Selenia MARA multi-microprocessor systems. In their approach the events monitored are memory accesses to specific locations. For each memory location an action is specified but is taken by hardware only if an event associated to the memory location is detected. PDAs are connected to the monitored buses of the target system. In their approach the monitoring system is not just a passive monitoring device, it can access the memory of the target system, can direct the bus to which it is attached, and can put the target processor into a hold state. Thus the monitoring system can interfere with the execution of the target system. The PDA allows the user to monitor memory and execute a variety of actions based on the location accessed and other conditions.

MARA is a multi-microprocessor architecture developed by Selenia SpA in 1979 for real-time process control. A MARA system consists of one or more nodes connected via serial links. Each node consists of up to 16 microcomputers which share memory and I/O interfaces through a nodal bus. These resources are called *nodal memory* and *nodal I/O interfaces*. Each microcomputer of a node consists of a microprocessor, a local memory, and I/O interfaces linked together through a local bus. Fig. 4.5 shows the architecture of a MARA node. A PDA can be connected to either a nodal bus or a local bus. If it is connected to a nodal bus, it monitors the nodal memory. If it is connected to a local bus, it monitors the local memory. Multiple PDAs can be used to simultaneously monitor the nodal bus and several local buses.

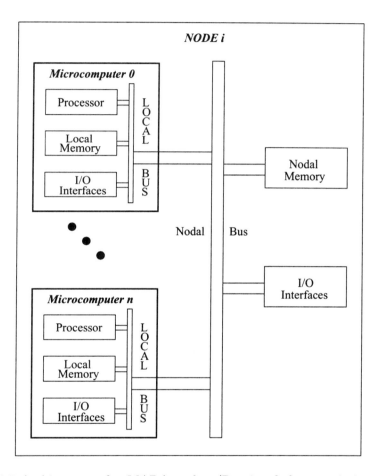

Fig. 4.5 Architecture of a MARA node. (Reprinted, by permission, from [230]. ©1986 IEEE.)

PAGE TAG

2	6
MOD	DSN

WORD TAG

4

CONDITION REGISTER

2	1	1	1	16	16	16
MOD	RD	WR	IR/OR	MSK	LB	UB

ACTION REGISTER

1	1	1	3	2
LIR	HLD	FIFO	CTN	TC

Fig. 4.6 Configuration of page and word tags and condition and action registers. (Reprinted, by permission, from [230]. ©1986 IEEE.)

At any given time the monitoring system only monitors a segment of memory called a *window*. A window consists of 1024 pages, each of which is 128 words of 2 bytes each. The PDA includes 1024 pairs of condition and action registers. The 1024 pairs are grouped into 64 sets with 16 pairs in each set. The condition register of each pair specifies monitoring conditions, and the action register specifies what actions will be taken if a specified condition in the condition register is met. Each page of the current window is associated with a page tag, and each word of the current window is associated with a word tag.

The page tag of a page specifies whether the page is to be monitored for every memory access to the page, not monitored at all, or only monitored for the specified conditions in the set of the condition registers pointed to by the page tag. Since the page tag only specifies which set of condition and action registers is associated to the page, the word tag associated to a word in the page specifies which pair of the condition and action registers is used for the word. Since there are only 16 register pairs in a set, only 16 different patterns of monitoring conditions can be specified for a page, or 128 words. Several words can have their tags pointing to the same pair of condition and action registers.

Fig. 4.6 shows the configuration of the page tag and word tag. A page tag is 8 bits long. A two-bit field, MOD of a page tag, is used to specify how the page is to be monitored. When MOD = 00, no event is monitored for the

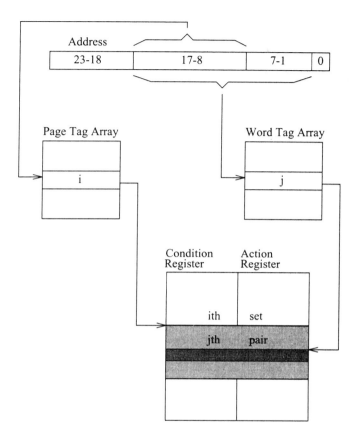

Fig. 4.7 Relationship between page and word tags and condition and action registers.

page; when MOD = 11, an event is generated upon every access to any word in the page; when MOD = 01 or 10, the set of condition and action registers pointed by the remaining 6 bits, called the descriptor set number (DSN), is used to specify the conditions and actions. A word tag is 4 bits long. The word tag points to a specific register pair in the condition and action register set pointed by the page tag of the page in which the word is located. In a window there are 1024 pages and 128 K words, so 1024 page tags and 128 K word tags are needed in a PDA. Fig. 4.7 shows the relationship between the page and word tags and the condition and action pairs.

The condition and action registers specify the monitoring conditions and actions to be taken. A condition register consists of seven fields as shown in Fig. 4.6. The MOD field, 2 bits, specifies how events will be generated. When MOD = 00, no event will be generated; when MOD = 11, an event is generated on every access to the associated words; when MOD = 01 or

10, the other fields in the register become effective. The single bit RD and
WR fields, when set, enable event generation on every read from or write
to the associated word, respectively. The mask field allows the user to select
certain bits of the word to be compared with the 16-bit lower-bound (LB) and
upper-bound (UB) fields. An event is generated according to the result of an
in-range or out-of-range comparison as selected by the 1-bit IR/OR field.

The action register in a condition and action pair specify what action will
be taken if an event is generated as specified in the condition register. The
action register consists of five fields. The local interrupt request field (LIR), if
set, specifies that an interrupt must be sent to the processor in the PDA. The
single-bit hold (HLD), if set, specifies that the processor mastering the current
monitored bus (which could be a target processor) must be put into a hold
state. The single-bit field (FIFO), if set, specifies that the current contents
of the target bus must be saved into the PDA's built-in 128-cell FIFO queue.
The other two fields enable counter/timers to be stopped or started. There
are seven counters/timers. The CTN field specifies which counter/timer will
be used. When one is programmed as a counter, it decrements when an event
is detected, and it sends an interrupt to the processor of the PDA when it
reaches zero. When one works as a timer, the 2-bit TC field specifies whether
to start, stop, or switch between the start or stop states of the timer.

Fig. 4.8 shows the architecture of the PDA. The computing element is
an 8080 processor with its own memory. It executes debugging commands.
The target interface logic (TIL) connects the PDA to the target buses. This
interface allows the PDA to access the target memory and to send interrupt
requests to the target bus. The I/O channel allows a host system to be
connected to the PDA. The FIFO queue and the counters/timers perform the
functions mentioned previously.

A MARA address (on either the nodal bus or a local bus) consists of 24
bits. Since a window starts at a page boundary, the current window being
monitored can be specified by the 16 most significant bits of the address. The
address relocation logic (ARL) compares these bits with the 16-bit current
window register (CWR). If a match occurs, the address will be passed on to
find the corresponding pair of condition and action registers for the accessed
word. That is, the page tag is searched, and then the condition and action
register set is found. The word tag is searched, and then the offset of the pair
is found in the register set. The contents of the condition register is sent to
the event detecting and processing circuitry (EDPC), which in turn compares
them with the state of the target buses. When a condition is met, it takes the
action specified in the action register.

4.3.2   Monitoring at Different Levels of Abstraction

In this section we discuss how to monitor at different levels of abstraction
using the above systems. Brantley, McAuliffe, and Ngo's monitor is mainly

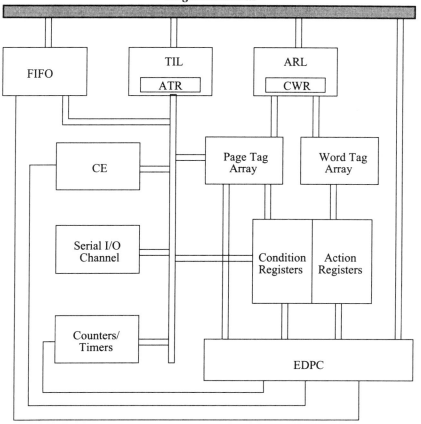

Fig. 4.8 Configuration of a PDA. (Reprinted, by permission, from [230]. ©1986 IEEE.)

used for performance monitoring. It counts the occurrences of events in order to compute the frequency of events. It helps little in debugging timing or logical errors. Liu and Parthasarathi's monitor can detect a specified signal pattern on the address and data buses and the read/write lines of the control bus. It then counts the number of clock cycles during which the pattern is being matched and the number of cycles during which the pattern is not matched. Only these two numbers are saved for later analysis. Lazzerini, Prete, and Lopriore's monitor allows the user to specify monitoring conditions and the actions to be taken for a selected segment of the target memory. The monitoring system can (1) count the occurrences of an event and measure the intervals between events, (2) collect data from the buses of the target system, (3) put the target processor(s) into a hold state, and (4) interrupt the processor in the PDA. It can be connected to the system bus or a local bus for monitoring activities between different processor-memory pairs.

Using Brantley, McAuliffe, and Ngo's Monitor

In Brantley, McAuliffe, and Ngo's monitoring system, each hardware component of the target system is instrumented to detect events and notify the monitor by sending signals, and the monitor counts the occurrences of events. The event signal can be used to analyze the utilization of various levels of the storage hierarchy, for example, the cache miss ratio or the memory service ratio between local requests and remote requests. This monitoring approach is very useful for system performance tuning, such as finding hot spots in memory and estimating the network latency by recording the times at which a remote memory request was sent and the reply was received. However, this approach may not be used to monitor the events at process and function levels as listed in Tables 2.1 and 2.2.

Using Liu and Parthasarathi's Monitor

Liu and Parthasarathi's approach can detect accesses to selected data, addresses, or blocks of addresses using its pattern register and mask register. It can help monitor events such as the access and usage of a memory location or a group of memory locations. It can also determine the amount of time during which an event is active or inactive. However, this monitoring approach cannot monitor events at the process or function level. One reason is that the monitor does not collect any other data except the contents of the two counters in the counter unit. Another reason is that a single-pattern register is not enough to specify all the patterns for the events at the process or function level.

CONDITION REGISTER

1	1	X	X	X	X...X	X...X	X...X
MOD		RD	WR	IR/OR	MSK	LB	UB

ACTION REGISTER

0	0	1	0	0	0	X...X
LIR	HLD	FIFO		CTN		TC

Fig. 4.9 The setting of the condition and action registers.

Using Lazzerini, Prete, and Lopriore's Monitor

In using Lazzerini, Prete, and Lopriore's approach to monitor process-level events, we first assume that the monitoring window is big enough to cover the code of the interrupt handlers and system call routines. We further assume that these handlers and routines are loaded permanently into the memory at a fixed location. We now divide the system calls into process-level related calls and unimportant calls. The process-level related calls are those that cause a process-level event to occur, such as a fork system call which causes a process creation event to occur. For the process-level related system calls and the interrupt handlers, we first find their memory locations. Then we assign their page tags and word tags to a pair of condition and action registers. The condition register is set to detect any memory accesses. The action register is set to latch the data on the target buses into the FIFO queue. Fig. 4.9 shows the setting of the two registers:

With the above setting, when a system call or an interrupt handler is executed, the executed instructions are collected into the FIFO queue. The computing element of the PDA can be programmed to save the collected data to a secondary storage. The collected data can be analyzed to derive the event(s) involved in each block of data. Thus events at the process level can be collected.

This system can only detect events that can be specified in terms of memory addresses, for example, whether a memory location is read or written. Using this system to monitor at the function level is difficult because in most systems a user process is not loaded into a fixed location. As will be discussed in Chapter 8, the parameters passed between the calling and called functions are saved in a stack that is in the user process's memory space. To collect the data for the function-level events, we need to latch the data from the target buses when the stack is accessed. If the process is located at a different location, we will not be able to identify where the stack is located.

4.4   Monitoring Distributed Systems

A distributed real-time system consists of a set of geographically dispersed computers that work together to achieve a common goal. Each computer, or a node, may be a single processor computer or a multiprocessor computer. To monitor this kind of system, there are several problems that need to be addressed. In this section we will discuss the hardware architecture for monitoring such systems and the issues involved.

In distributed systems, monitoring must be distributed to each node of the monitored system to avoid high perturbation of the data paths of the monitored system. This is accomplished by attaching a monitor to each node of the system. The monitor detects events and records the data on that node. Since all the nodes work together toward a common goal (i.e., they are not independent of each other), the global state needs to be constructed for systemwide testing and debugging.

To construct the global state, the data collected at each individual node must be transferred to a central location where the global state can be built. There are two options for transferring data to the central location. One way is to use the network of the target system so that the monitoring system shares the network with the target system. This approach can interfere with the communication between the target nodes. To avoid such interference, an independent network for the monitoring system can be used, allowing the monitoring network to have a different topology and different transmission speed from the target system. Since the monitoring network is not logically or physically connected to the target system, the target system will not be affected.

To construct the global state, the recorded time for the events on different nodes must have a common reference so that for a given time we can order events in a time sequence and combine the local states. Therefore a global common time reference is needed for all the nodes. Generally, each monitoring node already has its own local physical clock to order the local events. However, due to the drifting nature of quartz-controller oscillators, no two physical clocks run at the exactly same rate. Therefore the clocks at monitoring nodes must be synchronized to provide a systemwide global time. The monitoring network mentioned in the previous paragraph can be used as the hardware medium for clock synchronization algorithms. The clock synchronization will not perturb the network of the monitored system. Fig. 4.10 shows the general architecture of a hardware monitoring system in a distributed environment.

The recorded event data on each node can be transmitted immediately to a central collector or stored locally and transferred later to the central location. Which method is appropriate for a monitoring system depends on how the collected data will be used. If the data is used in an on-line fashion for dynamic display or monitoring system safety constraints, the data should be transferred immediately. This may require a high-speed network to reduce the latency between the system state and the display of that state. If the data is used in an off-line fashion, it can be transferred at any time. If the data is transferred immediately with a high-speed network, little local storage is needed. The data may also be transferred after the monitoring is done. This implies that each node should have mass storage to store its local data. The network can be slow in speed. There is a disadvantage with this approach. If the amount of recorded data on nodes is not evenly distributed, too much data could be stored at one node. Building a sufficiently large data storage for every node can be very expensive. Thus, if the data is used in an off-line fashion, it is suggested that a moderate speed network be used as long as it is fast enough for clock synchronization; a local storage then temporarily stores the collected data as a buffer. The data is transferred to the central station as they are collected in such a way that the clock synchronization is not hampered.

Fig. 4.10 shows an architecture of a typical distributed hardware monitoring system. In this architecture each node of the target system is attached with a monitoring node. The monitoring is designed in such a way that it does not interfere with the execution of the target node. Such a monitoring node generally consists of a probe, a detector, a filter, a recorder, a clock, and a synchronizer. The probe interfaces with the buses of the target node's processor in order to latch the signals on the buses. The detector detects events from the latched signals. The filter selects the events of interest. The recorder saves the data pertaining to the detected event. Each node has a local clock for recording the time at which events occur. The clock is synchronized with the clocks on other nodes by the synchronizer. The monitoring nodes are connected together through an independent and separate network. A central station is also connected to the network for global processing. The monitoring network controls the clock synchronization and the data transmission so the target network is not affected with by these activities. The mentioned functional blocks can be implemented in hardware, software, or a combination of the two, excepting the probe which must be in hardware. In Chapter 8 we will introduce a noninterference monitoring architecture for distributed real-time systems.

Observant readers must have noticed that none of the monitoring systems mentioned in this chapter deals with issues such as global processing, clock synchronization, and separate networks for monitoring distributed real-time systems. In the next chapter on hybrid monitoring, we will introduce several distributed hybrid monitoring systems. It will be seen that the architecture of distributed hybrid monitoring systems is very similar to that of hardware monitoring. The same problems we discussed for distributed hardware monitoring also exist in hybrid monitoring. The solutions proposed in the hybrid monitoring systems can also be applied to hardware monitoring. In the next chapter we will introduce several networks and clock synchronization

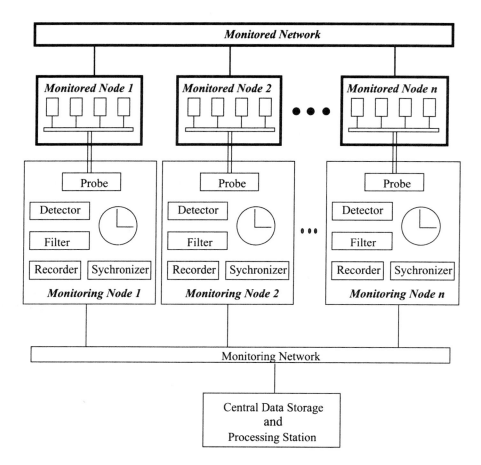

Fig. 4.10 Architecture of a distributed hardware monitor.

algorithms used in hybrid monitoring systems implemented for distributed
real-time systems.

4.5 Summary

In this chapter we discussed hardware monitoring for real-time systems and
introduced several proposed and/or implemented monitoring systems. An
advantage of hardware monitoring is that there is no or minimal interference
with the execution of the target system. The disadvantages are that it is costly
to built and that the systems become target-processor dependent. For hard
real-time systems with stringent timing and safety constraints, the advantage
of hardware monitoring overrides the disadvantages, since no interference to
the execution of the target system is allowed in these systems.

There are currently four hardware monitoring approaches. The first approach uses a phantom memory, which has the same range and the same
word size as the target memory, so it can mirror the contents of the target
memory in real time [308]. To enable the phantom memory's mirroring the
target memory in real time, the transactions appearing on the target buses
between the target processor and the target memory are detected and executed against the phantom memory. In this approach, besides the phantom
memory, little storage is needed for the collected data since only useful data is
saved. This approach assumes that the memory of the target system contains
all the information that needs to be collected.

The second approach uses a pattern-matching device to compare the signals on the target buses with the specified patterns [397, 230]. The signals
of interest are recorded and used to derive high-level information. This approach does not require the target memory to contain all the information
needed. However, it does require that all the information to be collected be
visible on the target buses so they can be derived from the recorded signals.
In contrast with the first approach, this approach will store not only the useful data but also unimportant data, since it collects data based on the signals
of the target buses.

The third approach also uses pattern matching for events. However, instead of collecting signals from the target buses, limited types of high-level
information are generated on-line in hardware, such as the number of occurrences of events and the interval between events are saved [50, 226, 230]. The
information generated is characterized as simple and fixed. Counters/timers
are employed in this system. This approach is suitable for monitoring system
performance, but it may not be used for debugging logical and timing errors
because it does not provide sufficient information. Little storage is required,
since only useful data is saved.

The last approach instruments the hardware components of the target
system to notify the monitor when events occur using special communication
lines. A hardware device counts the occurrences of events [50]. This approach

may not be appropriate for collecting information used for debugging logical
and timing errors because not enough information is collected. A variation of
this approach instruments the hardware components to notify occurrences of
events and collect the signals on the target buses when an event is reported.
In this way information is derived from the collected signals and the number
of the different kinds of events that can be recorded is limited.

In distributed real-time systems each node of the target system needs
to be monitored; the global state is constructed from the data collected at
each node. The node can be a single-processor computer or a multiprocessor
computer. To monitor each node, any of the approaches mentioned above can
be employed. To construct the global state, the data collected from individual
nodes is transferred to a central location where the global state is constructed.
To avoid any interference with the target network, a separate monitoring
network, is set up for the data transmission. The monitoring network can
also be used for synchronizing the clocks to a global time reference.

Exercises

1. Describe the procedure used to implement hardware monitoring.

2. How can hardware monitoring minimize the interference to the monitored systems compared to other monitoring techniques?

3. What is bus-snooping? How can bus-snooping be applied to hardware
   monitoring?

4. What kinds of run-time information can be collected using hardware
   monitoring?

5. What are global states? How can the global state of a distributed real-
   time system be collected and then constructed?

6. How does networking affect the collection data needed to construct the
   global state?

7. Describe the four kinds of hardware monitoring approaches addressed
   in this chapter.

8. Designing a hardware interface (refer to Fig. 4.2.). Assume that the target node's memory is designed as follows: The communication interface
   is memory mapped so that the address COMM_INTERFACE is used
   to read and write to the communication interface. A send instruction
   has the following format:

   ADDRESS   DATA
   COMM_INTERFACE command to send a message
   COMM_INTERFACE address of receiver

COMM_INTERFACE length of message
COMM_INTERFACE message
COMM_INTERFACE :
COMM_INTERFACE :
COMM_INTERFACE message
COMM_INTERFACE error checking code

The message can be one to 1019 words long (The total length of the message is the length of the data + 4). Design a hardware interface that records all the messages sent. Assume that a high-speed memory is used to buffer the messages and that a disk is used to save the data permanently. Ignore how the data is retrieved from the disk.

(a) How big should the buffer be? If you decide that only the first four words need to be saved, how big should the buffer be? State your assumptions concerning disk speed, memory speed, and the time required to set up a send message.

(b) Design an interface for reading the disk at the target node.

(c) Design an interface for reading the disk at a separate computer.

(d) If a processor has a prefetch buffer and you wish monitor the execution of that instruction, how do you know if the instruction was executed?

Chapter 5

Hybrid Monitoring

One of the drawbacks of the hardware monitoring approach is that as integrated circuit techniques advance, more functions are built on-chip. So desired signals may not be accessible. What information is recorded may not be sufficient to determine the behavior inside the chip. For example, increasingly sophisticated caching algorithms implemented for on-chip caches may no longer enable the information collected from external buses to be used to determine what data needs to be stored. Prefetched instructions and data may not be used, and some events can only be identified by a sequence of signal patterns rather than by a single address or instruction. Therefore hardware-passive bus snooping may not be effective. To avoid extraneous triggers generated by unused prefetched instructions and to be able to detect important sequences of events, the design complexity of a hardware monitor becomes very high. Hybrid monitoring is an attractive compromise between intrusive software monitoring and expensive nonintrusive hardware monitoring. It minimizes perturbation by allowing hardware to perform the majority of the monitoring tasks. In this chapter various hybrid monitoring techniques are introduced.

5.1 Introduction to Hybrid Monitoring

Hybrid monitoring uses both software and hardware to perform monitoring activities [152, 149, 329, 263, 262, 142, 186, 185, 235, 245, 246]. In hybrid monitoring, triggering is accomplished by inserting instructions into the target systems (instrumenting) to start recording in hardware. Software thus specifies the events to be detected in the monitored target programs, and hardware identifies and processes the events. Perturbation of the monitored system is greatly reduced by using hardware to store collected data into a separate storage. Execution perturbation is minimal if a single instruction triggers the monitoring hardware to record all necessary data. Thus a careful design of support hardware can greatly reduce perturbation at a modest cost.

The hardware monitor can be designed as a permanent part of the target system during the design phase, or it can be a separate device or coprocessor integrated into a target system during the testing and debugging phase. The former approach is addressed by Haban et al. [152, 149] and Reilly [329]. The latter is addressed by Mink et al. [263, 262] and Gorlick [142]. As suggested by Mink et al. in [262], manufacturers could provide a monitor as an option.

Current hybrid monitoring techniques use two different triggering approaches. One has a set of predefined addresses to trigger event recording. The monitoring unit is mapped into memory addresses. Each address represents an event. When a predefined address is detected on the system address bus, the monitoring device records the address and the data on the system data bus. This approach is called *memory-mapped monitoring*. It is employed in [152, 329, 262]. The other approach uses the coprocessor instructions to trigger event recording. The recording unit acts as a coprocessor that executes the coprocessor instructions. This is called *coprocessor monitoring*. This approach is employed in [142].

In memory-mapped monitoring, the steps for monitoring can be summarized as follows:

1. Define the event classes to be monitored, and allocate a memory address for each class.

2. Insert into the target program instrumentation code that will write to the memory locations allocated in step 1.

3. Compile the target program with the instrumentation code and construct a monitoring symbol table for the instrumentation code.

4. Link and load the object code of the instrumented target program so that the embedded code will trigger event recording when it is executed.

5. The hardware monitoring device snoops the address bus and matches the bus signal to the address assigned to the event class.

6. The monitoring device assembles the keywords of the detected event with a time stamp and other control information and saves them in data storage.

In coprocessor monitoring, the procedure of monitoring can be described in the following steps:

1–3. Same as the first three steps described above.

4. Link and load the object code of the instrumented target program so that the object code will send monitoring coprocessor instructions to the monitoring device.

5. The monitoring device acts as a coprocessor and executes the instructions.

6. The monitoring device assembles the keywords of the detected event
   with a time stamp and other control information and saves them in
   data storage.

5.2 Monitoring Uniprocessor Architectures

To monitor a single-processor system, both triggering methods mentioned
above can be employed. Fig. 5.1 shows the hardware architecture of a monitoring system for single-processor systems. The hardware monitoring unit is
connected to the external bus of the monitored system. This unit should be
directly connected to the monitored processor, bypassing the cache and the
memory management unit. If memory-mapped monitoring approach is employed, the hardware unit monitors the address bus for predefined addresses
that represent occurrences of an event of interest. If the coprocessor monitoring approach is employed, the hardware unit is accessed as a coprocessor
of the processor of the monitored system; that is, the processor controls the
coprocessor's activity.

In either case the hardware unit consists of a bus interface module and
an event recorder. The bus interface module encapsulates the monitored
system's bus activity so that the event recorder is independent of the bus
structure of the monitored system. The event recorder consists of a clock and
timer, overflow counter and control, trigger recognizer and data collector, and
event data storage. The clock and timer are used to stamp each event with
the current time. Since the order of the recorded events is the same as the
order of the recorded sequence, the time stamps here are only used to record
execution times. The overflow counter counts the number of events that have
not been recorded due to buffer overflow. Thus the user knows if events were
not recorded. It can also be used to help determine the buffer size needed to
avoid overflow.

In a memory-mapped system, the trigger recognizer and data collector
monitor the address bus of the monitored system for predefined addresses.
In a coprocessor monitoring system, the trigger recognizer and data collector
execute the coprocessor instructions sent by the target processor. In either
method they will check whether the detected event is enabled or not. If not,
they continue monitoring events. If the event is enabled, they assemble the
keywords of the event, overflow control, and current time together as an event
entry and save it in the data storage. The data storage can be constructed
with a high-speed FIFO buffer and memory. The FIFO buffer temporarily
stores data during event bursts that memory cannot handle. A secondary
storage for data may necessary in applications where massive amounts of
data need to be recorded and stored.

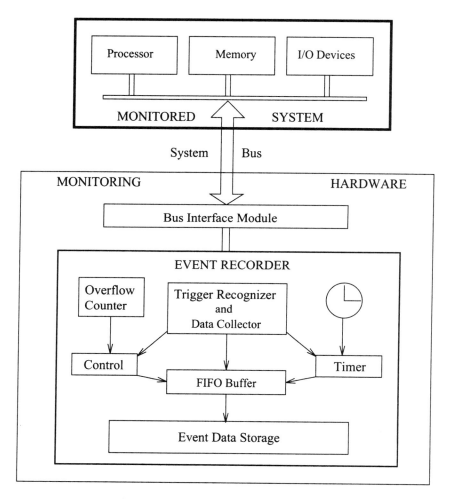

Fig. 5.1 Architecture of a uniprocessor monitor.

5.3 Monitoring Multiprocessor Architectures

In multiprocessor systems, processors may share memory and other I/O devices. A single monitoring unit can be used as the target of all write instructions from all the processors in memory-mapped monitoring. With coprocessor monitoring, a single unit can be used to execute coprocessor instructions from all the processors. As shown in Fig. 5.2, the monitoring hardware is the same as the hardware used in a single-processor system. Only the number of processors in the target system is different. Besides the trigger recognizer and data collector, each component in the monitoring hardware performs the same functions it performed in the single-processor system.

Since it is necessary to know which processor generated a recorded event, processor IDs must be recorded in addition to the other information that is recorded. This can be implemented by instrumenting the monitored system in such a way that the processor's ID is collected by the trigger recognizer and data collector along with other key data. For example, in memory-mapped monitoring, each processor maps the monitoring node into a different range of memory addresses. Thus a recorded address not only contains the event type but the processor ID can be found from it.

In the following discussion, different implementations of memory-mapped and coprocessor monitoring approaches are introduced.

5.3.1 Memory-Mapped Monitoring

The Test and Measurement Processor (TMP)

Haban and Wybranietz's DTM system [152, 149] is a typical example of memory-mapped monitoring in a distributed environment. Each monitored node is a multiprocessor computer. A test and measurement processor (TMP) is attached to each monitored node to record event traces on the node. All the TMPs are connected by a separate network to reduce the perturbation to the target system. Each event of interest is assigned a physical address. The TMP is designed to recognize the occurrence of a write operation to that address and capture the data written to it. Thus the target system is instrumented to write the keyword of an event to its corresponding address. The TMP snoops the address bus to capture addresses. When a predefined address is detected, the TMP stamps the event with the current time and saves the data being transmitted on the data bus. Fig. 5.3 shows the integration of a monitored system and TMP nodes. TMP is designed for distributed systems. It can be used to monitor multiprocessor systems by removing the network interface and network related functions in the monitoring network. A TMP can be permanently built into the monitored node. This is emphasized by drawing the TMP in the box of its target node.

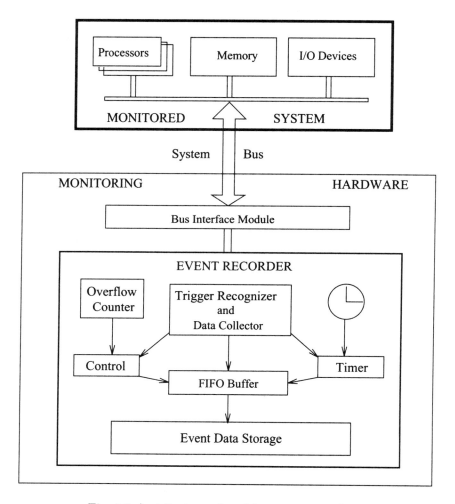

Fig. 5.2 Architecture of multiprocessor monitor.

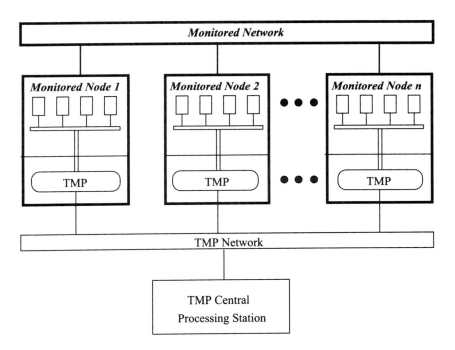

Fig. 5.3 Integration of a monitored system and TMPs. (Reprinted, by permission, from [152]. ©1990 IEEE)

TMP Architecture

A TMP consists of a bus interface module, an event processing unit (EPU), a general-purpose processor, its local memory, and I/O devices. Fig. 5.4 shows the architecture of a TMP. The bus interface module is target-system dependent, and it encapsulates the details of the target system so that the other components of the TMP can be independent of the target system. The processor is used to process collected events. The memory is used for storing collected events and as a working space for the processor. It cannot be accessed by the target processor. Some I/O devices are used to display the behavior of the target node on screen or print on printers. A hard disk can be used to store a large amount of collected data.

The EPU consists of a comparator, a clock and timer, an overflow control, and an event buffer. The clock and timer provide the time reference for events. The resolution of the clock guarantees that no two successive events have the same time stamps. The clock and timer do not interfere with the timer in the target system in any way. The comparator is responsible for checking the target system's address bus for designated events. Once such an address is detected, the matched address, the time, and the data on the target system's data bus are stored in the event buffer.

Overflow control is used to detect events lost due to buffer overflow. The TMP software should be aware of overflows to avoid presenting incorrect information. The overflow control can be implemented in two ways. In the first approach, an overflow counter counts the number of events lost. The value of the counter is stored with the first event that was stored in the buffer after the overflow. Thus the TMP software knows how many events were not recorded. In this method several bits are needed to store this number. For example, if 16 is estimated to be the maximum possible lost events, then 4 bits are needed to store the number. This method is employed in [152, 149].

It is very hard, if not impossible, to guess what the lost events are, so the exact number of the lost events may not be helpful in testing and debugging. Thus a second method uses a single software bit flag for every event event entry in the buffer to indicate an occurrence of overflow. It is set when overflow occurs and is reset after the next event is stored in the buffer. Thus every event is recorded with the flag field as zero if no overflow has occurred. In this way the TMP software is informed of overflow and only one bit is needed for each event.

Event Generation and Data Collection

In a memory-mapped monitoring system, each event is assigned an address. The trigger for recording information pertaining to an event of interest consists of a write instruction which is inserted at a well-chosen point in the target program(s). The write instruction stores a value to the address assigned to the event that is monitored by the hardware monitoring unit. This

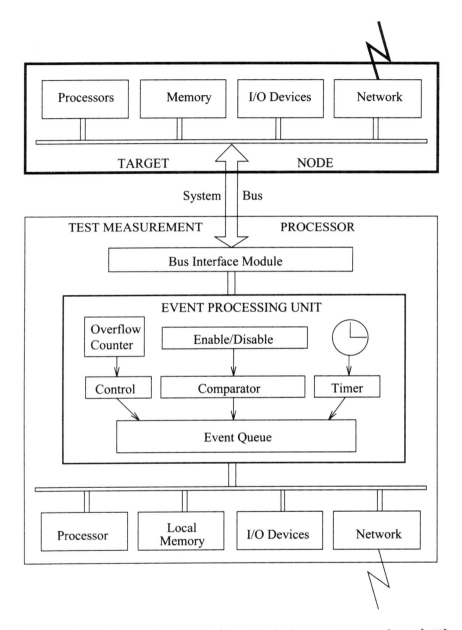

Fig. 5.4 Architecture of a TMP. (Reprinted, by permission, from [152]. ©1990 IEEE)

section will discuss event address assignment and monitoring at the process and function levels.

The addresses assigned to events should not interfere with the target memory. The address range for events should be programmable so that the TMP can adapt to different hardware environments. For multiprocessor nodes a different range of addresses can be assigned to each processor. Thus it can be determined which processor generated the event from the recorded address. For example, for an assignment of 16 processors and 256 events, the least significant 8 bits (bits 0 through 7) can be assigned to the 256 different events, and the next 4 bits (bits 8 through 11) can be assigned to the processors. Thus the address 3CF27945 hexadecimal represents event 45 hexadecimal generated by processor 9. It can be seen from this example that only part of an event address needs to be saved and that the processor ID can be easily generated by hardware with a comparator. The other bits can be discarded.

Each event is triggered by a write instruction that sends the event address to the system bus. The comparator in the EPU will watch for this address through the bus interface module and mark it as an event. The format of the write instruction is

store event_addr, value

Event_addr represents the event, and the value of the store instruction serves as a parameter of the event. For example, the send message event may have an address SEND, and the value specifies the sending process ID. For events with more than one parameter, several such instructions may be needed, with one parameter per instruction.

State transition events (i.e., assign, preempt, block, and resume) can only be collected by instrumenting the kernel, since those events are not visible to user processes. For example, to record the *assign* event, the following instructions may be inserted into the kernel:

store X_ASSIGN, process_ID
store X_ASSIGN, priority

Here X represents processor X. This processor address should be decoded in hardware. To record the *block* event, the following may be inserted:

store X_BLOCK, process_ID
store X_BLOCK, waiting_q_ID

To monitor execution behavior at the process level, the events listed in Table 2.1 need to be recorded while the target program is executing. The kernel needs to be instrumented to trigger events such as interrupts, which are not visible to the user processes. Since the user processes cannot detect interrupts, the kernel has to be instrumented to trigger the recording of interrupt events. The kernel should store the port ID of the interrupt and interrupted process's ID and then execute the interrupt routine.

In wait and signal events of semaphores, the value of a semaphore may not be accessible to user processes in some systems. For those systems the kernel needs to be instrumented to store semaphore values and trigger event monitoring. However, in most cases what matters is whether the process that called the wait operation can continue or has to wait for the semaphore to be released. That is, the exact value of the semaphore is not important. Thus we can remove the semaphore value from the process-level event list. To determine whether or not the calling process was blocked on the semaphore, we can check whether there was a BLOCK event on the waiting queue of the semaphore right after the wait operation was called. If there was one, it means the process was blocked on the semaphore. If there was not such an event, the semaphore's value was positive, and the process was continued with no blocking.

Another event needing attention is *process termination*. A process terminates normally by executing an exit system call, or abnormally if it is killed by its parent or the kernel. The process can be instrumented to record a normal termination. The kernel can also be instrumented to record such events. However, for abnormal termination the process cannot detect such an event by itself, and hence it cannot record such an event. Thus the kernel has to be instrumented to send the instructions for this event to the monitoring hardware.

All other events can be recorded by instrumenting the user processes. For example, the send event needs three parameters: the sender's ID, the receiver's ID, and the message ID. The instructions for a send event can be the following:

> store X_SEND, sender_ID
> store X_SEND, receiver_ID
> store X_SEND, message_ID

To monitor the function-level events listed in Table 2.2, user processes need to be instrumented to trigger function call and return events. To record function call events, the following code can be inserted into the calling function right before the function call:

> store X_F_CALL, calling_function_ID
> store X_F_CALL, parameter_1
> store X_F_CALL, parameter_2
> ...
> store X_F_CALL, parameter_n

To record function return events, the following instructions can be inserted in the called function right before the return statement:

store X_F_RETURN, called_function_ID
store X_F_RETURN, parameter_1
store X_F_RETURN, parameter_2
...

store X_F_RETURN, parameter_n

For function call events, only passed-in parameters need to be recorded; for function return events, only returned parameters need to be recorded.

The store instructions are simple memory write instructions. These instruction sequences used to trigger monitoring are not atomic. For example, while the three instructions for the send operation are being executed, they may be preempted by another process, and the new running process may also send a message to another process. This can be problematic as shown in the following example: Suppose that process p_i sends a message to p_j. When p_i executes this send system call, three event triggering instructions should be executed:

1 store X_SEND, p_i
2 store X_SEND, p_j
3 store X_SEND, msg_1

Because these instructions are not atomic, they can be preempted. Let us assume that the message is preempted by process p_m after the first instruction. If process p_m sends a message to process p_n, then another three instructions are executed:

4 store X_SEND, p_m
5 store X_SEND, p_n
6 store X_SEND, msg_2

Thus the collected data will be

1 store X_SEND, p_i
4 store X_SEND, p_m
5 store X_SEND, p_n
6 store X_SEND, msg_2
2 store X_SEND, p_j
3 store X_SEND, msg_1

How can the source of these parameters be distinguished? There are two possible solutions. The first treats the instructions for an event as a critical section that must be executed exclusively in relation to the instructions for other events. This guarantees that the instructions for an event will not be interrupted by other events. Semaphores can be used for this mutual exclusion. A binary semaphore X_bin_sema is declared for each processor X.

It is shared by all of the events on that processor. The instructions for each event use wait and signal operations as follows:

> wait(X_bin_sema)
> store X_SEND, sender_ID
> store X_SEND, receiver_ID
> store X_SEND, message_ID
> signal(X_bin_sema)

A variation of this method disables all of the interrupts on the processor while it is executing the instructions of an event group. Since no user process can disable all the interrupts, it implies that the kernel has to be instrumented to guarantee the atomic execution of the instructions. This solution is adopted in [152, 149]. This solution would not be desirable in real-time environments because it can cause the system to miss important interrupts or not service important interrupts promptly.

The second solution is to allow event sequences to be interleaved during event collection. During reconstruction of the system's behavior, those preempted events can be re-constructed by software if enough information is collected. Process state transition events can be used to determine which process was in execution, when it was preempted, and when it was resumed. For the above interleaving example, there must be a preempt event in which p_i was preempted, and before the event of line 2 there must be a resume event in which p_i was resumed. Thus we can infer that the first and the last two lines are the parameters of a single send event.

Interleaving between events on different processors is much easier to handle because the processes can be distinguished by the processor addresses. For example, assume in the previous example that the first send was generated by processor X and the second by processor Y (p_m and p_n were on processor Y), then the collected data would be in the following sequence:

> 1 store X_SEND, p_i
> 4 store Y_SEND, p_m
> 5 store Y_SEND, p_n
> 6 store Y_SEND, msg_2
> 2 store X_SEND, p_j
> 3 store X_SEND, msg_1

It is obvious that the two events can be separated by the processor addresses. The procedure for postprocessing events can be summarized as follows:

1. Separate events generated by different processors based on processor addresses.

2. Separate events caused by different processes based on resumed events, i.e., which process was in execution.

3. Link interrupted instruction sequences together.

Haban et al. [152, 149] employed this approach to implement a general method that can be used with any computer system and applied it to their incremental architecture for distributed systems (INCAS) multicomputer environment for collecting Kernel and process level events. Each TMP consists of a M68000-based processor with 1 Mbyte of local memory, dual RS232 ports for local interactions, a network interface to other TMPs and an event processing unit (EPU). The EPU consists of a local event buffer, a comparator, a clock, and an overflow counter. The event buffer is a FIFO queue with a depth of 16. Each entry in the buffer consists of 84 bits, 4 for the processor ID; 8 for events, 32 for event parameters; 36 for the time-stamp; and 4 for control (CPU mode, overflow marker).

Mink, Carpenter, Nacht, and Roberts [263, 262] use memory-mapped monitoring to implement the trace measurement system (Trams) for measuring the performance of MIMD multiprocessor systems. It uses software triggering and hardware recording of time and processor identification. Users embed triggering write instructions in their programs. Users can specify the data to be recorded. This hybrid monitoring architecture has been designed into a VLSI chip set that integrates the Trams' functions of software triggering and hardware recording with a pattern-matching hardware monitor that is used to measure architectural performance. This chip set is designed for centralized data collection in a tightly coupled system or a measurement node associated with each processor in a loosely coupled multiprocessor.

Reilly [329] proposed a monitoring system developed by DEC for extracting information from a parallel processor in order to debug, find the hardware bottlenecks, and determine the software performance. The monitored programs are first instrumented by the programmer, then the monitoring hardware recognizes the event signals generated during the execution of the monitored programs.

5.3.2   Coprocessor Monitoring

In commercial aviation all aircraft are equipped with a flight recorder that constantly records vital information on the aircraft. This idea is adopted by Gorlick in real-time systems monitoring. Gorlick [142] proposed a hybrid technique for monitoring and recording the behavior of real-time systems with minimal overhead. A "flight recorder" is attached to the target processor through a coprocessor interface. Instrumented programs send information on the events of interest to the flight recorder through the coprocessor interface. The flight recorder is connected to the target processor like a floating point coprocessor. The difference between this approach and the memory-mapped approach is that coprocessor instructions are used as the triggers instead of a set of special addresses.

Flight Recorder Architecture

The flight recorder consists of an event manager, a general-purpose processor, a clock, a set of registers, memory, and its own I/O devices and network connection. The registers can be accessed by the target processors directly through the coprocessor instructions defined in the target processors. The memory and the I/O devices are local to the flight recorder, and so are independent of the target processors. To minimize interference, the flight recorder is connected to a separate network. The processor of the flight recorder is used to process data and communicate with other flight recorders in constructing the system behavior for distributed environments. The event manager is used to decode and execute the coprocessor instructions. Fig. 5.5 shows the architecture of the flight recorder.

The flight recorder models the target system's behavior as a sequence of events. The target system to be monitored is instrumented using two types of event-related monitoring coprocessor instructions. The instructions are divided into data instructions and event instructions. The data instructions are used to send event-related information to the registers of the flight recorder. They also can be used to send control data to the flight recorder to enable or disable events; this will be discussed in detail shortly. The event instructions are used to inform the flight recorder of the occurrence of an event. When the flight recorder receives these instructions, it will save the information pertinent to the events.

The events recorded can be divided into three types. The first type is privileged kernel events used to record events that occur when the target processor is in the supervisor mode. These events can only be enabled or disabled by the kernel. Since the target processor must be in the supervisor mode to record these events, user processes executed in the user mode cannot generate kernel events by accident. The second event type can be used for both kernel and user-level events; the mode of the target processor is not significant. However, only the kernel can enable and disable an event of this type. The last type is used for users' processes that can be enabled or disabled by both the kernel and user processes. Events can be enabled or disabled by the target processors. The total number of events to be monitored is application dependent. According to [152, 149], 256 types of events are sufficient for most systems.

The enabling and disabling of events are controlled by a subset of the registers in the flight recorder. They are called *filter registers*. Each event is assigned a bit in the filter registers, which indicates if an event is enabled or disabled. For example, 256 events can be covered with eight 32-bit registers, R_0 to R_7. The first 64 events can use R_0 and R_1 for the privileged kernel events. The next 64 events can use R_2 and R_3 for mixed events. The remaining 128 events can use R_4 through R_7 for the user events. The target processors can read any register but can only write to registers R_4 through

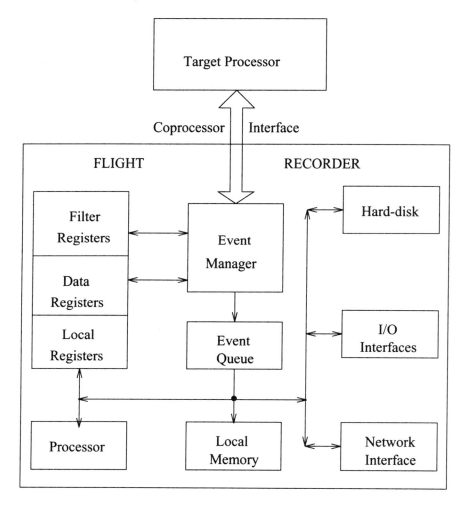

Fig. 5.5 Architecture of the flight recorder. (Reprinted, by permission, from M. M. Gorlick, The flight recorder: An architectural aid for system monitoring, *Proc. of ACM/ONR Workshop on Parallel and Distributed Debugging*, Santa Cruz, CA, pp. 175-183, May 1991. ©1991 Association of Computing Machinery, Inc.)

R_7 without restrictions. However, the target processors can only write to the first four registers when the target processor is in the supervisor mode.

The instructions for accessing the filter registers have the following form:

> load_filter R_i, (addr)
> store_filter R_i, (addr)

The first instruction loads the filter register R_i with the contents of the target processor memory location *addr*, and the second stores the contents of filter register R_i in the target processor's memory location *addr*.

Each event has a unique identifier. The target processor sends this identifier to specify the event to be recorded. This number is also used to find the corresponding entry in the filter registers. For 2^n events, n bits are used to encode the ID number. For the above example, 8 bits are necessary to uniquely identify 256 (2^8) events. The three most significant bits can be used to identify the filter register and the other five bits to identify the bit in the filter register. For this configuration it would be trivial to design necessary circuitry for determining whether an event is enabled or disabled.

An event can occur more than once. For each occurrence the target processor notifies the flight recorder by sending an event instruction along with the event ID to the flight recorder. This instruction is then decoded by the event manager. The event manager checks the filter to see if the event is enabled. If it is, the event manager assembles all the related information for the event and puts it into the event queue. The event is time-stamped by the event manager using the onboard clock. The ID of the processor that generated the event is also included. The event instruction has the following form:

> mark event_ID

Besides the event ID, time stamp, and processor's ID, an event can also have other key data. For example, in direct message passing, a send operation's destination and the ID or the contents of the message sent can be recorded. A subset of the registers in the flight recorder is used for such data. The target processor can access these data registers using data instructions. Before the target processor notifies the flight recorder of the occurrence of an event, it can save the the keywords of the event to the data registers. For example, four 32-bit registers D_0 to D_3 may be used for the keywords of events. In other words, an occurrence of an event can have up to 128 bits for its parameters. The data instruction for accessing the filter registers may have the following form:

> load_key D_i, (addr)
> store_key D_i, (addr)

The first instruction loads the filter register D_i with the contents of the

Bits 24 - 31	Bits 16 - 23	Bits 0 - 15
Event ID	Processor ID	Time-Stamp (high bits)
Time Stamp (low bits)		
Data Register D_0		
Data Register D_1		
Data Register D_2		
Data Register D_3		

Fig. 5.6 Event entry structure. (Reprinted, by permission, from M. M. Gorlick, The flight recorder: An architectural aid for system monitoring, *Proc. of ACM/ONR Workshop on Parallel and Distributed Debugging*, Santa Cruz, CA, pp. 175-183, May 1991. ©1991 Association of Computing Machinery, Inc.)

target processor memory location *addr*, and the second stores the contents of filter register D_i in the target processor's memory location, *addr*. Upon receiving the event instruction from the target processor, the event manager appends the contents of the data registers to the data block in the event queue. Thus, as shown in Fig. 5.6, a block of data is associated with the occurrence of each event. Because instructions may be interrupted, the filter registers and data registers must be saved during context switches.

Event Generation and Data Collection

State transition events – that is assign, preempt, block, and resume – can only be collected by instrumenting the kernel, since these events are not visible to user processes. To record the *assign* event, the following instructions are inserted into the kernel:

> load_key D_0, process_ID
> load_key D_1, priority
> mark ASSIGN

to record the *block* event, the following are inserted:

> load_key D_0, process_ID
> load_key D_1, waiting_q_ID
> mark BLOCK

All of the above events can only be triggered by the kernel. To avoid any generation of such events by the user, they should only be assigned kernel IDs. Thus the target processor must be in supervisor mode when such events are recorded, and users cannot disable these events.

To monitor execution behavior at the process level, events listed in Table 2.1 need to be recorded while the target program executes. As discussed earlier, events like interrupts, semaphore values, and process terminations are not discernible to the user processes. To monitor these events, the kernel needs to be instrumented.

The remaining events can be recorded by instrumenting user processes. For example, a send event can be recorded by inserting the following code right before the send system call:

$$load\_key\ D_0,\ sender\_ID$$
$$load\_key\ D_1,\ receiver\_ID$$
$$load\_key\ D_2,\ message\_ID$$
mark SEND

These instructions can also be incorporated into the send system call in order to make them transparent to the user. The process level events can be assigned IDs of any of the three types. The instructions for kernel- and process-level events can be permanently built into the kernel so that it generates a constant perturbation. This ensures that the target system will present the same behavior after the embedded code is removed.

To monitor the function-level events listed in Table 2.2, user processes need to be instrumented to trigger function calls and return events. These must be either mixed mode or user mode. To record function call events, the following code can be inserted in the calling function right before the function call:

$$load\_key\ D_0,\ calling\_function\_ID$$
$$load\_key\ D_1,\ parameter\_1$$
$$load\_key\ D_2,\ parameter\_2$$
...
$$load\_key\ D_n,\ parameter\_n$$
mark F_CALL

To record function return events, the following instructions can be inserted in the called function right before the return statement:

$$load\_key\ D_0,\ called\_function\_ID$$
$$load\_key\ D_1,\ parameter\_1$$
$$load\_key\ D_2,\ parameter\_2$$
...
$$load\_key\ D_n,\ parameter\_n$$

mark F_RETURN

For function call events, only passed-in parameters need to be recorded; for function return events, only returned parameters need to recorded. The total number of passed and returned parameters are application dependent. However, it has been suggested in [114] that the number of formal parameters in routines should not be more than five for clarity and simplicity. Thus five data registers should be sufficient in the flight recorder for function-level monitoring.

It is important to recognize that the time recorded is the time at which the event instruction was executed not the time at which the event occurred. This time is recorded because the event instruction may be interrupted before the event occurs. For example, we can record a send event using the following code:

$$1 \text{ load\_key } D_0, \text{ sender\_ID}$$
$$2 \text{ load\_key } D_1, \text{ receiver\_ID}$$
$$3 \text{ load\_key } D_2, \text{ message\_ID}$$
$$4 \text{ mark SEND}$$
$$5 \text{ send(Receiver\_ID, message)}$$

The time at which the send is called is of interest. However, because the execution of the above 5 lines is not atomic, the process could be preempted (or interrupted) after line 4 and before line 5, when the send is called. Thus the time recorded by the flight recorder is the time at which the "mark SEND" instruction was executed, not the time at which the send was called. When the send was called depends on how long the process was preempted. Thus the time recorded for each event should only be interpreted as the time at which the mark instruction was executed.

5.4 Monitoring Distributed Systems

5.4.1 Distributed Monitoring System Architectures

In distributed systems, monitoring must be distributed to each node of the monitored system to avoid high perturbation of the system's data paths. This is accomplished by attaching a monitor to each node of the system. The monitor detects triggers and records data generated by the node. The recorded event data can be stored local to each node or transmitted to a central collector. There are problems with this approach. If the recorded data is not distributed evenly, too much data could be stored at one node. To build a sufficiently large data storage for each node would be very expensive. One way to solve this problem is by transmitting recorded data at each node to a central location. Then the data storage of each node is replaced with a network interface that sends data to the central storage. To reduce perturbation,

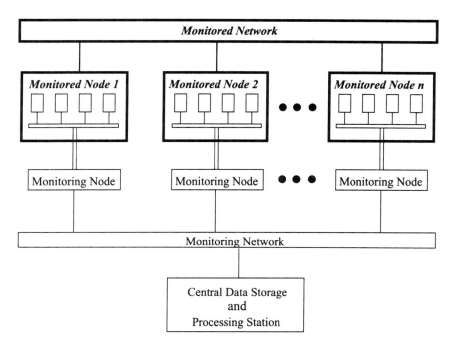

Fig. 5.7 Architecture of a distributed monitor.

a separate dedicated network is used for the collected data.

Each monitoring node has its own local physical clock to order the events on the node. However, due the drifting nature of quartz-controlled oscillators, no two physical clocks run at exactly the same rate. Therefore, the clocks at monitoring nodes must be synchronized to provide a systemwide global time. The monitoring network can be used as hardware medium for the clock synchronization algorithms. The clock synchronization then will not perturb the network of the monitored system. Fig. 5.7 shows the general architecture of a monitoring system in a distributed environment.

Each node of the monitored system can be a single processor or a tightly coupled multiprocessor system. Trigger recognition and data collection hardware at an individual node is the same as in a single processor or a multiprocessor system except that the clocks needs to be synchronized and a separate network is needed for data transmission to the central data storage and clock synchronization. Thus all the hardware techniques discussed above can be employed for distributed systems with little modification.

Haban and Wybranietz's DTM system [152, 149] employs a memory-mapped monitoring approach to monitor a program's execution in a distributed environment. The monitoring system consists of a set of TMPs attached to target nodes and a separate network. Each distributed target node has a TMP for event detection and collection. The collected event data with intraprocess relationships is locally processed, whereas event data pertaining to interprocess relationships is sent to the central monitor for global processing.

The topology of the TMP network does not have to be the same as the target's topology. Each monitoring node is responsible for collecting and processing events on its corresponding target node. The TMP central processing station is used to collect and process global information from individual TMPs. A TMP sends global information to the central processing station through the TMP network. Thus communication between TMPs does not interfere with the network of the target system. Fig. 5.3 shows the integration structure of the system.

Mink, Carpenter, Nacht, and Roberts [263, 262] employ a token ring for the monitoring network in their multiprocessor performance-measurement system. The token ring connects all the monitoring nodes attached to target nodes to a central station. It used a simple token-arbitrated protocol with the central station for the master as the only destination for all data on the network. When a monitoring node receives the token, it places its data on the network and passes the token. If it does not have data to send, it simply passes the token. The central station is the only originator of tokens, and it detects the loss of a token.

To provide a high-speed network for transmitting the collected data, the network path is designed for byte-serial rather than bit-serial operation. Eight lines are therefore needed for transmitting the data. In addition three control lines are needed for the token signal, clock synchronization, and the reset signal. The bandwidth of the network is 80 Mbytes per second.

5.4.2 Global Time and Clock Synchronization

In distributed environments, each monitoring node has its own local clock. The physical clock of each node totally orders the events on each node. However, as was mentioned earlier, due the drifting nature of quartz-controlled oscillators, no two physical clocks run at exactly the same time rate. This means that a completely accurate global clock cannot be implemented without additional hardware support.

In Haban and Wybranietz's DTM system two different versions of clock synchronization are implemented. The first version uses a physical global clock that triggers the time counters in the TMPs. This version is only used if the global clock is several feet away from the TMP nodes. The other version uses a central machine to synchronize all the clocks by running an algorithm similar to the TEMPO algorithm [148]. It does this by computing the clock difference with respect to each local timer using, the equation

$$D = \frac{D_1 - D_2}{2}$$

D_1 is the difference between the local node's message receiving time stamp and the central node's message sending time stamp, and D_1 is the difference of the central node's acknowledge receiving time stamp and the local node's acknowledge sending time stamp.

5.5   Summary

In hybrid monitoring the target system to be monitored is instrumented with triggering instructions to send event information to the monitoring hardware unit. Those triggering instructions can placed in the code by hand or generated automatically by compilers or monitoring tools. When instrumented programs are executed, the monitoring hardware identifies and processes the events of interest. Hybrid monitoring not only reduces the complexity of hardware-only monitoring but also minimizes the perturbation of software monitoring. Thus the goal of a hybrid approach is to provide hardware assistance that minimizes interference yet maximizes flexibility. The execution overhead of those instructions for both kernel and process-level monitoring can be so low ($< 1\%$) that they can be included in the production software.

Exercises

1. Describe the general procedure used to implement hybrid monitoring approaches.

2. How does the hybrid monitoring approach combine hardware and software monitoring approaches?

3. Describe the two different triggering approaches currently used for hybrid monitoring.

4. Compare the hardware devices used by the hardware monitoring approach and the hybrid monitoring approach.

5. What different triggering methods should be used when monitoring single processor systems and multiprocessors systems?

6. How does the hybrid monitoring approach reduce the amount of memory needed when collecting the run-time information?

7. For processors that have an on-chip cache, do different cache write-back schemes work better than others with memory-mapped monitoring?

8. Does a hybrid monitor with memory-mapped monitoring use less hardware than a similar hardware monitor that snoops the system bus of a processor that has no on-chip cache or prefetch buffer?

9. Show how a programmable logic device (PLD) could be used to implement the address decoding logic in a hybrid monitor. Use 0xF000 as the address decoded.

10. How could you make the monitor in the previous question program-mable? That is, the monitor would work with the same address and data bus but would trigger on different addresses. What steps are required, and what hardware would be needed?

11. In Section 5.3 it is mentioned that with memory-mapped monitoring, a single monitoring unit can be used for a shared memory multiprocessor. Explain why this is possible, and why it would not be possible with a pure hardware monitor.

12. How useful is a monitor that cannot record all events? That is, are there situations where it doesn't matter if all the data was collected? If you answered yes, not all data is important, how does the monitor know that what was missed was not important? If you answered no, is all data collected useful?

13. This chapter mentions that to monitor interrupts, the kernel must be instrumented. Using your favorite operating system try to instrument a typical interrupt. Explain the main difficulties encountered when instrumenting the operating system.

Chapter 6

Debugging Distributed Real-Time Systems

Debugging is the process of detecting, locating, analyzing, isolating, and correcting suspected faults. Debugging approaches use static and dynamic analysis techniques. Static analysis is used to verify the design specification and the source code to detect program anomalies, whereas dynamic analysis is used to analyze the program's execution behavior.

The most straightforward way to implement distributed debugging is to associate a sequential debugger with each target process and collect information from each distributed debugger. This implementation would be adequate if bugs occurred only inside the nodes. However, processes executing on different nodes have interprocess relationships that would not be detected with such an implementation. In addition, because real-time systems cannot be stopped or repeated, conventional interactive debuggers are not suitable for such systems. Therefore a dynamic approach featuring real-time monitoring is necessary.

In this chapter issues associated with analysis, monitoring, and debugging DRTSs will be examined. Section 6.1 examines static debugging techniques and a variety of approaches that have been proposed. Section 6.2 examines debugging DRTSs in relationship to the standard cyclic debugging techniques and shows why techniques designed specifically for DRTSs are needed. Section 6.3 presents a variety of issues related to monitoring, including deterministic replay, real-time debugging, scheduling, and process migration. Section 6.4 summarizes the main issues for debugging DRTSs.

The relationship between monitoring and debugging is described by McDowell and Helmbold [250], and by Plattner [308]. In addition McDowell and Helmbold [250] discuss the problems associated with debugging concurrent computing systems, including the probe effect, nonrepeatability, and the lack of a synchronized global clock. They survey three general solutions: traditional breakpoint style debugging, event monitoring, and static analysis. Each debugging technique has a tutorial treatment with a discussion of related work. McDowell and Helmbold conclude with a comprehensive comparison of different debugging techniques and systems.

6.1   Static Analysis and Debugging Techniques

Static analysis uses formal specification and verification to locate erroneous code before program execution. In general, static analysis is supported by a formal specification language that precisely specifies the system properties, a formal design method that systematically develops the system, and a formal verification method that logically proves the correctness of the developed system with respect to the specification. Among the principle characteristics of DRTSs (i.e., interprocess communication, interprocess synchronization, and timing constraints), the timing constraints are the most difficult to verify because reasoning about time requires nonmonotonic and continuous properties that are usually nonspecifiable and nonverifiable. Therefore, for static analysis to be suitable for finding the stringent timing requirements of DRTSs, it must be able to specify and verify the system properties in terms of time.

In static analysis some system characteristics are predictable and fixed, and some are predictable but not fixed and need to be constrained by setting upper and lower bounds. Some characteristics are totally unpredictable and remain unknown until run-time.

Some examples of predictable characteristics are:

- Period of periodic processes.

- Procedures for handling aperiodic processes.

- Process priorities.

Some examples of constrained characteristics and their bounded values are:

- Arrival time of aperiodic processes. A range is assigned before execution.

- Frequency of aperiodic processes. An upper bound is assigned before execution.

- Amount of interprocess communication. An upper bound is assigned before execution.

- Transmission delay for interprocess communication. An upper bound is assigned before execution.

The unpredictable characteristics are:

- Number of external interrupts.

- Number of context switches due to interrupts.

- Number of cycles taken by DMA cycle stealing.

Hsieh [172] provides a static approach that treats the timing analysis of cyclic concurrent programs as a set of cooperating sequential processes. The processes perform a sequence of atomic operations. The execution times of the atomic operations are independent of the synchronization needs of the concurrent programs. GR0 path-expressions are used to describe the synchronization and concurrence of the atomic operations. The behavior of a program is represented as a partial ordering of atomic operations in graph form. The timing analysis is performed on this graph using a critical path analysis method. His main concern is to determine whether a program can satisfy a given set of timing constraints.

Harter [187] proposes a timing analysis approach for level-structured systems. He assumes that the target system employs a multiple priority scheduling mechanism, is level structured, has a known number of processes, and has preset process priorities. The response time of a process is computed by including the delay time caused by the interruptions from higher-priority processes. In other words, the execution time of the higher-priority processes is treated as a net increase in the execution times of the processes at lower priority levels. Since the priorities of the processes and the number of processes in the system must be known in advance, this approach may not be suitable to dynamic scheduling systems in which the priority of a process may vary with time.

Jahanian and Mok [179, 180] present a formal logic RTL (Real-Time Logic) for specification and analysis of real-time systems. An event-action model is used to specify the timing behavior of a system. RTL formulas are used to express both the timing specification of a system and the safety assertions about the system. Time is captured by a function that assigns time values to events. Timing constraints are reflected as restrictions on this function. The specification of a system, given in terms of the event-action model, is transformed into a set of formulas of RTL that can be used to derive the safety assertions to be analyzed. If the safety assertions are derivable from the formulas, then the system is considered safe. Thus their work focuses on determining the consistency of safety assertions with respect to a timing specification expressed in Real-Time Logic.

Leveson and Stolzy [218] employ time Petri nets to model real-time systems for safety analysis. Minimum and maximum times are defined as the range of delays of each transition in the time Petri nets. Their goal is to derive timing constraints in order to avoid high-risk states in determining the runtime checks needed to detect timing failures. In performing a safety analysis, the reachability graph for the Petri net model of the system is constructed to determine if the system will reach a high-risk state. Once a high-risk state is detected, the system design is modified using one of the many ways discussed by the authors to eliminate them. After such modifications, run-time faults and failures are identified to determine which functions are critical and need to be made fault tolerant.

Ostroff [298] presents an approach for checking properties of real-time systems. In his approach real-time systems are treated as a set of interacting real-time discrete event processes. The notions of a timed transition model (TTM) and a parallel composition of TTM's are used as a computation model for real-time systems. Real-time temporal logic (RTTL) is used for specifying the properties to be verified. Verification is performed by a set of procedures working on the reachability graph of the system modeled in TTM. The lower and upper bounds of transitions of TTM are measured with respect to the clock. A procedure is used to check the real-time response property described in RTTL against the reachability graph of the TTM model.

Razouk and Gorlick [327] extend interval logic to real-time interval logic for dealing with the problems in distributed real-time systems. Their main concern is verifying that the execution of a program, as characterized by the execution traces, is consistent with its formal description of the desired behavior, which is expressed in the real-time interval logic. The extensions, as claimed by the authors, include the ability to deal with real-time, more powerful interval specification mechanisms, a limited form of quantification, and the direct expression of event predicates. Their work focuses on verification of timing constraints using the program execution traces. The authors do not mention how to use the history trace to help the user debug programs.

Jahanian and Goyal [177] use real-time logic to dynamically check timing constraints. Their approach is a formal technique for exception handling in real-time systems. Computation is viewed as a sequence of events that defines points in time at which events occur. A timing property is modeled as a relationship among events specified in RTL. Three classes of properties are identified and expressed in RTL and three corresponding algorithms for detecting violation of the properties are presented.

The disadvantages of static analysis are that the set of examined states is large and the complexity of computation high (often exponential). In addition static analysis has inherent limitations in dealing with asynchronous interactions between real-time controlling processes and real-world controlled processes. In other words, the behavior of DRTSs cannot fully be modeled or described until programs are running. For example, assumptions made during the design phase may be violated at run-time because of unpredictable race conditions among software processes due to unpredictable communication delays. In addition, when designing DRTSs, it may be necessary to assume an upper bound on processor-to-processor communication delays or to require a deadline on the execution of a task. However, violation of such assumptions must be detected dynamically. Since debugging DRTSs must account for the behavior of both the controlling processes and the controlled processes, the run-time information is extremely important. Therefore static analysis is not sufficient for debugging DRTSs. Nevertheless, static analysis plays an important role in the debugging phase, especially in reducing specification errors and design errors that appear in the early part of the design life cycle. The information from static analysis provides test data and debugging and monitoring guidelines for the dynamic debugging process [250]. For example, the program segments that do not need run-time support and have been analyzed and verified to be without errors can be exempted from monitoring. Conversely, the information gained from dynamic debugging can be used to reduce the computational complexity of static analysis by restricting the program states analyzed. In general, a debugging approach combining static analysis tools and dynamic debugging tools can assert structural and logical correctness at the static analysis level and allow the dynamic debugging to concentrate on functional and timing errors.

6.2 Dynamic Analysis and Debugging Techniques

The traditional dynamic method for debugging sequential software has no timing constraints. The program is executed until an error manifests itself; the programmer then stops execution, examines the program states, inserts assertions, and then re-executes the program in order to collect additional information about the error causes. This style of debugging is called *cyclic debugging*. Three techniques are used to perform cyclic debugging: memory dumps, tracing, and breakpoints:

1. *Memory dumps.* The memory dump technique provides the lowest level debugging information. Once the system is terminated abnormally or by programmer request, the program status, including program object code, register contents, and memory contents, is dumped into a file. This technique provides sufficient information to find the error. Unfortunately, programmers must have a strong background in machine-level language to examine the dumped code. Even so, the process is tedious and error prone.

2. *Tracing.* The tracing technique utilizes special tracing facilities embedded in the compiler or operating system to continuously track and display every step of the program's execution, including control flow, data flow, variable contents, and the function calling sequence. The advantage of tracing is that users can interactively suspend program execution to examine the changes of program states at any point in time. With hierarchical levels of abstraction support, users can examine arbitrary details of the program state during execution by traversing between levels and focusing on suspect program segments. Tracing gives programmers a sense of the step-by-step flow of the program's execution.

3. *Breakpoints.* The breakpoint technique utilizes predicates that are inserted either by the programmer or by the system to suspend program execution. The predicates can be conditions regarding data values, system times, or code segments. Once a predicate is satisfied, the program execution is suspended

and the relevant run-time information, such as variable values, stack contents, and register values, can be displayed. After the programmer examines the displayed information, program execution can be resumed.

If monitoring and other modifications are used, many of the approaches used in cyclic debugging can be used to dynamically debug DRTSs. Before examining how this can be done in the next section, we note here the types of program errors that can occur. They include errors due to deadlock, communication, synchronization, and scheduling.

Errors related to deadlock can be summarized as follows:

- Waiting for a process that is deadlocked with another process.

- Waiting for a message that has never been sent or is stuck somewhere in the network.

- Waiting for the use of mutually exclusive resources.

Errors related to communication are:

- Cannot locate the server before a time-out has occurred.

- Request lost.

- Reply lost.

- Acknowledgment lost.

- Server crashed.

- Client crashed.

- Server received duplicate messages.

Errors related to synchronization are:

- Logical clock incorrectly synchronized with the physical clock.

- Starvation caused by mutual exclusion.

Errors related to scheduling are:

- Time-outs.

- Missed deadlines.

- False starts.

- Execution delays.

As mentioned earlier, debugging DRTSs is difficult because of the timing constraints and the interprocess communication and synchronization of distributed real-time systems. Bugs located at the interprocess level are not easily isolated because few methods exist to depict the relationship between processes. Furthermore the correctness of a distributed real-time system depends not only on the logical results of the computation but also on the times at which the results are produced [369]. Thus the systems might not only commit computation errors, (i.e., the system produces incorrect results) but also timing errors, (i.e., the system produces results that do not conform to the timing constraints). Cyclic debugging is effective in debugging non real-time sequential software. The most straightforward approach to employ cyclic debugging in debugging DRTSs is by connecting non-real-time sequential debugging tools to each distributed process. However, there are four reasons why the cyclic approach is nearly impossible:

1. The need for continuous operation and asynchronous process interaction will rule out interactive debugging. Interactive debugging requires that program execution be suspend while the programmer examines the program states. But while the processes are halted, the physical clocks are still running. This can cause the suspended processes to miss their physical deadlines. This problem can be avoided by providing a logical clock for each asynchronous processing node that stops whenever processes on the node are halted. Thus logical time rather than physical time is used to measure the time-dependent operations. Therefore a process can miss its physical deadline but still meet the logical deadline. However, in DRTSs the real-world controlled processes must use physical clocks, so they cannot be stopped. Even if the real-world inputs were simulated to allow logical clocks, the approach would only be good for the testing and debugging phase, not for run-time debugging because the controlled processes cannot use a logical clock.

2. Lack of a global clock reference and a global state will rule out the sequential approach of simply connecting sequential debugging tools together. Processes in distributed real-time systems are distributed in different nodes and are executed in parallel. Therefore the state of the whole system is the union of the states of all nodes, and the time of the whole system has to be synchronized by a global time reference. This is difficult to achieve when debugging DRTSs because tracing and breakpoint facilities must be coordinated. When a process is halted by a breakpoint, the remaining processes must be either halted immediately by receiving a broadcast blocking message from the system or continue their execution until they are blocked by the halted process. However, the broadcasting messages are received at different times, so the global state of the entire halted system will not be accurate because processes are not halted at the same time. Also the clocks must be synchronized after every process interruption. This additional overhead is usually not acceptable in DRTSs. Other approaches such as Lamport's "happening-before" relation [207] cannot be used to fully describe the timing

behavior because the relationship only describes the event sequence, not the current time. Without a synchronized global state and a global clock, the total ordering and precise timing of an event occurrence cannot be determined because the precise sequence of two events occurring on two distinct nodes is nondeterministic. Therefore, in order to measure the accuracy of the global state in relation to the time of events on different nodes, a global time reference is needed.

3. The nondeterministic and nonrepeatable nature of DRTSs rules out cyclic debugging. Cyclic debugging is based on repeatability. Thus tracing facilities should exhibit the same program information every time they trace the same program with the same inputs. However, due to the nondeterministic characteristics of DRTSs, the tracing facilities may reveal different information about the same program for different traces, so errors cannot be reproduced. But reproducing errors is the cornerstone of cyclic debugging. One solution is to monitor the program execution and then to process the recorded information so that the execution of the monitored programs can be repeated.

4. Stringent timing constraints rule out the intrusive monitoring approach. In addition to the computation errors of conventional systems, DRTSs may have timing errors. Therefore both the attributes of system states and the times at which the system states occur need to be collected in order to debug timing errors. During monitoring, any attempt to gain information regarding program execution will affect the run-time behavior of the monitored programs. This is called the *probe effect* [250]. Since cyclic debugging needs instrumentation to reveal the program's status, this will affect the program's behavior, especially its timing behavior. In DRTSs, stringent timing constraints prohibit any interference with the execution of a target program because the overhead caused by the attempt to collect run-time information will change the target system's behavior. Errors that occurred with no interference may not manifest themselves when there is interference. On the other hand, some errors may be introduced because of the existence of interference. For example, in cyclic debugging, halting a process after a single step or at a breakpoint may cause other processes to miss their deadlines or have other problems.

6.3   Debugging Approaches with Monitoring Support

Information gained from monitoring can be used in many ways to help the debugging of distributed and/or real-time systems during or after the execution of the target program being monitored. We can classify debugging approaches with monitoring support as follows:

1. *Real-time display.* The execution of a target program is monitored and displayed, all in a continuous real-time mode (e.g., the execution of a program is monitored and displayed in real-time). This allows real-time browsing of program execution, but only limited debugging information can be provided. In this approach the target program cannot be suspended or repeated, and

no modification to the target program is allowed.

2. *Real-time debugging.* The execution of a target program is monitored, analyzed, and debugged, all in a continuous real-time mode. For example, a real-time debugger will terminate the execution of a process as soon as the debugger detects that a process will miss its deadline; then, if it is possible, the debugger reschedules this process to another processor in order to keep the system running correctly. In this approach the execution of the target program cannot be suspended or repeated, but it can be modified automatically in real-time during execution.

3. *Interactive debugging.* The execution of a target program is monitored and will be suspended for debugging if a predefined situation is encountered, such as a breakpoint. After bugs are fixed, the execution of the target program and the monitoring activity are resumed. In this approach the target program can be suspended and modified, but the execution is not repeatable. This approach is not suitable for real-time systems because the real-time processes cannot be stopped for debugging.

4. *Deterministic replay.* A trace or log of the program execution is recorded during the execution and can be replayed deterministically after the execution. In this approach the target program cannot be suspended during the monitoring but it can be replayed after the monitoring. That is, the replayed execution of the target program can be suspended for examination. Since this replaying is based on the execution trace, if any modification has been made to the program, the procedure of execution and monitoring has to be repeated in order to obtain the latest execution trace.

5. *Dynamic simulation.* A trace or log is recorded during a target program's execution and is used for dynamic simulation to evaluate the run-time behavior of target program in a different run with different test data. In this approach the execution of the target program is not suspended, and no modifications are allowed during the monitoring. However, the execution is repeatable and allows the replayed execution of the target program to be suspended for examination. This approach also accepts modifications to the program and simulates the new run-time behavior of the modified program without re-execution. This approach is particularly useful for testing.

Obviously a real-time display is only useful for browsing; it does not provide many aids to debugging. Likewise interactive debugging is not useful for real-time systems, since they cannot be stopped for debugging. The remaining three debugging approaches are suitable for debugging distributed real-time systems. Since dynamic simulation is very similar to deterministic replay, we will only discuss deterministic replay and real-time debuggers. In summary, deterministic replay is an off-line approach that enables one to debug a system by replaying a system's run-time behavior after the system's execution, whereas real-time debugging is an on-line approach that enables one to debug a system in real-time during the system's execution.

6.3.1 Deterministic Replay

After run-time data has been collected via monitoring, the next issue is how to utilize the event trace to facilitate debugging. Currently the most effective way of using the event trace is deterministic replay, which is very useful in exhibiting the program states repeatedly. The program errors can be displayed and examined in conjunction with the program states that have lead to the errors. Deterministic replay can be used to replay the event sequence that led to a deadlock so that the cause of the deadlock can be determined, or it can be used to replay the precedence and timing relationship between relevant processes and events so that the data dependency analysis can be performed. Because time-critical information has been saved during monitoring, additional instrumentation can be added to the replayed program without affecting the information replayed. Therefore breakpoints can be safely used in replay to reveal more information tailored to the programmer's needs. The principle advantage of using the deterministic replay in DRTSs is that it allows cyclic debugging without program re-execution. For a distributed system, replay is useful for repeatedly viewing the same interprocess-dependent information. The replay of interprocess-dependent information such as interprocess communication and synchronization provides an environment that allows debugging a single process in isolation. This is done by a controlled environment that simulates the rest of the processes execution and exhibits only the execution thread of the single examined process. For a real-time system, replay is useful for repeatedly viewing the same time-dependent information and the external I/O and interrupt information. The time-dependent information such as time stamps of events as well as the time between events provide a consistent database that allows timing analysis methods to perform deterministically. The external I/O and interrupts information provide the information needed to simulate the asynchronous process interaction between the controlling computer system and the controlled real-world.

A deterministic replay method is described by Tai, Carver, and Obaid [382]. When debugging an erroneous execution of a concurrent program P, with input X, it is often necessary to repeat the execution in order to collect additional debugging information. However, the re-execution of P with the same X may not to produce the same sequence of events (SYN-sequence). Thus deterministic debugging is proposed to enable a deterministic re-execution of a concurrent program based on the recorded SYN-sequence of a previous execution of P. The probe effect caused by monitoring the SYN-sequence is the main concern of this approach because it will slow down the execution of concurrent programs.

LeBlanc and Mellor-Crummey [212] present instant replay as a general solution for reproducing the execution behavior of tightly coupled parallel programs. During program execution the relative order of significant events is saved, but the data associated with such events is not saved. This approach uses less time and space to save the information needed for the program replay than other methods. Instant replay is independent of any particular form of interprocess communication used, but the interference caused by software instrumentation methods may restrict the capability of instant replay to debug parallel real-time systems.

A hardware monitoring and replay mechanism to deal with the testing and debugging of real-time software systems is presented by Tsai et al. [398]. They decompose the testing and debugging activity into three phases: (1) monitoring and data collection, (2) postprocessing, and (3) replay. The main objective of their approach is to ensure minimum interference of a target system's execution while providing the user with a comprehensive testing and debugging environment. Based on this approach, a noninterference monitoring architecture is implemented to collect program execution data without affecting the execution behavior of the target system. A replay mechanism is used to control the reproduction of program behavior and the examination of the states and behavior of the target system.

Another issue in debugging distributed systems is that when a breakpoint halts one process, the other processes in the system may not be able to halt at the same time because of communication delays. This causes an imprecise global state. Manabe and Imase [241] propose how to set breakpoints and halt the system in the replay phase to form a global state for distributed computing debugging. The principle of their approach is to find the first global state that satisfies a global condition set by predicates and to consider problems of halting at this global state. Two algorithms in conjunction with corresponding predicates are introduced in their paper. An algorithm called Conjunctive Predicate is used to halt the first global state that satisfies the predicate, and the other algorithm called Disjunctive Predicate is used to halt the global states other than the first global state.

6.3.2 Real-Time Debugging

Real-time debugging is used to verify that constraints are met and to use information gathered to reduce the constraints, since most of the bounded values are based on worst case assumptions. In addition, run-time analysis can be used to examine how unpredictable characteristics affect the system. Run-time analysis needs to be based on the run-time information gained during a target program execution. Such information includes the program itself and the target system on which the program is executing. This information must be monitored during program execution. That is, the monitoring system needs to collect not only program information but also the target hardware information.

A real-time debugger uses information such as the CPU utilization and various process queues to analyze the process status, fix bugs, and modify the program in real-time without halting the execution of the target program.

For example, a real-time debugger can locate processes that are going to miss their deadlines and then kill them in order to save CPU time for other processes; or it can compute the available CPU time during dynamic scheduling to allow more processes that were unscheduled with static scheduling to become scheduled; or it can evaluate resource utilization including CPU utilization, bus traffic, and I/O utilization so that a process that is going to miss its deadline can be migrated to another processor with a smaller load. In real-time monitoring the monitor works as a real-time control system, while the target system being monitored works as a controlled system. The requirement of real-time monitoring is that the time required for monitoring an event must be less than the intervals between events. For example, if events occur every 20 clock cycles, then the monitoring system must complete its monitoring activity within 20 clock cycles after detecting the event. Otherwise, some monitoring information will be lost or the program will be disrupted. In addition a real-time monitor must not change the behavior of the real-time system being monitored. That is, it must not cause any timing constraint violations.

6.3.3   Related Work

We now review various approaches to dynamically debugging.

Ogle, Schwan, and Snodgrass [294] present an ER information model based on a relational database approach for program monitoring and debugging. Two declarative languages are used in this model, the attribute language and the view language, to specify what to monitor and what action should be taken for a detected event. The attribute language is used to specify the attributes of an object to be monitored, such as the size of a waiting queue or a real-time constraint. The view language is used to specify the events to be monitored and the actions to be taken when an event is detected, such as migrating a process to another processor to balance the work load if the number of processes in a waiting queue exceeds the size defined by the attribute language. The declarative specification in the attribute language and the view language will be compiled to low-level event collection and analysis mechanisms and linked with the target program's object code and the monitor's object code for run-time monitoring and dynamic adaptation. The dynamic adaptation addressed in their paper is subject to the problem of load balancing between resource requests and consumption. If a resource is found to be overused, the dynamic adaptation can either slow down the resource request rate or reroute processes to a similar resource.

Raju, Rajkumar, and Jahanian [316] propose run-time monitoring for an environment with real-time tasks running on a multiple processor system. Their method detects, as early as possible, events that violate timing constraints so that the process with the violation can be terminated and release resources for other processes. There are three main issues covered in their paper: partial evaluation of timing constraints among events in order to detect violations earlier, minimizing message passing between monitors in order to reduce interprocess communication overhead, and performing clock synchronization in order to compare time stamps tagged from different clocks. The evaluation of timing constraint violations is based on a real-time logic (RTL) model using a graphical representation called a *constraint graph*, which can be used to denote the type of timing constraints (delay and deadlines) and to derive violations (missed deadlines) between the occurrences of time-related events. To ensure that monitoring is performed in real-time, the monitoring activities are treated as part of the application and needs to be scheduled with other application processes and must meet timing constraints as well.

Haban and Shin [150] show how the monitoring information can be used to dynamically schedule processes that cannot be scheduled with the static scheduling algorithm, and vice versa. The information can also be used to identify a process that is schedulable under a static scheduling algorithm but will miss its deadline during execution. Most of the scheduling work known today assumes that the task execution time is known a priori, and the scheduling algorithm is based on the worst-case execution time of each task. Since the worst execution time is usually longer than the actual time, some unschedulable tasks may be completed in time during actual execution. Haban and Shin handle the above problems by employing a real-time monitoring approach to analyze the monitored results. They then fed the analyzed results back to the host operating system for dynamic scheduling of tasks and verification of the monitored tasks.

Lyttle and Ford [232] present Rockwell's Ada symbolic debugging system (ASDS) which supports unobtrusive stand-alone monitoring with monitoring control software and event detection hardware to collect the low-level signals directly from the buses. Without modification of the monitored target programs, the monitoring control software in ASDS is used to define monitoring conditions and the actions to be taken whenever the conditions are met, while the event detection hardware is used to record incoming event addresses, bus signals, and target control signals. Besides the traditional techniques used by a symbolic debugger such as breakpoints, traces, and memory dumps, ASDS can resume the real-time execution of the monitored target programs by reconstructing the state of the target system based on the execution histories recorded before the target program was suspended for examination.

6.4 Problems Facing Monitoring Supported Debuggers

In this chapter we have examined a variety of static and dynamic debugging approaches. For DRTSs, monitoring is especially important. The challenges of monitoring-supported debugging is how to gather enough debugging information without causing intolerable monitoring interference. There are three challenges:

1. *The criteria for events of interest.* Programmers have to carefully define the events to be collected to prevent missing important information. Unfortunately, programmers need an a priori knowledge of which events will contribute to possible program errors. The most straightforward way to overcome this problem is to collect all events. However, this creates increased perturbation. This dilemma can be solved by using nonintrusive monitoring to passively collect all events occurring during program execution. If intrusive monitoring is used, then a comprehensive perturbation analysis must be performed to predict the degree of intrusion, and adjustments must be made during replay.

2. *The memory requirements for event trace.* The memory for storing event traces must be large enough and fast enough to store all the information. To quickly store the information, entire event logs should be put into main memory, which increases the bandwidth and decreases latency and makes the approach infeasible for large-scale software. As an alternative, a shadow memory separated from main memory could be used. Here a dedicated area of main memory is used to store the event trace, and its contents will be flushed out to the shadow memories periodically. The shadow memories can use a memory hierarchy to balance the speed and cost of the monitoring system. But this approach still intrudes on the program execution because the monitor shares the main memory with the target processor. This problem can be solved using hardware devices to fetch data directly from the buses rather than from main memory.

3. *The method of event presentation.* The presentation of monitored data both in terms of storage and display must be efficient and correct. But the challenge is how to abstract data from the voluminous event traces and display it in a meaningful way. Data filtering, hierarchical architecture, and program visualization provide the answer. A great deal of arbitrary data that is irrelevant to the program's execution is collected along with the events of interest during program monitoring. Data filtering eliminates unnecessary data from the event logs. The filtered event traces are then reorganized into a hierarchical architecture to form levels of abstraction that allow programmers to traverse arbitrary levels of detail tailored to their needs. Program visualization is the most efficient way to display multiple threads of control flow because it displays the interaction between processes graphically. For programmers it is easier to understand the global operation using graphical information as opposed to textual information.

6.5   Summary

Debugging is the process of detecting, locating, analyzing, isolating, and correcting suspected faults. Debugging approaches use static and dynamic analysis techniques. Static analysis is used to verify the design specification and the source code to detect program anomalies, whereas dynamic analysis is used to analyze the program's execution behavior.

The disadvantage of static analysis is that the set of examined states is large, and the complexity of computation is high. Furthermore static analysis has inherent limitations in dealing with asynchronous interactions between real-time controlling processes and real-world controlled processes. In other words, the behavior of DRTSs cannot fully be modeled or described until programs are running. Since debugging DRTSs must account for the behavior of both the controlling processes and the controlled processes, the run-time information is extremely important. Therefore static analysis is not sufficient for debugging DRTSs.

The traditional dynamic method for debugging sequential software is to execute the program until an error manifests itself; the programmer then stops execution, examines the program states, inserts assertions, and re-executes the program in order to collect additional information about the error causes. This kind of cyclic debugging is effective in debugging non-real-time sequential software. However, it is almost impossible for cyclic debugging to be employed for distributed real-time systems due to the fact that DRTSs require continuous operation, global clock and state, nondeterministic execution, and stringent timing constraints.

Several debugging approaches with monitoring support have been developed. They can be classified into real-time display, real-time debugging, interactive debugging, deterministic replay, and dynamic simulation. A real-time display is useful for browsing, but it does not provide many aids to debugging. Interactive debugging is not suitable for real-time systems that cannot be stopped for debugging. The remaining three debugging approaches can be used in debugging distributed real-time systems. Dynamic simulation is very similar to deterministic replay. Deterministic replay is an off-line approach that enables one to debug a system by replaying a system's run-time behavior after the system's execution, whereas real-time debugging is an on-line approach that enables one to debug a system in real-time during the system's execution.

Exercises

1. Define the terms debugging, static analysis, and dynamic analysis.

2. Why is it not possible to directly apply conventional distributed system debugging techniques to distributed real-time systems?

3. In static analysis, what kinds of system characteristics are predictable? What characteristics are unpredictable?

4. What are the advantages and disadvantages of static and dynamic analysis? How can the two approaches complement each other?

5. What is cyclic debugging? What are the three techniques mainly used when performing cyclic debugging?

6. Why is cyclic debugging not suitable for debugging distributed real-time systems?

7. Besides the errors listed in the chapter, give other types of errors related to deadlock, communication, and synchronization.

8. How many different debugging approaches with monitoring support exist? Which is the most suitable for distributed real-time system debugging?

9. List the main difficulties faced when attempting to debug distributed real-time systems.

10. Static analysis allows one to detect errors in code before it is executed. Are there errors that theoretically could be detected statically but in practice are not detectable?

11. What difficulties are posed when dynamically debugging a real-time single-processor system as compared to a single-processor system that is not real time? What techniques could be used to overcome these difficulties? What are the limitations of these techniques?

12. What difficulties are posed when dynamically debugging a distributed system as compared to a single-processor system? What techniques could be used to overcome these difficulties? What are the limitations of these techniques?

13. The need for dynamic debugging is partly due to poor design, sloppy coding, and bad habits. Doing it right the first time is much cheaper than debugging. Examine your programming style. Do you add comments to your code? Do you use enumerated types? Do you jump into the coding process too quickly without a clear idea of what you're trying to achieve and how you will achieve it? Think about the bugs that continually crop up in the code you write or work with. What can you do to reduce these bugs?

Chapter 7

Specification Techniques

7.1 Real-Time Processes

Real-time systems such as flight control systems, space shuttle landing control systems, aircraft avionics control systems, robotics, patient monitoring systems, and nuclear power plant control systems are often required to interact with an independent external environment. A typical real-time system must monitor and control this environment, exhibit predictable time-dependent behavior, and execute on a system with limited resources. Typically real-time systems consist of controlling subsystems (the computer controllers) and controlled subsystems (the physical environment). The interactions between the two subsystems are described by three operations: sampling, processing, and responding. The computer subsystems continuously sample data from the physical environment; the sampled data is processed immediately by the computer subsystems, and a proper response is sent back to the physical environment. All three operations must be performed within time constraints. Thus real-time systems are characterized by time-related correctness related to an event's start time, end time, and its duration. These time constraints distinguish real-time systems from non-real-time systems. For non-real-time systems, time affects the performance but not the correctness. For real-time systems, time plays a critical role; a delay or a failure of a system to respond may result in severe damage to the controlled subsystems or even fatal disasters.

A real-time system can be specified as a set of real-time processes and the interactions among these processes. A process is called a *real-time process* if the correctness of the process depends on when the process begins or how long the process executes. This time information can be defined for the whole process or for parts of the process.

Real-time processes can be further classified as *periodic*, *aperiodic*, or *communicating processes*. Each type of process requires different timing constructs. Periodic processes are activated at regular intervals. They usually perform a cyclical function, such as collecting data values at predetermined times or performing routine maintenance chores. The behavior of these processes are usually known a priori. A typical periodic process may sample execute a loop every N units of time. Periodic processes are characterized by a start time, maximum execution time, deadline, and laxity, where laxity refers to the time when a process must have completed its execution. A process with all of these characteristics that executes only once is still considered periodic. In contrast, aperiodic processes are usually involved with external real-world events, such as commands from human operators or a change in a sensor value. These events are frequently aperiodic and unpredictable. Because the events activate the execution of the process, these processes are aperiodic as well. So, besides the characteristics of a periodic process, aperiodic processes are characterized by their arrival time. Aperiodic processes can be described using a stimuli-response model. How the stimuli is handled can be specified in advance by the procedure handling the response. However, the arrival time of the stimuli is unknown before execution. In general, the use of aperiodic processes distinguishes hard real-time systems from other systems.

Except for the arrival time, one can model an aperiodic process as a periodic process. Since the types of stimuli and the corresponding procedures used to respond to the stimuli are known a priori, one can create a dedicated process that will look for the arrival of stimuli periodically. For example, a CPU checks for interrupts before the execution of every instruction. If there are interrupt requests from other devices (stimuli), then an interrupt handling routine will be executed to service the interrupt. In this case the arrival time of the interrupt cannot be predicted, but the types of interrupts are known and can be checked for periodically. In addition the responding procedures are all predefined. For processes with burst events, a different model may be necessary.

A real-time process that is not classified as periodic or aperiodic may be classified as a communication process. A real-time communication process specifies the timing constraints associated with interprocess communication. Constraints that may be specified include how soon a message should be received after it is sent, how long a sending process will wait for a reply after a message has been sent, how long a receiving process will wait for a message, and how long a receiving process many process a message.

Obviously the notion of time is important to real-time systems. There are four time-related tasks that a real-time system must be able to perform [58]:

- Time stamp events.

- Delay processes.

- Time-out processes.

- Specify deadlines and schedule processes to meet the deadlines.

To time stamp events a system must have access to a clock or have the ability to measure the passage of time, so that time can be specified by an absolute time or by an elapsed time relative to the start of an activity. However, although all nodes in a distributed system may have access to a clock, it is difficult to synchronize the clocks. Synchronization is important because if two processes are working with timing constraints but have separate clocks, the worst-case timings must be adjusted to account for slower clocks and clock skew. A real-time system must also be able to delay a process so that a process can queue on a future event instead of using a busy wait. The time-out task is useful for detecting the nonoccurrence of an event. A time-out limits the amount of time a process will wait for an event. In addition to being logically correct, real-time programs must satisfy timing constraints imposed by the physical environment. These are referred to as the deadline specifications. A deadline refers to constraints such as the minimum and maximum execution time. Deadline scheduling refers to arranging (scheduling) the execution of processes to meet timing constraints.

7.2 Specification of Real-Time Processes

The analysis of real-time systems is supported by a formal specification language that precisely specifies the system properties, by a formal design method used to develop the system, and by a formal verification method used to logically prove the correctness of the developed system with respect to the specifications. Usually we model a real-time system as a set of tasks. Each task is characterized by two events, the beginning event when a task begins its execution and the ending event when a task completes its execution. A task remains in execution between the two events. In addition tasks in real-time systems usually have timing constraints such as those defined in [96]. Dasarathy has classified the timing constraints of real-time systems. Three such constraints are (1) the maximum timing constraint, which is the maximum amount of time that may elapse between the occurrence of two events; (2) the minimum timing constraint, which is the minimum amount of time that must elapse between the occurrence of two events; and (3) the duration timing constraint, which is the maximum lifetime of a task. With regard to the principle characteristics of real-time systems, the timing constraints are the most difficult to verify because reasoning about time requires non-monotonic and continuous properties that are usually nonspecifiable and nonverifiable. Therefore, for analysis methods to be suitable for analyzing the stringent timing requirements of real-time systems, the methods must be able to specify and verify the system properties in terms of time.

Periodic processes must specify and analyze the following timing properties:

- Start time.

- Worst-case execution time.

- Laxity.

- Deadline.

Besides these periodic timing properties, an aperiodic process must specify and analyze the arrival time.

Communication processes must handle the following timing properties:

- Maximum receiver waiting time (how long a receiving process will wait for a message).

- Minimum communication delay (how soon a message can be received and processed by a receiving process after it is sent).

- Maximum communication delay (how long a message can be received and processed by a receiving process after it is sent).

- Maximum sender waiting time (how long a sending process will wait for a reply after a message has been sent).

In the following sections we will introduce several techniques for modeling and specifying real-time systems. First, Petri nets will be introduced in Section 7.3. Petri nets are a dynamic modeling technique that has gained popularity in modeling and analyzing concurrent systems. Several time-related extensions of Petri nets will be introduced for modeling real-time systems. Then a set of logic-based real-time specification languages, including temporal logic and its extensions and real-time logic, will be introduced in Section 7.4. Many techniques based on state transition systems have been developed, and explicit representations of timing constraints have been added to the state transition systems. We will examine those state transition systems and their extensions in Section 7.5. Section 7.6 will introduce process algebra and its extensions. Finally, in Section 7.7 we will introduce synchronous programming languages.

7.3   Timed Petri Nets

Petri nets are a particular kind of directed graph [279]. A Petri net can be specified by a 4-tuple, (P, T, F, M) where

- P is a set of places, $P = p_1, p_2, ..., p_m$,

- T is a set of transitions, $T = t_1, t_2, ..., t_n$,

- F is a set of arcs that connects places and transitions,

- M is a set of markings, $M(p_1), ..., M(p_j), ..., M(p_m)$, where $M(p_j)$ denotes the number of tokens in place p_j and $M(0)$ denotes the initial marking.

In Petri nets, rectangles represent transitions, and circles represent places. Transition t_j is said to be enabled if each input place p of t_j has at least $w(p, t_j)$ tokens, where $w(p, t_j)$ is the weight of the arc from p to t_j. A net is an ordinary net if all its arcs have a weight of one. A transition is fireable once it is enabled. The firing of transition t_j is instantaneous and will remove $w(p_i, t_j)$ tokens from each of its input places p_i and put $w(p_k, t_j)$ tokens into each of its output places p_k.

In Petri nets modeling, places can represent conditions, and transitions can represent events. A token arriving at a place can be interpreted as a true condition. Consequently the input and output places of a transition, t, can be interpreted as the pre-conditions and post-conditions of t. The firing of a transition can be interpreted as an event occurring at an instant in time. Therefore t is enabled when its pre-conditions are true and its post-condition becomes true after t's firing. Besides the above interpretation of places and transitions, places can also represent signals, with transitions representing tasks that process the signals. Consequently the input and output places of a transition can be interpreted as its input and output signals, respectively.

Petri nets have gained popularity in recent years because of their usefulness in modeling and analyzing concurrent systems. However, the concept of time is not explicitly provided in Petri nets, which limits their usefulness for real-time systems. Many efforts to extend Petri nets can be found in the areas of temporal behavior analysis and performance evaluation, and we would like to compare these extensions of Petri nets in this section. Most of the extensions have been achieved by imposing additional timing constraints onto the enabling and firing rules of the original Petri nets. Therefore we will compare these extensions in terms of timing constraints and enabling and firing rules.

7.3.1 Petri Nets Enabling and Firing Modes

We classify enabling rules as two types: *typeless enabling rules* and *typed enabling rules*. Typeless enabling rules treat all tokens as the same. Therefore, for the enabling of a transition t_j, one only considers the presence of tokens in each input place of t_j. In contrast, typed enabling rules treat tokens individually so that each token may possess different attributes. Therefore, for the enabling of a transition t_j, one not only considers the presence of tokens but also the types of tokens, that is, t_j is not enabled until each input place of t_j has the right combination of token types.

Based on the classification of typeless and typed enabling rules, we classify firing rules as typeless firing rules and typed firing rules, respectively. The result of a typeless transition firing is implicit, which means tokens will be removed from each input place of t_j and added into each output place of t_j

based on the arcs' weights. Petri nets use the typeless enabling and firing rules. In contrast, the firing of a typed transition t_j will remove specific colored tokens from each input place of t_j and add specific colored tokens into each output place of t_j. As a result a table is needed to specify what combinations of input colored tokens can be used to enable transitions and what combinations of colored tokens should be removed from input places and be added into output places after the firing. Colored Petri nets are a typical example of nets that follow both typed enabling and firing rules.

We also define two firing modes based on how soon an enabled transition must fire: weak and strong firing modes. The weak firing mode does not force any enabled transition to fire. In other words, an enabled transition may or may not fire. The weak firing mode is used in Petri nets modeling. The strong firing mode forces an enabled transition to fire as soon as it is enabled. The strong firing mode is used in conflict-free firing Petri nets [279]. The strong firing mode is not suitable for some nets with conflict-free structures because this mode will result in a contradiction.

7.3.2   Time-Related Extensions

The time related extensions of Petri nets primarily impose additional timing constraints onto transitions or places. The imposed timing constraints can be represented as constants or functions. For example, a constant is used for a single delay [167, 318, 321], and a function is used for a time pair consisting of lower and upper bounds [218, 255]. Other functions include stochastic Petri nets that treat a timing constraint as a probability function of the transition firing rate [229, 306] and ER nets that treat a timing constraint as a function of colored tokens in input places [117, 136].

Timed Petri nets were first proposed by Ramchandani [321] who analyzed the timing of asynchronous concurrent systems. Timed Petri nets were derived from classical Petri nets by associating a finite fire duration with each transition of a net. Timed Petri nets follow the strong firing mode: A transition t_j, with a delayed time T_{del}, will immediately fire when the necessary tokens have arrived at time T_0, and the firing is delayed T_{del}. Before T_0 the arriving tokens are not preserved and can be used to enable other transitions if t_j is in a conflict structure. During the time period from T_0 to $(T_0 + T_{del})$, the tokens are preserved for t_j so that no other transitions can use these tokens. At time $(T_0 + T_{del})$ the tokens will be removed from t_j's input places and output places. Timed Petri nets are capable of specifying timing requirements for the components of a systems with a fixed execution time (or time delay).

Ramamoorthy and Ho [318] extended the use of timed Petri nets to the area of performance evaluation. Stochastic Petri nets (SPNs) are mainly used for performance evaluation. In contrast to the constant delay used in timed Petri nets, SPNs use an average delay that is a probability function based on a transition's firing rate.

Peng and Shin used generalized stochastic Petri nets (GSPNs) to model the real-time control activities of a distributed system [306]. The modeled activities in GSPNs are combined into a sequence of homogeneous continuous-time Markov chains (CTMCs) in order to analyze the probability of missing deadlines.

Timed and stochastic Petri nets are mostly used for simulation-based performance evaluation. The performance is evaluated by finding a minimum cycle time for completing a firing sequence (where each transition fires at least once) that leads back to the initial marking, namely finding the minimum cycle time for the execution of a periodic process.

Time Petri nets were introduced by Merlin and Farber [255] for analyzing the recoverability of communication protocols. Time Petri nets are similar to timed Petri nets except that time Petri nets use a time pair instead of a single delay. A transition in a time Petri nets is associated with (TC_{min}, TC_{max}), where TC_{min} represents the minimum delay and the TC_{max} represents a time-out. If a transition t_j is enabled at time T_0, then t_j cannot fire before $(T_0 + TC_{min})$ nor after $(T_0 + TC_{max})$. Since time Petri nets follow a strong firing mode, if the firing does not take place during the time period from $(T_0 + TC_{min})$ to $(T_0 + TC_{max})$, then t_j must fire at $(T_0 + TC_{max})$.

Leveson and Stolzy [218] employ time Petri nets to model real-time systems for safety analysis. Minimum and maximum times are defined as the range of delays of each transition in the time Petri nets. Their goal is to derive timing constraints so that they can avoid high-risk states and determine the run-time checks needed to detect timing failures. To perform the safety analysis on a system, the reachability graph for the Petri net model of the system is constructed to determine if the system will reach a high-risk state. Once a high-risk state is detected, it is eliminated by modifying the system design using one of the many techniques discussed by the authors. After these modifications, run-time faults and failures are identified to determine which functions are critical and need to be made fault-tolerant.

Berthomieu and Diaz propose an enumerative method to analyze the temporal behavior of a concurrent system [40]. Through the technique of reachability analysis used in time Petri nets, Berthomieu and Diaz propose an enumerative analysis method to exhaustively model and validate behavior such as undecidability and boundness.

Temporal Petri nets use temporal logic to explicitly express certain temporal properties of Petri nets (e.g., fairness and liveness). Other examples include specifying a transition that will eventually fire at every marking that is reachable from the current marking. Unlike other time extensions of time-related Petri nets, which express and analyze the timing behavior directly on the net, temporal Petri nets use temporal logic to express and analyze temporal behavior. In other words, a temporal Petri net is a Petri net used in conjunction with temporal logic formulas: Temporal Petri nets = (N, F), in which N is a pure Petri net and F is the temporal logic formula used to constrain the temporal properties of N. To verify a temporal Petri net, N and F are treated as a unit. Since temporal Petri nets follow linear-time propositional temporal logic, given a marking M, the modeling and analysis of temporal properties are confined to a linear firing sequence, as denoted in [377]. This technique suffers from the same high complexity problem of other linear-time propositional temporal logic pertaining to concurrency analysis.

We summarize the above extensions of Petri nets by distinguishing their difference in firing modes. Timed (stochastic) Petri nets use the strong firing mode in which a transition is forced to fire immediately after it is enabled. Firing of a transition will last for a period of time, and tokens will be preserved during the firing period. Time Petri nets use the strong firing mode in which a transition is forced to fire at time $T_0 + TC_{max}$ if the transition has not fired or been disabled by firing due to another transition. In time Petri net modeling, tokens will not be preserved because the firing of a transition is instantaneous.

7.4 Temporal Logic

Temporal logic, especially propositional temporal logic [242, 297, 7], is a natural way to express the qualitative temporal behavior of real-time systems. Examples of these expressions include "Every stimulus p must be eventually be followed by a response q." Propositional temporal logic can be classified as *linear-time* propositional temporal logic such as PTL [127] or as *branching-time* propositional temporal logic such as CTL [112]. It is mentioned in [8] that linear-time temporal logic is used to express the linear structures of states, whereas branching-time temporal logic is used to express the hierarchical structures of states.

The linear structure represents a linear state sequence of a system execution. For example, a linear-time propositional temporal logic formula, $\Box(p \to \Diamond q)$ can be interpreted as "Every stimulus p must be followed by a response q." The hierarchical structure represents all possible state sequences or paths $\cup P$ of a system's execution. Branching-time propositional temporal logic is built on top of linear-timer propositional temporal logic with additional path quantifiers. For example, a branching-time propositional temporal logic $\forall \sigma \Box(p \to \exists \Diamond q)$, $\sigma \in \cup P$, can be interpreted as "Every stimulus p is possibly followed by a response q." Linear-time propositional temporal logic is not suitable for concurrence structures due to the high complexity in model checking [358]. Branching-time propositional temporal logic is designed reduce the complexity of model checking concurrent systems, but it is confined to systems with fair execution sequences. For example, CTL cannot express the fairness of concurrent programs [84].

Unfortunately, unrestricted propositional temporal logic is insufficient for expressing quantitative temporal requirement such as "Every stimulus p must be eventually (always) followed by a response q within five time units." To overcome this shortcoming in expressing quantitative temporal requirements, quantitative extensions of both linear-time and branching-time propositional temporal logic have been proposed. They have different syntax, but they both have a method to reference the time of states (events) and logic formulas to specify the timing constraints that correlate the times of different states (events). There are three typical methods used to extend the quantitative expression of linear-time propositional temporal logic. One is the use of explicit clock variables, such as a global clock used in TPTL [7], XCTL [160], and RTTL [296]. Another uses bounded temporal operators such as the one used in metric TL [202]. The last method uses a time function such as the one used in RTL [179, 180].

For expressing a temporal requirement that "Every stimulus p must be eventually followed by a response q within 5 time units," TPTL [4, 5] utilizes freeze quantifiers for binding a variable to the corresponding time when a proposition holds. Thus the TPL formula for the above requirement is $\Box x.(p \rightarrow \Diamond y.(q \wedge y \leq x + 5)$, where x is bound to the clock reading when proposition p holds and y is bound to the clock reading when proposition q holds. The two variables x and y are compared when proposition q holds.

XCTL [160] utilizes a global state variable for referencing the time when the proposition holds. Thus the XCTL formula for the above requirement is

$$\Box(p \wedge (x = T) \rightarrow \Diamond(q \wedge T \leq x + 5)$$

where T is the clock variable whose reading is assigned to x when p holds, and T continues to increase its reading, and the reading of T is used to compared with $(x + 5)$ when q holds.

Metric TL [202] utilizes bounded temporal operators to restrict the time spanning between two propositions. Thus the metric TL formula for the above requirement is $\Box(p \rightarrow \Diamond[0,5]q)$, where $[0, 5]$ is used to restrict the modal operator $\Diamond$ of the time period spanning between p and q.

Real-time logic (RTL) [179, 180, 176, 268, 182, 178] is a formal RTL for specification and analysis of real-time systems. An event-action model is used to specify the timing behavior of the system. RTL formulas are used to express both the timing specification of the system and safety assertions about the system. Time is captured by a function that assigns time values to the occurrences of events. RTL utilizes additional quantifiers rather than modal operators, and events are referenced by an event occurrence function, $@(E, i)$. The symbol $@$ is the time function that will return a clock reading for the time when event E occurred the ith time. Thus the RTL formula for the above requirement is

$$\forall i \exists j \forall t @(p, i) = t \rightarrow @(q, j) \leq t + 5$$

The specification of a system, given in terms of the event-action model, is transformed into a set of formulas in RTL that can be used to derive the safety assertions. If the safety assertions are derivable from the formulas, then the system is considered safe. Thus their work focuses on determining the consistency of safety assertions with respect to a timing specification expressed in RTL.

Real-time temporal logic (RTTL) and timed transition model (TTM) are approaches for checking properties of real-time systems. In these approaches, real-time systems are treated as a set of interacting real-time discrete event processes. The notions of a timed transition model (TTM) [298] and a parallel composition of TTM's are used as a computation model for real-time systems. Real-time temporal logic (RTTL) [297, 296] is used for specifying the properties to be verified. Verification is performed by a set of procedures working on the reachability graph of the system modeled in the TTM. In modeling the real-time properties, a global clock is assumed to tick indefinitely. The lower and upper bounds of transitions of the TTM are measured with respect to the clock. A procedure is used to check the real-time response property described in RTTL against the reachability graph of the TTM model.

The quantitative extension of branching-time propositional temporal logic is analogous to those found in linear-time propositional temporal logic. For example, RTCTL [113] utilizes a bounded temporal operator.

TRIO [117, 273, 137] is an executable specification language based on a temporal structure. It is used for real-time systems, and it allows the specification of quantitative time properties (e.g., the time between the occurrence of certain events). TRIO's formal semantics can accommodate a variety of time structures, from dense to discrete and finite. Finite time structures are used to execute the TRIO specifications. The definition of a state in TRIO includes the time-dependent predicates and variables, and the valuation functions associated with every TRIO formula. A time-dependent predicate models events. A time-dependent variable represents numeric values of physical or other quantities that may change over time. The valuation functions are divided into time-dependent and time-independent functions. TRIO can use these states to check the satisfiability of properties specified.

Event-based real-time logic (ERL) [72] is a modification of interval temporal logic. It is used to verify the behavior of a program's execution. With an event-based conceptual model in mind, ERL provides a high-level framework for specifying timing properties of real-time software systems. In a testing and debugging approach, ERL also specifies the expected behavior (specification) and actual behavior (execution trace) of a target system. It can also verify that a program meets its specifications.

Real-time interval Logic [327, 285, 275] extends to real-time interval logic in order to handle the problems associated with distributed real-time systems. Their main concern is verifying that the execution of a program, as characterized by the execution traces, is consistent with its formal description of the desired behavior, which is expressed in the real-time interval logic. The extensions mentioned by the authors include the ability to handle real-time systems, more powerful interval specification mechanisms, a limited form of quantification, and the direct expression of event predicates. Their work focuses on the verification of timing constraints using program execution traces. The authors do not mention how to use the history trace to help the user debug programs.

7.5 Timed State Transition Systems

Many techniques based on state transition systems have been developed to handle both functional and time specifications [163, 92]. The extensions to state transition systems include adding typed data, predicates, hierarchies of modules, and explicit representations of timing constraints. In this section we examine extensions concerning concurrency, communication, synchronization, and the representation of timing constraints.

STATEMATE [158, 234, 159] is a set of graphical tools for specifying, analyzing, designing, and documenting large and complex reactive systems. STATEMATE specifies and analyzes a system under development (SUD) from three separate but related points of view – structural, functional, and behavioral. STATEMATE provides three graphical languages – module charts, activity charts, and state charts to support the three views, respectively. The module charts construct a structural view by hierarchically decomposing a SUD into a set of physical components called modules and identifying the information that flows between them. The activity charts construct a functional view by constituting the activity hierarchy and flow information of SUD. The state charts construct a behavioral view by specifying control activities between any levels of the activity hierarchy for specifying when, how, and why things happen to the SUD over time.

State charts [158] are a graphical language for STATEMATE [158, 234, 159] and are used to depict the system behavior over time. State charts combine and extend conventional finite state machines and state transition diagrams. They are extend because conventional state diagrams are unstructured and sequential in nature and suffer from state explosion, which makes state diagrams inappropriate for complex systems. State charts overcome the shortcoming of state diagrams by supporting hierarchical structures and transition levels, and they can enter states at any level. In addition, state charts decompose states in an AND/OR fashion and feature an instantaneous broadcast mechanisms for communication.

Mode charts [182, 178] are similar to state charts but include the notation of time in the state-based transition systems. A transition in mode charts is associated with a pair of times – a delay and a deadline, which denote the shortest amount of time an event must wait before it can occur and the longest amount of time an event may wait. Requirements specified in mode charts can then be transformed into real-time logic (RTL), which is an assertion language for verification.

Communicating real-time state machines (CRSMs) [347] are an extension of state machine for communicating synchronously over unidirectional channels. Transitions of CRSMs are guarded commands that have the same semantics of Hoare's CSP semantics [165]. The guarded commands in CRSMs can be input/output for sending or receiving messages, or internal commands for computation and physical activity in the CSP. The time-related extension of CRSMs over the state machine is that the command execution and synchronization are associated with continuous time.

RSL [3] is the requirements statement language used by SREM (software requirements engineering methodology). RSL provides a language that is operationally modeled by a structured finite-state machine. RSL uses requirements networks, or R-nets, to structure the description of the processing. Each R-net can be modeled by an equivalent graphical representation. Performance requirements, such as accuracy and response time, are expressed using paths through R-nets. A processing path is defined by attaching named nodes, called validation points, onto the R-net graph and then defining the path in terms of a sequence of these *validation points*. Maximum and minimum response times can be given for a specified path. Accuracy requirements are expressed in terms of data recorded at the validation points. One of the advantages of RSL is that it comes as part of the SREM environment and has several supporting tools available to support generation and verification of software requirements. Both static structural and behavioral inconsistency errors can be detected. Data flow consistency checking and traceability of system-level requirements to processing (software) requirements are available. However, RSL also has some deficiencies. Stimulus response networks are not hierarchical, and modularity is limited. In addition distributed systems are difficult to describe because the state machine model assumes that a message is completely processed before the next message arrives.

RTRL (real-time requirements language) [96] similarly models a system by making each port of the system a finite-state machine. A requirements engineer specifies behavioral transitions that occur based on the stimuli received and the system's current state. Timing constraints are specified by defining timers. RSL was developed at GTE Laboratories and is used in conjunction with the RLP (requirements language processor) and the ATE (automatic test equipment). The RLP processes the requirements, locates any lexical, syntactic, or semantic errors, and detects inconsistencies, ambiguities, and redundancies in the resulting database. The ATE can generate test paths and report failures if the implemented system does not meet specifications.

PAISLey, the process-oriented, applicative, interpretable specification language [440, 441] is designed to enable the development of an executable model accompanied by specification methods, analysis techniques, and software tools. PAISLey combines formal representations of both data manipulation and control. In addition to general functional programming features, PAISLey uses cyclical processes and exchange functions to handle real-time systems. In PAISLey, processes are specified by a set of all possible states and a successor function on those states which defines the successor state for each state. It goes through an infinite sequence of states asynchronously with respect to all other processes. The processes are cyclical. In PAISLey, timing properties are verified using timing assumptions and assertions. A timing assumption is a property that is directly enforceable by means of implementation decisions. A timing assertion is a timing requirement that is not directly enforceable. The goal of validation is to establish that the assumptions imply timing assertions. Timing constraints are part of the PAISLey syntax and semantics. Timing assumptions and assertions are specified in the form of upper and lower bounds on a function evaluation time. Testing a timing assertion is achieved by simulating the performance of the specified system and checking if the assertion holds. Timing assumptions are inconsistent when the lower bound of a function is greater than the upper bound of the function that called it.

7.6   Timed Process Algebra

Process algebra is a powerful mechanism for expressing concurrent systems. Programs are specified in algebraic languages providing sequential and parallel composition of processes, nondeterministic choice, hiding (program abstract), and recursion (loop). Labeled transition systems provide the semantics for process algebra specifications, where the states are process expressions and the labels are actions or communications between processes. We can view process algebra as a descendant of automata theory. However, instead of examining the execution trace of a single automation, process algebra examines the behavior of systems of communication automata. The most distinguishing feature of process algebra is an equation-based calculus for reasoning about processes. The algebraic laws of these calculi define the actions of operators and allow the transformation of one system into another. Lastly, process algebra defines various notions of equivalence of systems (bisimulation, trace equivalence, observational equivalence, failure equivalence, etc.). Properties of process algebra specification can be verified through reasoning in the corresponding calculus or by an analysis of the labeled transition system that is the model of a specification. An implementation can be shown correct relative to a specification by proving that the proper congruence or equivalence holds between them. Properties of a specification may also be stated and proved in terms of a modal logic.

Process algebra has been extended to include the notion of time by allowing labels to be taken from the time domain [24, 290, 197]. In a timed system a process changes state by either executing some atomic action assumed to take no time or by letting time pass. Time passes only if all component processes agree to do so.

Timed CSP [339] is an extension of Hoare's Communicating Sequential

Processes (CSP) [165, 166]. The Oxford University timed CSP group has been working on this theory for years and has associated proof systems, temporal logics, and refinement models. Timed CSP is able to specify and verify the behavior of objects and the occurrence and availability of certain events. The language of timed CSP extends CSP by adding the timed operators delay and time-out. In other words, the interpretation of the untimed CSP operators needs to be considered in a timed context. CSP's notation for a delay is "$a \rightarrow P$," which means that a system is initially prepared to engage in event a and then behave as P. The process "$at \rightarrow P$" denotes that the system will behave as P exactly t units of time after the synchronization of event a. The notation of a time-out uses the operator $\triangledown$. Thus "$Pt \triangledown Q$" denotes that the control is transferred from P to Q if no communication occurs before time t.

Timed CCS [437] and temporal CCS [269] are both extensions of Milner's calculus of communicating systems (CCS) [261]. Timed CCS extends untimed CCS by adding additional time delays that are modeled by a set of events indexed by a given time domain. This time domain is treated as a subset of the alphabets of the CCS, which results in the same syntax as the untimed CCS. Temporal CCS provides a time notation similar to timed CCS. Both timed CCS and temporal CCS are able to deal with discrete and dense time domains.

Calculus communicating shared resources (CCSR) [131, 132, 133, 215] is an extension of CSP. CCSR can model time constraints, interrupts and resources that cannot be modeled in CSP. For example, using CCSR one can quantify the time needed to execute a command and the time available to the command for accessing resources such as processor and I/O channels

Language of temporal ordering specification (LOTOS) [47, 46] is a formal description method whose operational semantics is defined by labeled transition systems. The timed version of LOTOS has additional time attributes for defining temporal restrictions on the execution of actions. Timing attributes are added to the actions of the untimed LOTOS by a set of allowed times and a delay statement. The notation for allowed times is denoted as $a5$, which means action a occurs at time 5, or $a1..5$, which means action a may occur at any time between 1 and 5. The delay statement is denoted as $delay5; a$, which means delay action a for 5 units of time. With the two time notations, LOTOS is able to represent a variety of timing constructs, such as fixed delays (an event must occur after a fixed of delay has elapsed), synchronous timings (an event must occur during a period of time), and fixed times (an event must occur at a given absolute time).

Algebra for timed processes (ATP) [291] is a behavioral description mechanism for timed systems. ATP can be transformed into a timed graph, which is a graph that evolves over time. This transformation makes existing model-checking techniques applicable to ATP. The operational semantics of ATP is defined by labeled transition systems. ATP extends this labeled transition systems and proposes a hybrid system with guarded commands and functions that are a generalization of timed graphs.

7.7 Synchronous Programming Languages

The design of synchronous programming languages is based on a "synchrony hypothesis" that assumes a controller can instantaneously react to an external event. The program reaction time of the controller is negligible compared with the reaction time of the controlled environments. This implies that the controller's reaction time to an event is always shorter than the minimum delay between two consecutive events. For example, it is assumed that a temperature controller written in synchronous programming language will never miss any temperature readings from the environment because the controller can react to the readings instantaneously.

RT-ASLAN [20] is a formal language for specifying real-time systems. It is an extension of the ASLAN specification language for sequential systems. RT-ASLAN supports the specification of processes in a real-time system through arbitrary levels of abstraction. A real-time system is modeled via a set of processes communicating via an interface process. Transitions in a process, can be periodic or nonperiodic. In addition a sequencing operator is used in the specifications of transitions to model precedence constraints. The interface process is considered to be an abstract data type representing the shared resource through which the processes communicate. Time is maintained by a process that increments a time variable after each tick transition. The ASLAN specification language is built on first order predicate calculus and employs the state machine approach to perform verification. To prove that a specification satisfies a critical requirement, ASLAN generates conjectures to be used in constructing an inductive proof the correctness of the specification with respect to the invariant and constraint assertions. The language processor for RT-ASLAN generates both critical functionality correctness conjectures and performance conjectures. Interface specifications are related to the communication mechanisms between processes. Communicating specifications use a cycle value for timing purposes. A cycle value means that the corresponding transition is supplied at regular intervals. Finally, transitions may have timing attributes, meaning their absolute execution time is at most the timing value.

LUSTRE [68, 154, 156, 155], ESTEREL [37, 48], and SIGNAL [216, 36] are all data-flow languages based on the synchrony hypothesis. Since the reaction time in these languages is assumed to be shorter than the minimum delay separating two consecutive external events, the only real-time problems for such synchronous languages is how to minimize and measure the reaction time, in other words, how to specify and evaluate the relationship between inputs (external events) and outputs (reactions). These languages generate efficient, linear sequential code for program reactions rather than unpredictable loop or recursion code. However, the synchrony hypothesis is not always realistic, and due to the linear code, most synchronous languages do not allow nondeterminism.

Lucid is a data-flow language based on modal logic. It deals with time in an implicit rather than an explicit way. Several researchers have proposed using the Lucid as the basis for the specification of real-time systems [116, 359]. Faustini and Lewis consider their proposal to be the first step in defining a nonprocedural language that allows the specification and formal verification of real-time computations. Statements in a Lucid program are theorems that can be derived from the axioms and rules of inference on which Lucid is based. Both approaches are very similar. Faustini associates with each stream a corresponding stream of time constants, or a time window of (infinity, infinity). All reasoning about time is carried out using interval arithmetic. Correspondingly Skillcorn and Glasgow use the behavioral semantics of operator nets to define two new operator nets "early" and "late". The earliest and latest time sequences correspond to the earliest and latest time at which the corresponding elements of the sequence on the original arc can be produced. In addition timing constraints are put on the inputs and outputs of the system. Lucid is executable, and it allows the performance equations to be solved for whichever values are dependent. Both studies consider the concept of real-time exception handling. When the output of an operator net does not occur within its time window, then a fault is generated as the output data object. This is an indication that the real-time specification cannot be met. Because Skillcorn and Glasgow's approach separates the real-time component of the specification from the operational part, it is possible to think separately about issues such as safety and liveness, on the one hand, and performance, on the other.

Real-time Euclid [196], an extension of Euclid, is a language for reliable real-time systems. Real-time Euclid includes features for handling reliability and schedulability problems. It defines every construct to be bounded by time and space. The programmers are responsible for specifying time bounds or time-out exceptions for all loops, wait statements, and device requests that must be appropriately handled by exception handlers. With these mechanisms real-time Euclid is potentially analyzable for guaranteed schedulability.

7.8   Summary

The applications of real-time systems are becoming increasingly important in everyday life. How to represent this kind of system has become a critical research problem. A real-time system can be specified as a set of real-time processes and the interactions among these processes. Real-time processes can be further classified as periodic, aperiodic, or communication processes. Periodic processes are activated at regular intervals. In contrast, aperiodic processes are usually involved with external events and are characterized by the event's arrival time. Communication processes are related to the timing constraints associated with interprocess communication. Many formalisms have been proposed to specify distributed real-time systems. A formal representation of the structure and behavior of distributed real-time systems will help us ensure the correctness of the system. The techniques introduced in this chapter include timed Petri nets, temporal logic, timed state transition systems, timed process algebra, and synchronous programming languages.

Petri nets have been widely used in modeling and analyzing concurrent systems. However, the concept of time is not explicitly provided in Petri nets. In this chapter we have discussed several time extension of Petri nets to deal with real-time systems. Most of the extensions have been achieved by imposing additional timing constraints onto the enabling and firing rules of the basic Petri nets. Therefore we have also compared these extensions in terms of timing constraints and enabling.

Temporal logic is another formal way to represent the qualitative temporal behavior of real-time systems. Temporal logic is classified as linear-time temporal logic and branching-time temporal logic. Linear-time temporal logic is used to express the linear structure of states, whereas branching-time temporal logic is used to specify the hierarchical structures of states. Various temporal logic discussed in this chapter includes real-time temporal logic, event-based real-time logic, real-time interval logic, and TRIO.

State transition systems have been a popular method to specify functional and time properties of software systems. We have discussed various extensions of state transition systems to represent concurrency, communication, synchronization, timing constraints in a distributed real-time system. The techniques discussed include STATEMATE, state charts, mode charts, communicating real-time state machines, RSL, RTRL, and PAISLey.

Process algebra is a descendant of automata theory, and it is a powerful mechanism for specifying concurrent systems. The most distinguishing feature of process algebra is an equation-based calculus for reasoning about processes. Various notions of equivalence of systems can be defined and verified through reasoning in the corresponding calculus. Process algebra has also been extended to express the concept of time. The examples discussed include timed CSP, timed CCS, CCSR, LOTOS, and ATP.

Several synchronous programming languages such as LUSTRE, SIGNAL, ESTEREL, RT-ASLAN, and Lucid, were also discussed as ways to specify real-time systems.

Exercises

1. Besides the examples given in the chapter, list other real-time system examples closely related to our daily lives.

2. What are the three interactions between the controlling and controlled subsystems?

3. What are real-time processes?

4. What timing properties are used to specify and analyze periodic processes? What about aperiodic processes and communication processes?

5. Describe places and transitions defined in Petri nets.

6. List various approaches of extending Petri nets in terms of time-related features.

7. Describe the differences between firing rules in Petri nets and their time-related extensions.

8. What are the differences between linear-time propositional temporal logic and branching-time propositional temporal logic? Which is more suitable to distributed real-time systems?

9. Describe the extensions that have been made to state transition systems in order to handle both functional and timing specification and analysis.

10. List the usage of process algebra and how timed process algebra contributes to real-time specification and analysis.

11. What are synchronous programming languages? Compare them with other data-flow programming languages.

12. Why are time-outs useful to a real-time system?

13. Define typeless enabling rules.

14. Define weak firing mode.

15. Why were time-related extensions for Petri nets developed, and what are these extensions?

16. Explain why temporal logic is useful. Give a concrete example.

17. How can analysis of a real-time system aid one in the design of a real-time system? What types of errors or design flaws will it detect or prevent?

18. The last section in the chapter discusses synchronous programming languages. Using a typical procedural language as an example, discuss what features you would like to see that would aid in the design of DRTSs. Could you implement these with a preprocessor or library of functions for the language?

Part II

THEORY AND PRACTICE

Chapter 8

A Noninterference Monitoring Approach

To monitor a distributed real-time system, three things have to be considered. First, the monitoring system should not interfere with the execution of the target system, since the target system would not exhibit the same timing and synchronization behavior if the monitoring system interfered with its execution. Second, the monitoring system should let the user define the information to be collected and control the monitoring. Third, the monitoring system should provide a global time reference in order to record the time of events occurred and the duration between events observed on different nodes.

This chapter first describes a hardware monitoring architecture that can monitor the execution of distributed real-time systems without interfering with their execution. Noninterference is achieved by detecting the states of the target system through the data, address, and control buses of the target processors. With this monitoring system the user can control the monitoring by defining the starting and ending conditions of the recording process. Therefore only data of interest is collected from the target system. A global time reference is provided by the monitoring system. This global time reference is realized by using the monitoring system's network to synchronize the local clocks of the monitoring nodes. The network of the monitoring system is independent of the target system, both in hardware and software. Thus it does not interfere with the execution of the target system.

After the description of the monitoring architecture, we will discuss how to monitor distributed real-time systems at the process and function levels using this monitoring architecture. We will see how to monitor and collect the process-level events listed in Table 2.1 and the function-level events listed in Table 2.2. We also show how to represent the execution behavior using the collected data.

8.1   A Noninterference Hardware Approach

The design of the monitoring system is based on the bus structure of the MC68000 processor. Using a different bus structure would require minor modification of the monitoring system architecture and the postprocessing mechanism. In this section, we will describe the architecture of the monitoring system and how it is used to monitor program execution. The detailed design of the monitoring system architecture is presented in [396, 397, 398].

"Noninterference" means that the execution of the target system is not affected by the monitoring and debugging activities. In a very strict sense, any breakpoint planted in the target software by the user to store transient data interferes with the execution of the target system because CPU time is stolen in order to perform the memory storage operations. Therefore, to create a noninterference testing and debugging environment, some auxiliary hardware is needed to assist the monitoring and recording of execution information.

The system we used for execution monitoring and data recording is a microcomputer-based module. It can monitor a real-time software system and collect process execution information without interfering with the target system's execution.

8.2   Overview of the Monitoring System

The monitoring system consists of a set of monitoring nodes connected via a communication network that is separate from the target system's communication network. The network topology of the monitoring system is independent of the target system's topology. Each node of the target system is attached with a monitoring node through the data, address, and control buses of the target processor. A monitoring node monitors its corresponding target node by sampling the signals on the buses. Fig. 8.1 shows the system overview of the monitoring system. Since the monitoring system has its own network, any communication among the monitoring nodes does not interfere with communication in the target system.

The architecture of the monitoring nodes, as shown in Fig. 8.2, consists of two key components: the *interface module* and the *development module*. The interface module is the front-end of the monitoring system and is specially designed to interface with the specific processor in the target system. It detects the events of interest and collects data concerning the events based on the predefined conditions set by the user. The development module is the host computer for the interface module. This module is a general-purpose microprocessor-based system that contains all the supporting software for the initialization of the interface module, clock synchronization and interprocessor communication of the monitoring system, and postprocessing activities.

The monitoring system provides a global time reference by synchronizing the local clocks built in the interface modules of the monitoring nodes. Since

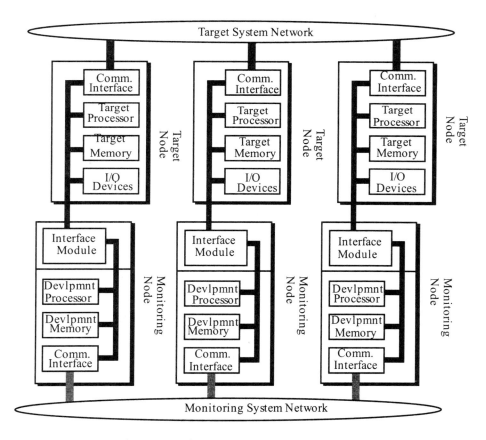

Fig. 8.1 Overview of the monitoring system's architecture.

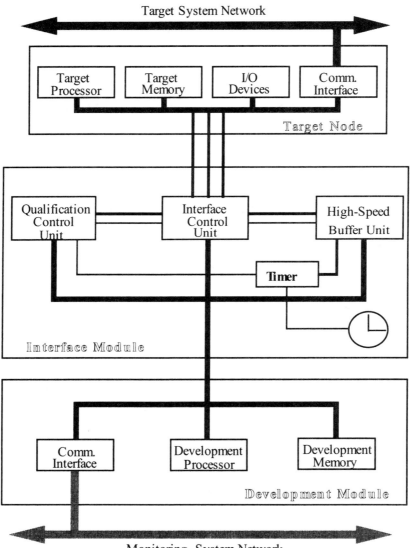

Fig. 8.2 Overview of a monitoring node.

this clock synchronization is controlled by the development modules via the monitoring system network, it does not interfere with the execution of the target system. The monitoring system watches program execution and collects execution information from the buses of the target system. Therefore it does not interfere with the execution of the target system either.

Referring to the architecture of the monitoring nodes shown in Fig. 8.2, the monitoring system monitors the state of the target node by sampling the signals on the buses of the target processor. It starts recording data from the buses when a "start" condition is detected and stops the recording when a "stop" condition is detected. The *qualification control unit* of the interface module is designed to detect start and stop conditions by comparing the state of the target node to the user-predefined starting and ending trigger conditions. In this section we will examine in more detail the design of the monitoring system. For information on the hardware implementation of the monitoring system, the reader should refer to [397, 398].

8.3   The Interface Module

The main function of the interface module is to compare the states of the target processor with the user-defined starting and ending conditions of recording process through the data, address, and control buses of the target processor. If a starting condition is matched, it begins to save signals on the buses of the target processor and stops the recording process when a stopping condition is matched. As shown in Fig. 8.2, the interface module consists of four functional units: (1) the *interface control unit* (ICU), (2) the *qualification control unit* (QCU), (3) the *timer* and the *local clock*, and (4) the *high-speed buffer unit* (HSBU).

The monitoring system is connected to the target system via the ICU. One of the functions of the ICU is to establish a connection between the target node and the monitoring system without creating electrical interruptions for the target processor. The other function is to sample the signals on the buses of the target processor during each bus cycle and transfer them to the QCU. The QCU compares the state of the target node with the preset trigger conditions and then produces a control signal to start or to stop data recording. If a starting condition is matched, the recording process will be started, and if an ending condition is matched, the recording process will be stopped.

Usually the bus speed of the target system is set as high as possible. To reduce the cost of storing high volumes of data, high-speed registers are used as a buffer between the target system's buses and the development module's memory. The latched data is first written into a high-speed buffer and then transferred into the development module's memory.

In a single-processor system, only one clock running in the system, but in a distributed system, each node has its own local real-time clock. To measure

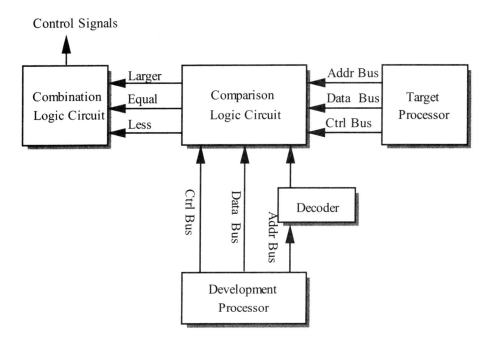

Fig. 8.3 The qualification control unit.

the time of an event and the interval between events, which may be observed from different nodes, it is necessary to provide a common time reference. The timer and clock in the interface module are used to stamp events with the time at which they occurred. All clocks in the monitoring system are synchronized by the development module through the network of the monitoring system. Thus the clocks are used as a global time reference to record events occurring at different nodes.

The QCU is a key component of the interface module that enables the user to control the monitoring. Fig. 8.3 shows the block diagram of the QCU. The development processor is used to set the QCU to the various conditions defined by the user. Besides the decoder, the design shown in Fig. 8.3 has two blocks. One is the comparison logic circuit, which is composed of a number of comparators. Each comparator can issue three basic condition signals, "equal," "greater than," and "less than" as a result of the comparison. The other circuit is the combinational logic that takes the basic conditions generated by the comparison unit and generates control signals for the recording process.

The QCU monitors the execution of the target node by sampling the states of the processor of the target node during each bus cycle. If the sampled state matches any of user-defined starting conditions, the combinational logic circuit produces a signal to start collecting data from the buses. The length of the execution history to be recorded is controlled by a trace counter that counts the number of cycles recorded or by the detection of an ending condition defined by the user. When a user-defined ending condition is matched with the state of the buses, or when a predefined length of the execution history has been recorded, the recording process is automatically stopped.

The QCU is actually a hardware implementation of software breakpoints defined by the user through the development processor. The comparison logic circuit in the QCU is primarily programmable logic, which gives the flexibility required to support general software breakpoint conditions. The specific timing constraint is a critical issue in the design of the QCU because the comparison must be completed within one bus cycle and the control signals must also be generated accordingly.

8.4 The Development Module

The development module is the central processing unit of the monitoring system, and it functions as a host machine for the monitor. It consists of the *development processor unit*, the *development memory unit*, and the *communication interface*. The development module is independent of the target processor. Independence is achieved by moving the target-dependent functions into the interface module. The development module provides an interactive interface to the user and is responsible for all the testing and debugging activities, including the following:

1. Initialization of the monitoring system.

2. Controlling the interface module to collect the target system execution history.

3. Synchronizing the local clocks in the interface modules through the monitoring system network.

4. Performing postprocessing and interpretation of collected data.

5. Performing timing analysis.

Timing analysis will be presented in later chapters. Postprocessing and interpretation are two very important system-dependent activities supported by the development processor unit. They process and interpret the recorded execution data. The other functions of the development module are as follows:

1. *Initialize the interface module.* On "system power-on" or "system reset," the development processor initiates a system hardware initialization and loads the check-point (breakpoint) conditions into the QCU.

2. *Provide data for global timing analysis.* For the timing errors that involve more than one target node, the development module will transfer the necessary data to a specified node where global timing analysis procedures are carried out.

3. *Provide a user-friendly interface.* The development module provides a user-friendly interface under various situations such as prompts for trigger condition setup or display messages on various system activities.

8.5   Process-Level Monitoring

In testing and debugging a distributed real-time system, different levels of abstraction of the execution information provide different levels of details as discussed in Section 2.2.1. Higher-level information refers to events such as interprocess communication and synchronization. In contrast, lower-level information refers to events such as the step-by-step execution trace of a process. In this section a monitoring method at the process level using the monitoring system described in this chapter is introduced. The next section will describe how to monitor at the function level using this monitoring system.

In Section 2.2.1 we identified a set of events that should be monitored at the process level. The events listed in Table 2.1 are given a code for each event in Table 8.1. The coding will be used in later sections of this chapter where we discuss postprocessing. To monitor these process-level events using the above monitoring system, two sets of trigger conditions are preset into the QCU of the interface module: starting trigger conditions which initiate the recording process, and stopping trigger conditions which terminate the recording process. The recording process begins when a sequence of one or more events occur and ends when the key values of the event(s) have been recorded. The control flow of the monitoring process is as follows: At the outset, the monitoring system is initialized and connected to the target system. The identified starting and stopping trigger conditions are initialized in the QCU. During program execution, the QCU watches the target system states. It initiates the recording process when a starting trigger condition is matched and terminates the recording when a stopping trigger condition is matched. The monitoring procedure can be summarized as follows:

1. Connect the monitoring system to the target system.

2. Load the trigger conditions.

3. Initialize the interface module.

4. Monitor execution behavior of the target system and record execution information pertaining to the process-level events.

5. Transfer the recorded data to secondary storage for postprocessing.

Code	Event	Key Values
E1	Process Creation	Parent Process Identification Create Call Time Node Identification
		Child Process Identification Creating Process Time Node Identification
E2	Process Termination	Parent Process Identification Resuming Time Node Identification
		Child Process Identification Terminating Time Node Identification
E3	Process Synchronization	Process Identification Operation (P/V) Semaphore Identification Value of the Semaphore Time Node Identification
E4	I/O Operation	Process Identification Operation (I/O) I/O Port Identification Message (I/O Buffer) Time Node Identification
E5	Interprocess Communication	Sending Process Identification Message Node Identification Send-Call Time Receiving-Acknowledgment Time
		Receiving Process Identification Message Node Identification Receive-Call Time Receiving-Message Time
E6	Wait Child Process	Parent Process Identification Child Process Identification Time Node Identification
E7	External Interrupt	Interrupted Process Identification I/O Port Identification Message (I/O Buffer) Time Node Identification
E8	Process State Change	Process Identification New State Transition Time Node Identification

Table 8.1 Coded process-level events and their key values.

To find the trigger conditions, let us first examine how an operating system kernel works. The kernel of an operating system can be considered to be an interrupt-driven program. Fig. 8.4 shows the general control flow of a kernel. When an interrupt (trap) occurs, the hardware transfers control to the operating system kernel and switches into the supervisor mode. The kernel determines what kind of interrupt (trap) has occurred. If an error occurs in the application process, the kernel terminates it and selects the next process to run. An application process requests system resources through the kernel by executing a system call with parameters that identify what is requested. When a system call is invoked, a software interrupt occurs, and control is transferred through a predefined interrupt vector to a system service routine. This system service routine executes the request on the user's behalf. The final interrupt option shown in the figure is an I/O interrupt, which causes the kernel to awaken the process that is waiting for this I/O device. After the kernel processes any of these interrupts, it transfers system control back to the user process.

To collect the events and their key values, the monitoring system can be set to detect the interrupts from the I/O devices and the software traps from the applications processes that request services from the kernel. As discussed in Section 2.2.1, to collect the key values for an event with subevents on two nodes, such as remote process creation events, the starting and ending conditions should include the interrupts from the interprocess communication devices.

The kernel provides many other types of system calls. To avoid latching data for unimportant system calls, we set the trigger conditions to identify the system calls that are related to the process-level activities. Based on the above discussion, we can summarize the following five conditions as starting trigger conditions:

> IF ((system call interrupt) AND (interrupt is process-level related))
>   OR ((system call interrupt) AND (I/O request))
>   OR (I/O completion interrupt)
>   OR (external interrupt from IPC device)
>   OR (program error interrupt)
> THEN trigger the recording process.

After the kernel services system calls or interrupts, it always switches the mode to user mode and then returns control to an application process. Thus the stopping condition for all the events can be

> IF (instruction changes the system mode to user mode)
> THEN stop the recording process.

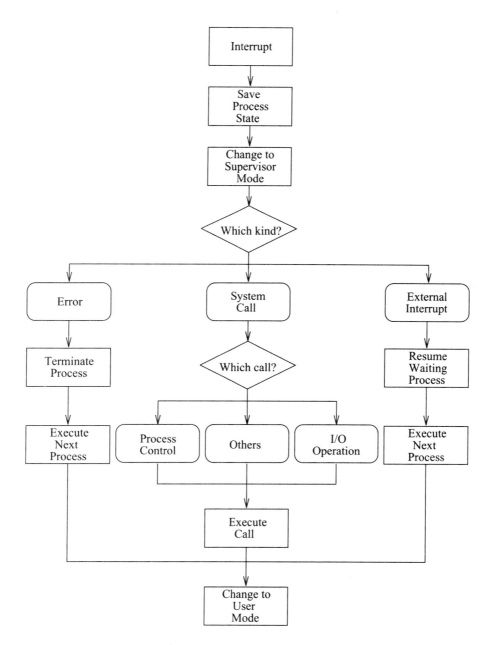

Fig. 8.4 An overview of interrupt processing.

To illustrate these ideas concretely, we will examine features of the UNIX operating system. The UNIX operating system has a user mode and a supervisor mode. The operating system kernel provides common services to user processes. User processes interact with the kernel by invoking a set of predefined system calls. On the VAX 4.3 BSD UNIX operating system, the system calls are implemented by the CHMK (change mode to kernel) instruction with a parameter that specifies the service requested. This privileged instruction causes a software interrupt (trap) and a switch to the supervisor mode. The trap handler determines which system call is requested and transfers control to the corresponding service routine. After the service routine is complete, a privileged instruction REI (return from exception or interrupt) is executed to return control to the user process and to switch to the user mode.

For example, a new process can be created by another process by invoking a "fork" system call. The fork system service routine assigns a unique identification number to the new process, allocates memory for it, initializes it, and sets up the relationship between the parent and the child process. If the key values from this fork event are recorded, then the event can be recreated later. The starting trigger for process creation events would be

IF ((process is forked) and (parameter=2))
THEN trigger the recording process.

And the stopping trigger would be

IF (execution of REI)
THEN stop the recording process.

For this and other events, the execution information pertaining to the process-level events is collected from the target system as a data block that contains the key values for the events. The development memory unit containing the collected data can be designed to be large enough to save the largest data block. When the QCU is waiting for the next trigger condition, the collected data in the development memory unit can be saved to secondary storage so that the development memory unit can be used to store new data. By considering the time for the operating system to perform a context switch before it can respond to the next interrupt, it is easy to calculate and allocate enough memory space in the development module to allow continuous data recording and system monitoring.

8.6 Function-Level Monitoring

The collected process-level data can be used to analyze the behavior among processes. This analysis can identify faulty processes or the processes responsible for the error. However, the process level may be too abstract for the programmer to remove bugs. To isolate faults to components at a lower level (i.e., functions or procedures), the system should be monitored at the function level. This process can be done in two steps. First, a set of faulty processes is identified using the data collected at the process level, then those processes are monitored at the function level where faulty functions are identified using collected data.

Before discussing monitoring at the function level, we should note the restrictions that we will make on the programming language in which the target program is written. The programming language is block structured; a block is a function or a procedure. The scope of variables is determined statically. A process consists of a set of functions (procedures), and the main program for the process is also a function. A function can activate other functions by a calling statement. A called function terminates by executing a return statement, and it returns control to the calling function. A calling function and a called function communicate via passing parameters. Parameters can be passed by value, result, or value-result. Cross-function gotos are not allowed. These restrictions are satisfied in most modern programming languages. If the language uses pass-by-reference for parameter passing, the approach discussed in the following for function-level monitoring may only be able to collect the pointers to the passed variables, not the value of those variables.

The events to be monitored at the function level appear in Table 8.2. A corresponding code is given for each event. These codes will be used in post-processing. To monitor these function-level events using our monitoring system, one must know how a block-structured program is executed. In a block-structured language, variables are allocated dynamically upon the entry into the block in which they are declared. An activation record is associated with the activation of a block or function. The activation record that is allocated to a run-time stack is a region containing the dynamic variables of the function. An activation record is allocated when a function is called and is freed when the function returns. An activation record for function P may contain the following:

1. A dynamic link (a pointer to the activation record of the caller of P).

2. A static link (a pointer to the activation record of the most recent activation of the function containing P).

3. A return address (in the caller of P).

4. Parameters passed to P by the caller (copy of actual parameters).

Code	Event	Key Values
F1	Function Call	Calling Function Identification Called Function Identification Passed-in Parameters Time
F2	Function Return	Calling Function Identification Called Function Identification Returned Parameters Time

Table 8.2 Coded function-level events and their key values.

5. Local variables for P.

6. A register save area and an area for temporary variables.

Local variables are referenced as offsets from the top of the stack. In a static block-structured language, the binding of names to declarations is based on the physical placement of blocks in the program text, not on the order of calls. The static link is used for this purpose.

To process a function call, the system must perform the following steps:

1. Allocate part of the called function's activation record (including storage for the parameters, return values of the called function, the saved area, and the dynamic and static links).

2. Set the dynamic link.

3. Set the static link.

4. Set the return address.

5. Transmit the parameters.

6. Push the new activation record onto the run-time stack.

7. Transfer control to the called function.

From these steps it can be seen that all of the key values pertaining to function call events are explicitly accessed, and thus they will appear on the buses of the target processor. If we latch the data from the target processor's buses during the execution of the above steps, these key values can be filtered from the collected data. Now the question is how to set up a trigger condition so that the signals on the buses are latched during the execution of the above steps.

The best trigger condition is one that is common for all function calls and will not be true for any other circumstances. Fortunately most processors have "call" instructions that are only used for function calls. However, this instruction is not executed at the beginning of the above procedure but as the last step, step 7. Thus we cannot use this call instruction as a starting trigger condition. Since this instruction is always the last instruction for processing a function call, we prelatch data from the buses and save the prelatched data when a call instruction is executed. If the prelatched data is long enough, they should contain all the key values for function calls. The following paragraph explains the idea.

Suppose that the above steps can be carried out in a maximum of N_1 instruction cycles of the target processor. That is, the data of N_1 instruction cycles preceding a call instruction should include all of the key values needed to record the call. Thus the monitoring system prelatches data from the target buses in a FIFO manner with a buffer of length N_1. When the execution of the call instruction is detected, the prelatched data is saved to the memory of the development module.

To find trigger conditions for function return events, let us examine the steps in a function return:

1. Store return values, if any, in its activation record.

2. Restore the run-time stack to its previous state.

3. Restore the registers and the status information.

4. Return control to the caller.

Just as with the function call, the data needed for the function-level information is included in this procedure, and step 4 is also carried out by a specific "return" instruction. Suppose that these steps can be carried out with a maximum of N_2 instruction cycles on the target machine. Then the same method used with the function call can be employed. Thus prelatched data of N_2 instruction cycles will be transferred to the memory of the development module when the execution of the return instruction is detected.

From the discussion above, we summarize the function-level monitoring as follows:

1. Set the prelatched data buffer length to $\text{MAX}(N_1, N_2)$.

2. Save the prelatched data with length N_1 when the call instruction is detected.

3. Save the prelatched data with length N_2 when the return instruction is detected.

8.7   Process-Level Data Processing

Generally, a distributed real-time system is very large, and therefore the representation of the execution behavior is very complicated. To reduce this complexity, the execution behavior is presented in different ways. The presentations are classified into two classes based on the types of errors: *logical behavior presentations* and *timing behavior presentations*. Logical behavior is concerned with the correctness of logical results of computation without concern for the times at which the results are produced, while the timing behavior is concerned with the correctness of the times at which results are produced. That is, the timing behavior is used to check whether the timing constraints imposed on the system are satisfied or not.

In this section we will discuss how to represent different aspects of the execution using the data collected at the process level. We will examine data structures and algorithms that are useful for this purpose. Given a log of collected data, we first discuss how to extract useful data to form process graphs that show the parent-child relationship between processes, P/V operation sequences on semaphores that show synchronization among processes, and process interaction graphs via message passing that show interprocess communication between processes.

8.7.1   Postprocessing at the Process Level

The execution data collected from the target system at the process level is called the process-level program execution log (PPEL), and it is voluminous and target processor dependent. Since the data is collected as blocks with the starting and ending conditions, they contain not only the key values of events of interest but also unrelated data. Therefore we first organize the collected data into an intermediate data set, the Integrated process-level execution log (IPEL). The IPEL contains only key values and control data needed to identify the process-level events, and it is constructed in such a way that higher-level logical views can be derived easily.

The IPEL consists of two related data structures, as shown in Fig. 8.5. The process creation tables (PCT) present the processes running on the nodes and their parents. Each entry of the PCT corresponds to a process in the system, and it contains the process identification (P-ID), the parent process identification (PP-ID), and the time at which the process was created. The event-chains (EC) for each node describe the events that occurred in the node. Each node of the EC, corresponding to an event, contains the key values of the event and two pointers. One pointer links all events in a node into a time sequence (time-link). The other pointer links all events related to an individual process (process-link). Since there is no process migration in the target system, the process link will not cross the event-chains of other nodes. Each process entry in the PCT is linked to the first node of the EC

related to that process. The PCT and EC of a node can be constructed by
its corresponding development module since they do not contain the data of
other nodes. The IPEL head table is used to connect all the PCT's and EC's
together. After the IPEL for a node is constructed, the IPEL head table can
be easily constructed.

In the following, we describe an algorithm for constructing the IPEL from
a given PPEL for a node. Records R_1, R_2, ..., R_n represent the data blocks
in the PPEL at the process level. The data structure of the IPEL's is shown
in Fig. 8.5. PCT(M) is the process creation table where M is the number of
processes on the computer node. Each node of the event-chain contains the
key values and the event code used to distinguish types of events.

Algorithm CIPEL (Creating IPEL).

A1:   Initialization: Set PCT(M) to empty.

A2:   Repeat the following steps (A3 to A5) for R_1 to R_n.
      Then terminate the algorithm.

A3:   Identify the event code E_i of the current record R_i.
      IF E_i is a creating process event THEN
            Get the time at which the process was created.
            Identify the process-id and its parent process-id.
            Add these values into PCT as the last entry.
      ELSE
            Get the time.
            Identify the process-id and other key values of E_i.
      ENDIF.

A4:   Save E_i and the key values into a Node.
      Link Node to the tail of the time-link of the Event-Chain.
      Adjust the process-link of Event-Chain.

A5:   Detect whether event E_i has caused other state transition events
      (e.g., "waiting" to "ready," "ready" to "running," or both).
      IF it has invoked other state transition events THEN
            Identify the process-id(s) and other key values of
                  the state transition event(s),
            Save the key values into Node(s), and
            Link Node(s) to the tail of the time-link of Event-Chain.
            Adjust the process-link of the Event-Chain.
      ENDIF.

END of Algorithm CIPEL.

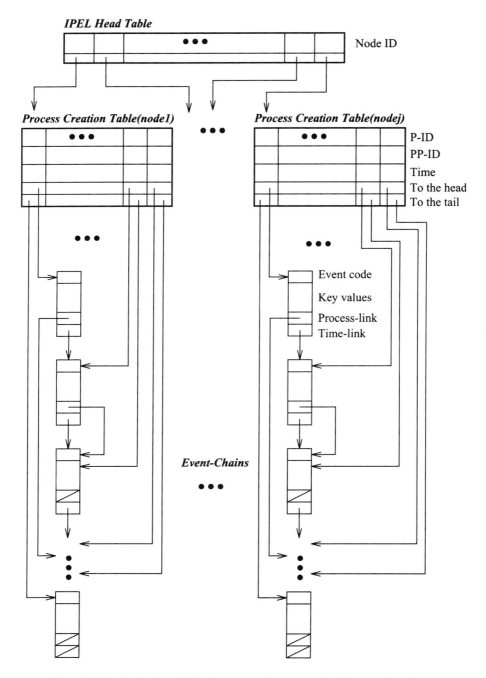

Fig. 8.5 Logical view of the integrated process-level execution log.

8.7.2   Logical Views at the Process Level

After the collected data are organized into an IPEL, we construct from the IPEL a set of process-level logical views, which assist in software testing and debugging. These logical views are process graphs, P/V operation sequences on semaphores, and the process interaction graphs derived from message passing. In the following, we first discuss how these logical views can help in debugging different logical errors and then describe how to construct these logical views from the IPEL.

The process graph (PCG) shows the parent-child relationships among all processes running in the system. A typical PCG is shown in Fig. 8.6. Nodes in the graph denote processes and directed edges represent the parent-child relationships between the processes. By providing the process parent-child relations, this graph can be used by the user to infer which processes may be responsible for the faults found in comparing the graph with the expected process graph. The following algorithm derives the process graph from the IPEL. It first searches the PCT's for the system process that created the application process. It then picks a process and links it to its parent if the parent exists in the tree; otherwise, it picks another process. This is repeated until all the processes are linked in the tree.

Algorithm CPCG (Constructing the PCG).

/* This algorithm is used to construct the PCG using the PCT's and the EC's. */

B1:   Set the system process that created the first application process as the root of the PCG and mark it as P_0.

B2:   Link the first application process as the child of the root.

B3:   Repeat Step B4 until all the processes are marked.

B4:   Select an unmarked process P_u in the PCT's
      IF P_u's parent is in the graph already THEN
            mark P_u and link it to its parent.
      ELSE
            Skip P_u.
      ENDIF

END of Algorithm CPCG.

The semaphore is a mechanism provided by the operating system for processes to synchronize with each other. The operating system provides semaphore services with P/V or wait/signal operations. The correct use of a

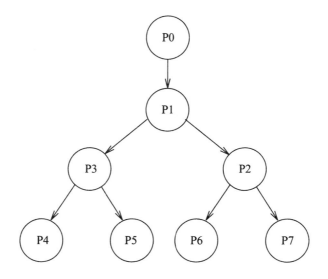

Fig. 8.6 A process graph.

semaphore is the responsibility of each individual process. Thus the programmer must be completely aware of the information shared among processes. Although there exist several models for typical process synchronization problems, such as the producer/consumer and reader/writer problems, process synchronization is still error-prone in distributed real-time systems.

It is very hard to detect synchronization errors by only examining the program source code. To find process synchronization errors, the examination of the run-time behavior of the participating processes is very helpful. To represent the synchronization behavior among processes using semaphores, a P/V operation sequence (PVOS) is constructed from the collected data for each node. Fig. 8.7 gives an example of P/V operation sequences. Each node of the sequence represents a P/V operation, and data stored for each operation includes the process ID that performed the operation, a field indicating whether a P or V operation performed, the semaphore ID on which the operation was performed, the value of the semaphore, and the time at which the operation was performed. All the nodes are linked together in a time sequence.

This operation sequence reflects the synchronizing behavior of the processes on semaphores. The user can check the P/V operation sequences to identify synchronization errors. For example, if a process executed a P operation for a critical section and no V operation was recorded when leaving the critical section, we would identify the process as a faulty process because it may have caused another process to be in the "waiting" state forever.

Below we describe an algorithm that derives the PVOS from the event-chain. The algorithm searches the event-chain of a given target node for P/V

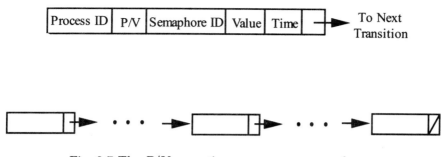

Fig. 8.7 The P/V operation sequence on semaphores.

operations and links them together.

Algorithm CPVOS (Constructing the PVOS).

/* This algorithm is used to construct the PVOS on semaphores for all the computer nodes. */

C1:   Repeat the following steps for all the computer nodes.

C2:   Node := the first node of the Event-Chain of a computer node. Set the head of the PVOS of the computer node to NULL.

C3:   Repeat this step until finding the tail of the time-link.
       IF Node.Code = "E3" THEN
            Link this node to the tail of the PVOS.
       ENDIF.
       Node := Node.Time-link.

END of Algorithm CPVOS.

In a distributed real-time system, interprocess communication between nodes has unpredictable delays because processes communicate with their environment asynchronously through I/O devices. In addition, because of the concurrent execution of processes, the events in a distributed system cannot be expressed in a total order fashion as in a single processor system. Some events may occur at the same time. Therefore, to help the user, a representation is needed for these concurrent behaviors.

When debugging infrequent and irreproducible errors that do not have an obvious cause, a common approach is to examine the traces of interprocess messages to see if any abnormality can be detected [146]. To do so, we use Lamport's "happen-before" partial relation [207] to construct a graph called process interaction graph via message passing (PIGMP) which presents the logical behavior in interprocess communication. With this graph, we can localize faults within processes by checking the messages and their sequences to identify faulty processes and unexpected sequences of messages.

In addition to the interprocess communication, there is also communication between the processes and the environment. A process sends its output to the environment, and it proceeds without waiting for any acknowledgment. If a process needs an input from the environment, it has to wait until the input becomes available. The environment generates an interrupt for each input, and it continues without waiting for the acknowledgment from the receiving process. Thus the input/output between processes and their environment can be modeled as asynchronous interprocess communications with the environment as a dummy process, $P_{external}$. This environment process can only perform two operations, send and receive.

As discussed in Section 2.2.1, an event in a distributed real-time system may be modeled as several subevents because these subevents may occur at different times. For example, a receive-message event in interprocess communication may be modeled as two subevents: The receiver executes the "receive" system call, and the receiver receives the message because the time at which the "receive" call was invoked could be different from the time at which the receiver actually received the message. This event decomposition is very helpful for timing analysis because we can determine how long the receiver was in a waiting state or how long the message had been available before the receiver was ready to receive it. However, for the purpose of logical behavior representation, such timing is not needed as long as the message was received by the receiver. Thus a receive-message event can be simply characterized by the receiver, sender, and message. Send events can be specified with the same data.

Fig. 8.8 gives a typical example of a PIGMP. Each column represents a process, and the environment is marked with $P_{external}$. Send/receive events for a process are totally ordered, and the send/receive events among processes are partially ordered. An arc between two processes represents communication with the source of the arc as the sender and the destination of the arc as the receiver. Each node specifies the sender and the receiver, and each arc is marked with the message in the communication. If a sender sent a message to a process that had been terminated, there would be a dangling arc from the sender. If a receiver waited for a message from a process that had been terminated, there would a dangling arc to the receiver.

The following algorithm derives the PIGMP from a given IPEL. The algorithm first deletes all the nodes except I/O event (E4), interprocess communication (E5), and external interrupt (E7) nodes. For interprocess communication events, it looks for both parties and links them together if they are found. For input and output events, it links the process with the dummy process for the environment.

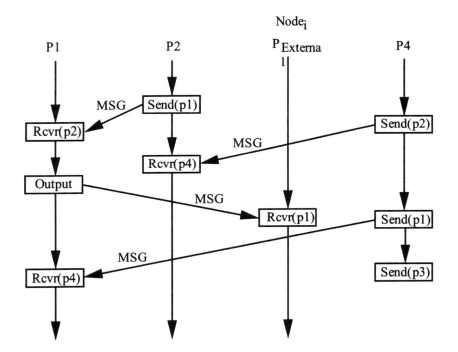

Fig. 8.8 The process interaction graph via message passing.

Algorithm CPIGMP (Constructing the PIGMP)

/* This algorithm is used to construct the PIGMP for interprocess communication from the IPEL. */

D1:   Use Process-Link to separate processes.

D2:   Delete all nodes whose code is not "E4," "E5," or "E7."
Combine all the subevents into one single event.

D3:   For all the nodes left, do the following:
IF the other side of pair of send/receive can be found THEN
       Link the pair with an arc marked with the message.
ELSE
       Draw an outgoing dangling arc if the node is a send.
       Draw an incoming dangling arc if the node is a receive.
ENDIF.
IF (the node is "input" with external interrupt)
        or (the node is "output") THEN
     Link it to $P_{external}$ with an arc
        marked with the message (I/O buffer).
ELSE
       Skip it.
ENDIF.

END of Algorithm CPIGMP.

8.8   Function-Level Data Processing

The data recorded at the function level, called the function-level program execution log (FPEL), has the same problem as PPEL's. That is, they are represented in the machine-level code, and the interpretation is target processor dependent. Also, besides key values, the FPEL contains unrelated instructions and data. Therefore it is necessary to filter out unimportant data and reorganize the remaining data so that logical representations can be easily derived.

In our approach, an intermediate data set called the integrated function-level execution log (IFEL) is derived from the FPEL. Each node of the IFEL represents a function-level event with its key values. A pointer is used to link all the events in a time sequence. Fig. 8.9 gives an example of an IFEL. The IFEL can be constructed by the following algorithm:

Algorithm CIFEL (Creating the IFEL).

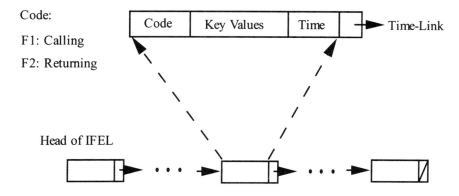

Fig. 8.9 An integrated function-level execution log.

/* This algorithm is used to construct the IFEL from the FPEL data set. Records $R_1, R_2, \ldots, R_n$ represent these data blocks. */

E1:   Initialization: Head-of-IFEL := Null.

E2:   Repeat Step E3 for R_1 to R_n.

E3:   Identify event F_i of the current record R_i.
       Get the time.
       Identify the function-id and other key values.
       Save F_i and the key values into Node.
       Link Node to the tail of the time-link of the IFEL.

END of Algorithm CIFEL.

From the IFEL a logical view called the function-calling tree (FCT) can be derived. The FCT shows the calling relationships between functions. It can be used to check the preconditions and the postconditions of each function using the passed-in and returned parameters. Thus it helps in localizing faults to individual functions. The function-calling tree (FCT), shown in Fig. 8.10, which is derived from the IFEL is a logical view of the function calling behavior of the program. The root of the tree represents the main function of the process. The other nodes in the tree represent the executions of functions with the key values of both calling and returning events. An algorithm for deriving the FCT from the IFEL is given below. It first constructs a node for the main function of the process, and then for each call event (coded F1; see Table 8.2), it fills a new node with the passed parameters and links the node to its calling function. If the next event is a return event, the returned parameters are saved into the node of the last call event because the return event must be the return of the function of the last called function. If the next

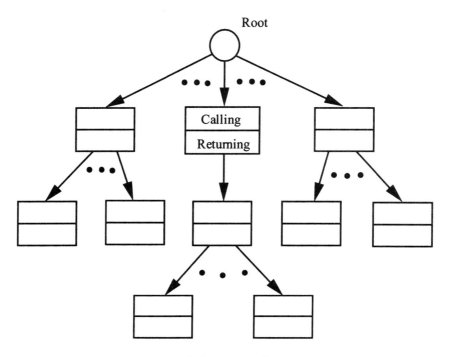

Fig. 8.10 A function-calling tree.

event is another call event, a new node is allocated and linked to its calling function, as mentioned above. This continues iteratively until all the events are processed.

Algorithm CFCT (Constructing the FCT).

/* This algorithm is used to construct an FCT from an IFEL. */

S1:   Initialization:
       Current-Node := Head-of-IFEL.
       Root := Null.
       Tree-Node := Root.

S2:   Repeat Step S3 until the tail of the IFEL is met.

S3:   IF Current-Node.Code = "F1" THEN
           Get a null New-Tree-Node.
           New-Tree-Node.Calling := Current-Node.
           Tree-Node.pointer := New-Node.
           Tree-Node := New-Node.

ELSE
        Tree-Node.Returning := Current-Node.
        Assign the parent node as Tree-Node.
ENDIF.
Current-Node := Current-Node.Pointer.

END of Algorithm CFCT.

8.9 Summary

In this chapter we first described our noninterference monitoring architecture for distributed real-time systems. In this architecture a monitoring node is attached to each node of the target system. All of the monitoring nodes are connected together via a network that is independent of the target network. In each monitoring node we employed a hardware device to snoop the data, address, and control buses of the target node for specified conditions. Once a condition is matched, a specified action can be performed by the monitoring node. Each monitoring node has a clock independent of the target node, and the clocks are synchronized through the monitoring network to provide a global time reference. Since the monitoring system does not use any of the resources of the target system, it does not interfere with the execution of the target system.

To collect the process-level events listed in Table 8.1, we identified starting and stopping trigger conditions that need to be detected by the monitoring hardware. Once a starting trigger condition is detected, the recording process latches all of the signals on the buses of the target processor until a stopping condition is detected. To collect the function-level events listed in Table 8.2, the data on the target processor buses is continuously latched into a fixed length buffer and saved into the monitoring memory when a trigger condition is detected. The length of the buffer is designed to be sufficient to contain all the key values for function-level events.

After the data is collected, we derive a set of graphs to represent different aspects of the execution behavior of the target system. At the process level, we construct a process graph that represents the parent-child relationship among processes, a P/V operation sequence on semaphores that helps in debugging synchronization errors, and a process interaction graph via message passing that allows the user to examine the messages and their logical sequences between processes. At the function level, a function calling tree is constructed that shows the calling relationship among functions. In this chapter we mainly discussed logical behavior representations that help in debugging logical errors. In distributed real-time systems we also need to represent timing behavior to help the user in debugging timing errors. In the next chapter we will discuss how to represent timing behavior from the collected data and how to debug timing errors.

Exercises

1. In Fig. 8.2, which provides an overall scheme of a monitoring node, a timer is used in the interface module. What is its purpose?

2. Describe how the triggering conditions are determined.

3. What is the integrated process-level execution log (IPEL) used for?

4. Why is the process graph (PCG) useful?

5. A function-calling tree (FCT) is useful for dynamically debugging programs written for single-processor functions. Write a program in PERL or any other language that will instrument a program that creates a calling tree. A basic program would simply dump out the sequence of functions called. A more usable program would indent the function names called so that the user could see how functions are nested.

6. The previous exercise simply asked for function names. Write a program that will instrument the program so that the data passed and returned to each function is written to a file as the program is executed.

7. A drawback of the previous two programs is that much of the data is output. The user may not know what to look for, and even if the user does know what to look for, it may be difficult to find. Thus dynamic error checking could reduce the number of problems and help the user find errors more quickly. Write a program that will instrument programs to dynamically check all variables passed into a function. Make it configurable so that a programmer can use it to specify the range of each variable. Compare your instrumentation program to writing strongly typed code that specifies ranges for variables and traps any violations.

8. Write a program that ensures that all variables in a program are initialized.

Chapter 9

A Graph-Based Timing Analysis

9.1 Causes of Timing Errors

The correctness of a real-time system depends not only on the logical results of the computation but also on the times at which the results are produced. The results must be produced within the specified timing constraints. The violation of a timing constraint may cause loss of life or property, depending on the application. Thus, in real-time systems, debugging timing errors is as important as debugging computation errors. In this chapter we first identify the basic causes for timing errors and then discuss how to graphically represent the timing behavior of real-time systems.

For the following discussion, we first define the terms and notations that we will use. A *timing constraint*, TC, is defined as a time restriction between the *starting event*, TC_{se}, and the *ending event*, TC_{ee}, which marks the beginning and ending of the timing constraint, respectively. The times at which the two events start and end are denoted TC_{st}, and TC_{et}, respectively. We call the processes that perform the starting and ending events the *starting process*, TC_{sp}, and the *ending process*, TC_{ep}.

We define the *relevant processes*, TC_{rp}, of TC as the set of processes that interact with the starting process or the ending process of the timing constraint directly or indirectly through message passing, semaphore synchronization, or I/O operations during the time interval from TC_{st} to TC_{et}. The environment is modeled as a dummy process, $P_{external}$, that interacts with the processes in the node through I/O operations. The I/O operations between the $P_{external}$ and the processes in the node are treated as asynchronous interprocess communication.

Timing constraints are classified into *interprocessor timing constraints* and *intraprocessor timing constraints* in a distributed real-time system. The intraprocessor timing constraints are those whose relevant processes are all on the same node. The interprocessor timing constraints are those whose relevant processes are dispersed on more than one node. Intraprocessor timing constraints are similar to those in a single processor system, where satisfaction of the timing constraints is not affected by other target nodes. For the interprocessor timing constraints, the nodes that contain the relevant processes are called *relevant nodes* and represented as TC_{rn}.

9.1.1 Three Basic Causes of Timing Errors

To identify the causes of timing constraint violations, we first take a look into the states a process can be in. After a process is created and before it terminates, a process may be in one of three states: running, ready, or waiting. A process state transition diagram in Fig. 9.1 shows the process states and the state transitions that can occur. After a process is created, the process is admitted and enters the *ready* state, where it waits to be executed. When the process is scheduled for execution or assigned to a processor, it enters the *running* state. When an interrupt occurs, the process goes back to the ready state and waits to be scheduled again. When the process has to wait for I/O processing to complete or an event to occur, it enters the *waiting* state, and it will go back to the ready state when the I/O processing has completed or the event has occurred. From this we can see that the process may be in one of the three states until it exits or terminates. Corresponding to these three process states, we can identify three *basic* causes of timing errors:

- Computation causes (corresponds to the running state).

- Scheduling causes (corresponds to the ready state).

- Synchronization causes (corresponds to the waiting state).

A basic cause of a timing error is a the timing constraint violation which is due to a combination of these three causes.

Computation can cause a violation of a timing constraint if the processes spend more time than expected on computation (here we refer to computation as the execution time of the program). That is, the relevant processes of the timing constraint spend more time in the running state than expected. *Scheduling* can cause a timing error if the process was not allocated enough CPU time. *Synchronization* may cause a timing error if the relevant processes wait for an event or a message that never occurs or is never received. A typical example of a timing error caused by synchronization is a deadlock, where a set of processes are in a circular waiting state forever.

9.1.2 Four Immediate Causes of Timing Errors

The causes of timing errors may be a combination of the three basic causes. We define immediate causes of a timing error as the most direct cause of the timing error. For instance, a deadlock will result in a timing constraint violation. However, this deadlock might be caused by an assignment to a

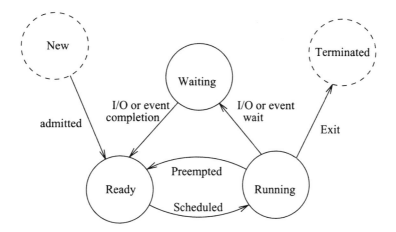

Fig. 9.1 Process states and their transitions.

variable or by the scheduling. Thus the source responsible for timing error is the assignment (or the scheduling), although we say that the deadlock is an immediate cause of the timing error. There are seven possible combinations of the three basic causes, as shown in Fig. 9.2, but not all the combinations need to be considered. Combination 4, scheduling and synchronization, can be discarded, since scheduling is a nonimmediate cause of the timing error in this combination. If the relevant processes are deadlocked, the scheduler cannot do anything directly to these processes. Scheduling might have caused this deadlock, but scheduling is not considered as an immediate cause of the timing error. For the same reason, combination 5 can be discarded too. When a process is in the waiting state, it cannot be executed. Computation cannot cause a process to leave the waiting state. Computation is not an immediate cause to the timing error in combination 5 either. Combination 7 is ignored, since it is simply a combination of 4 and 5.

For combination 6: scheduling and computation, two cases may be considered. In the first case, the timing error can only be corrected by both reducing the execution time and allocating more CPU time to the relevant processes. In other words, even if the CPU(s) had only been allocated to the relevant processes, the timing constraint would still be violated because the computation of the program would take more time than the timing constraint, or even if the computation time was reduced to zero, the timing constraint would still be violated because the relevant processes stayed in the ready state (waiting for CPU) longer than the timing constraint. In the second case, the timing constraint can be met by either reducing the computation time or allocating more CPU time to the relevant processes.

From the discussion above we conclude that there are four possible immediate causes of a timing error:

Number	Computation	Scheduling	Synchronization
1	0	0	1
2	0	1	0
3	1	0	0
4	0	1	1
5	1	0	1
6	1	1	0
7	1	1	1

0: without   1: with

Fig. 9.2 Combinations of the basic causes.

- Computation.

- Scheduling.

- Synchronization.

- Combination of computation and scheduling.

From the user's point of view, a timing error may occur in two ways. One way is that the ending event of the timing constraint occurred and was observed. The other way is that the ending event did not occur and therefore was not observed. If the problem is due to the synchronization, the ending event will not occur. Computation may also prevent the ending event from occurring, for example, if there was a dead loop in a relevant process. However, we assume that the ending event does not occur only when the synchronization is an immediate cause of the timing error. That is, if a timing error is caused by the scheduling and/or the computation, the ending event of the timing constraint always occurs.

9.2   Representations of Timing Behavior

The timing behavior of the system can be represented by the relationship between events and the times at which the events occurred. As discussed in Sections 9.1.1 and 9.1.2, the process states and the duration of the states are very helpful in debugging the timing errors. To represent both the interactions among processes and the states and the state durations of processes, we construct *colored process interaction graphs* (CPIG). The events of a process are depicted in a column. Each node of the graph represents an event, and a vertical arc represents the interval between events in a process. An arc between two columns represents an interaction between the two corresponding processes. We use three colors to represent the three different states. The CPIG includes all the processes and all the events in the target system. The user can browse through this graph to observe the interactions between processes and the timing behavior of the whole system.

The CPIG includes all the processes and events in the target system for the user to observe the behavior of the whole system. Because of that, it tends to be very large and complex. In many cases the user may want to study the behavior relevant to an individual timing constraint. For example, the user may want to find whether the computation or scheduling is a cause of a timing constraint violation. For this purpose the CPIG is not appropriate. To help the user in studying the behavior pertaining to individual timing constraints, we derive a *dedicated colored process interaction graph* (DCPIG) from the CPIG. The DCPIG contains information relevant to the immediate causes of the given timing constraint. With this graph the user can find the causes of the timing error with little distraction.

The CPIG and DCPIG reflect the timing behavior of the target program under the given hardware environment of the target system, such as the number of the processor. However, in some cases a program may violate a timing constraint no matter how many processors are available. For example, the program may need more time than specified by the timing constraint. To find the computation cause of the timing error a *program graph* (PG) is derived from the DCPIG of the timing constraint. With this graph the user can check the execution time on the longest path to see whether the timing constraint is violated due to computation.

In this section we use an example to show the differences among the CPIG, the DCPIG, and the PG. Then in the remaining sections of this chapter we discuss timing analysis using these graphs. In the next chapter we will describe algorithms for deriving these graphs and other graphs for debugging distributed real-time systems.

Suppose that the program shown in Fig. 9.3 has been monitored using the monitoring approach introduced Chapter 8. In Fig. 9.3 each column represents the code for a process noted on the top of the column. Processes P_1, P_2, and P_3 run on $node_i$, and processes P_4 and P_5 run on $node_j$. For clarity, we only show the statements monitored in the program. Two timing constraints are specified on the system:

1. P_1 should perform the *output* operation within TC1 time units after P_1 creates P_2.

2. P_4 should send message Msg5 to P_1 within TC2 time units after P_4 receives message Msg2 from P_3.

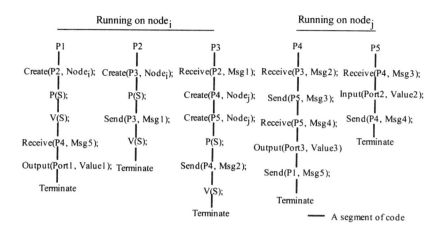

Fig. 9.3 A program example used for timing analysis.

After postprocessing the collected data of the program, the CPIG is constructed as shown in Fig. 9.4. With this CPIG we can see that process P_0 (a system process like shell on UNIX) was created at t_0, which in turn created process P_1 at t_1. P_1 was first executed at t_2, and it created P_2 at t_3 which in turn created P_3 at t_4. Since processes P_1, P_2, and P_3 were on the same node, each new process was created immediately. In contrast, process P_3 executed the create call at t_{11}, however, process P_4 was not created and did not become ready for execution until t_{12} because P_3 and P_4 were not on the same node (i.e., $node_i$ needed to send the process creation request for P_4 to $node_j$ via communication lines). Another example of an error caused by communication delay can be seen at the point where P_4 sent a message to P_2 at t_{28} and P_2 did not receive the message until t_{33}. Process synchronization via semaphores can be seen in this example as well. Process P_1 executed a P operation at t_7 with no success because P_2 had held the semaphore since t_5. When P_2 released the semaphore at t_9, P_1 was released from the waiting queue and changed to the ready state.

Fig. 9.5 and Fig. 9.6 are the DCPIGs of timing constraints 1 and 2, respectively. For timing constraint 1, the starting event is the create call at t_3 and the ending event is the output at t_{35}. All the processes but P_0 are the relevant processes of the timing constraint. P_0 is not a relevant process because it did not interact with P_1 (the starting and ending process) between t_3 (the starting point of the timing constraint) and t_{35} (the ending point of the timing constraint). The DCPIG of the timing constraint 2 can be interpreted in the same way. From the two DCPIGs we can determine that constraint 1 is an interprocessor timing constraint and that $node_i$ and $node_j$ are the relevant nodes while constraint 2 is an intraprocessor timing constraint on $node_j$.

Fig. 9.7 and Fig. 9.8 are the PGs for the timing constraints 1 and 2,

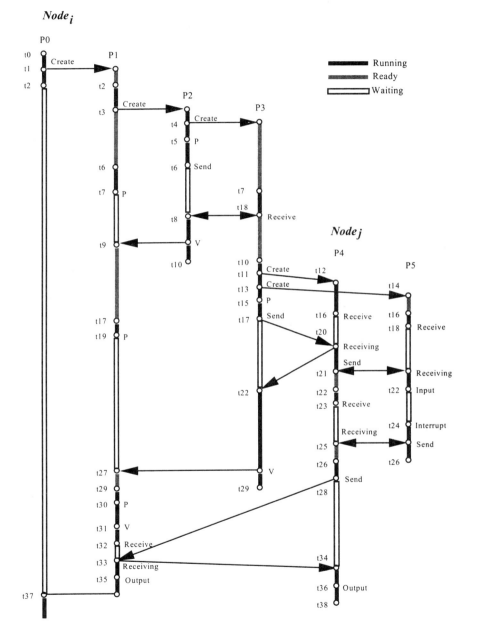

Fig. 9.4 A colored process interaction graph.

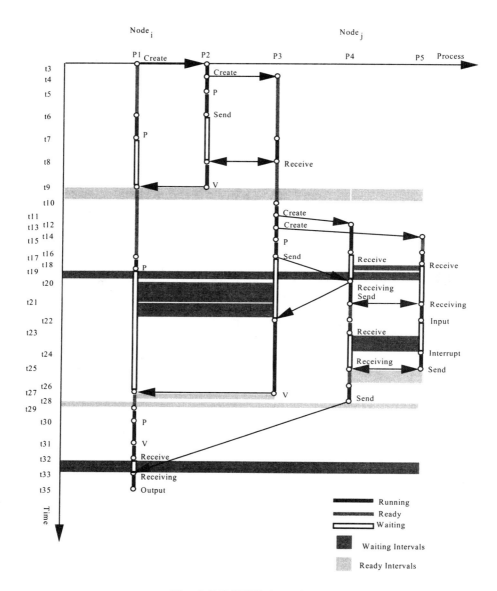

Fig. 9.5 DCPIG for TC1.

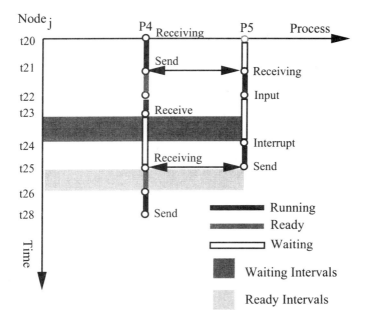

Fig. 9.6 DCPIG for TC2.

respectively. Each edge in a PG is referenced by a number and marked with the process ID and the amount of time the process was in execution. For example, edge 9 in Fig. 9.7 represents the execution time in the amount of $(t_{16}\text{-}t_{12})$ of process P_4.

9.3 Timing Analysis of Synchronization Causes

There are six possible reasons for a set of processes to be in a waiting state for an unlimited time. The first reason is that the processes are involved in a *deadlock* situation. The second is that they are involved in a synchronization in which one partner has terminated. This is called *distributed termination.* For example, if a process was waiting for a message from another process that had terminated, the process would be in the waiting state forever. The third reason is that the processes are involved in a synchronization in which a partner failed to synchronize. For example, a process never released a semaphore, or a partner in an interprocess communication does not have the requested send/receive operation. We call these *missed operations* because the requested operations are not executed. The fourth reason is *starvation.* This can happen when semaphores are used for process synchronization. A process requesting a semaphore never acquired it because processes with a higher priority had continuously used the semaphore. Finally, in a distributed

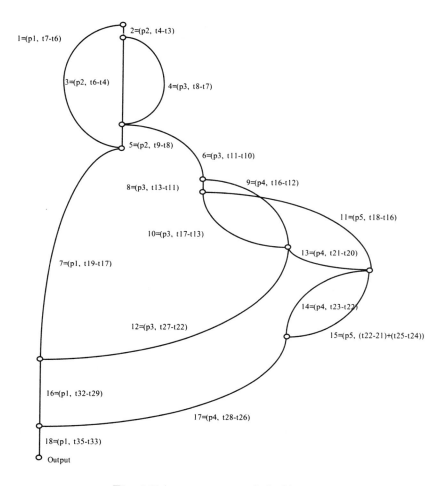

Fig. 9.7 A program graph (PG) for TC1.

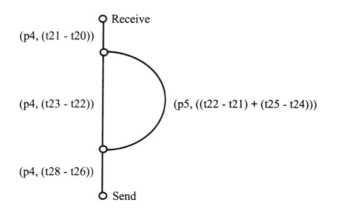

Fig. 9.8 PG for TC2.

real-time system, a process can also wait for a message for an unlimited time if there is a *loss of message* or a *communication deadlock*. For example, a message can be lost during data transmission. A communication deadlock could occur if every node waits for the next node to find an available slot in the communication buffer until a message is sent. All of the above six cases leave the involved processes in the waiting state forever. Thus, if any of the above six reasons is a cause of a timing error, the ending event of the timing constraint would not occur or it could be observed. Thus we have the following:

Theorem 9.1 *If the ending event, TC_{ee}, of a timing constraint is observed, then deadlock, distributed termination, missed operations, starvation, lost messages, and communication deadlock cannot be a cause of the violation of the timing constraint.*

In this section we discuss how to analyze the collected execution history of a system in order to determine possible synchronization causes of timing errors.

9.3.1 Analysis Procedure for Synchronization Causes

A distributed termination occurs when a process is trying to send to or receive from another process that has been terminated. In most cases it is easy to determine if distributed termination occurred by checking whether a process's partner has terminated. However, in a distributed real-time system, a receiver could execute the receive call at the same time as an expected sender that is located on a different computer node terminates, or in synchronous communication a sender could send a message at the same moment that the receiver terminated. Note that in these two cases, missed operations could also be the cause of the timing error. With the following analysis technique, we report distributed termination if the above cases occur.

Deadlocks can be detected by determining if the processes are circularly waiting for each other or not. For example, assume that three processes communicate using synchronous message passing. If every process is programmed to send a message to the next in a circle before it tries to receive, the three processes would be deadlocked, waiting for acknowledgment in a circle forever. However, in distributed systems two processes could be mutually waiting for each other for a period of time but not deadlocked. For example, a process sends a message to another process on a different node, while the receiver executes the receive call before the message arrives at the receiving node. Thus the sender waits for the acknowledgment from the receiver, and the receiver waits for the message from the sender. Until the message arrives, both the processes wait for each other. However, they are not in deadlock.

Detecting distributed termination and deadlocks is relatively simple, as noted above. However, determining the other four synchronization causes is almost impossible. That is because monitoring the execution of a program cannot be infinite; thus whether an event would happen in the future cannot be determined from the limited collected program execution history. Therefore, whether a partner process would execute the requested operation in the future (missed operation), whether the "starved" process would obtain the semaphore (starvation), and whether the message "lost" (loss of message) or "locked" in the communication buffer (communication deadlock) would be received cannot be determined from the collected data. For this reason, instead of reporting missed operations, starvation, communication deadlocks, and loss of messages, we provide the user with the information on the execution, and the determination of the problem is left to the user.

Missed operations could happen in both interprocess communication and synchronization. In interprocess communication, if the expected receiver (or sender) does not execute the receive call (or the send call), the sender (receiver) would wait forever for the acknowledgment (message). In this case the partner either terminated after the send/receive call was made or was still live at the end of the collected history. In direct message passing the process must explicitly name its partner, so we can find the anticipated partner and find the status of the partner. In interprocess synchronization, if a process has executed a P (wait) operation but no V (signal) operation was executed, all the other processes requesting that semaphore would wait forever. In most applications the total number of P operations on a semaphore is designed to be equal to the number of V operations to be executed on the same semaphore. Thus one may count the number of P and V operations. If the executed P operations were more than the executed V operations, one may consider a missed operation as the possible cause.

Starvation only occurs in interprocess synchronization. A process requesting a semaphore has to wait because other processes with a higher priority have continuously accessed the semaphore. An indication of possible starvation is that some processes (at least one) were waiting for a semaphore that had been requested and acquired by other processes with a higher priority than the waiting processes.

Loss of messages and communication deadlocks only occur in interprocessor communication. Messages are lost during transmission or are deadlocked in the buffers of the IPC devices. In both cases the sending processes must have sent the message, and some of the receiving processes are in the waiting state. If the waiting processes are prolonged for an unreasonable stretch of time, one may consider loss of message and communication deadlock as possible causes. Whether the waiting is unreasonably long is a decision for the user to make. Without the knowledge of the communication network, it is virtually impossible to distinguish between the loss of messages and the communication deadlock from the collected data.

We can summarize our timing analysis procedure for synchronization causes as follows: If the ending event of the timing constraint in question is not observed, the synchronization analysis is performed. We first detect distributed terminations and exclude the detected processes involved in distributed terminations from the waiting process set to be considered for other synchronization causes. Then a deadlock detection procedure detects the processes that are waiting for each other circularly and excludes those processes from the waiting process set. If there are still processes left in the waiting state after the distributed termination and deadlock detection, we detect starvation and missed operations. Finally, we conclude that any processes left in the waiting process set have a lost message or are in communication deadlock.

9.3.2   Distributed Termination

To detect distributed terminations, we first put all the processes in the waiting state into variable W_STATE. If W_STATE is empty, it is determined that synchronization cannot be a cause of the timing error. If W_STATE is not empty, we then use the following procedure to detect distributed terminations: This detection procedure searches for the partners of the waiting processes to determine whether they have terminated. To do this, it constructs process-waiting chains. If a waiting chain ends on a process that has terminated at an earlier time, we report a distributed termination and put the processes in the waiting chain into D_TERM. If a waiting chain ends on an active process, we leave them in W_STATE for other synchronization detection algorithms to examine.

Algorithm DISTRIBUTED-TERMINATION-DETECTION:

/* This algorithm detects the distributed terminations. The set
variable WAITING and D_TERM are used to contain the processes
that are being processed and the processes that are in distributed
terminations, respectively. W_STATE is used to contain the processes that are in the waiting state, but neither in deadlocks nor in
distributed terminations. */

ST0: For each process in all the PCT's
      IF the last node of the process is a state transition event
           IF the new state is waiting
                Insert the process into W_STATE;
           ENDIF
      ENDIF
ST1: Set WAITING and D_TERM to null;
      Select one process in W_STATE as current process P.
ST2: Repeat until every process in W_STATE is marked;
      IF P $\in$ D_TERM or P has terminated in an earlier time THEN
           D_TERM:=D_TERM $\cup$ WAITING $\cup$ { P };
           WAITING=null;
           Mark P;
           Select another unmarked process in W_STATE as P
    ELSE
           IF P is not in W_STATE THEN
                Set WAITING to null;
                Select another unmarked process as P;
           ELSE
                Put P into WAITING;
                Mark P;
                IF P is waiting for a message/reply THEN
                      Select the partner as P;
                ELSE
                  IF P is waiting for semaphore S THEN
                      Search the PVOS of S for P'
                          which was occupying S;
                      Set P' as P;
                  ELSE
                    IF P is waiting for an I/O THEN
                      Set WAITING to null;
                      Select an unmarked process as P;
                  ENDIF
                ENDIF
              ENDIF
           ENDIF
      ENDIF

ST3: IF D_TERM is null THEN
        Report "No distributed termination";
    ELSE
        W_STATE=W_STATE - D_TERM;
        Report "Distributed termination:" D_TERM;
    ENDIF

END of Algorithm.

We can compute the complexity of the algorithm as follows: The first and third steps cost a constant time. Suppose that we have N processes in the system. Searching for all the waiting processes takes N steps to check the last state of each process. For the second step, within the repeat loop, the partner for a direct communication can be found in a constant time by searching the IPEL. If P is waiting for a semaphore S, we need at most $N - 1$ steps to search the PVOS of semaphore S for P' that has occupied S. That is because, after P' occupies S there are at most $N - 1$ processes in the list waiting for the semaphore S. Since a process would not be in the WAITING set again if it has been marked, the second step will repeat N times for the N processes. Thus the complexity of the algorithm is $N * (N - 1) = O(N^2)$.

9.3.3 Deadlocks

There are various deadlock detection algorithms in the literature [135, 307, 353, 354]. Here we present a deadlock detection algorithm [307] using the IPEL and the P/V operation sequences. In this algorithm all semaphores and messages in the system are considered to be shared resources. To detect deadlocks, we search for process-waiting chains among the waiting processes. If a process-waiting chain becomes a circle, there is a deadlock, and the processes involved in the deadlock are reported. If a waiting chain ends with a process that is not in the waiting state, then the processes in the waiting chain are not involved in deadlocks. If a waiting chain ends with a process that has been in a deadlock, then the processes in the waiting chain are added to the deadlock.

Algorithm DEADLOCK-DETECTION.

/* This algorithm detects deadlocks. The set variables WAITING and BLOCKED are used to contain the processes that are being processed and the processes that are in deadlocks, respectively. W_STATE contains the waiting processes. */

ST1: Set WAITING and BLOCKED to null;
    Select one process in W_STATE as current process P.

ST2: Repeat until every process in W_STATE is marked;
  IF P is in WAITING or BLOCKED THEN
    BLOCKED:= BLOCKED ∪ WAITING;
    WAITING=null;
    Mark P;
    Select another unmarked process in W_STATE as P
  ELSE
    Mark P
    IF P is not in the waiting state THEN
      Set WAITING to null;
      Select another unmarked process as P;
    ELSE
      Put P into WAITING and W_STATE;
      IF P is waiting for a message/reply THEN
        Select the partner as P;
      ELSE
        IF P is waiting for semaphore S THEN
          Search the PVOS of S for P'
            which was occupying S;
          Set P' as P;
        ELSE
          IF P is waiting for an I/O THEN
            Set WAITING to null;
            Select an unmarked process as P;
          ENDIF
        ENDIF
      ENDIF
    ENDIF
  ENDIF
ST3: IF BLOCKED is null THEN
    Report "No deadlock";
  ELSE
    W_STATE=W_STATE - BLOCKED;
    Report Processes in BLOCKED are deadlocked.
  ENDIF.

END of Algorithm DEADLOCK-DETECTION.

This procedure is similar to the procedure for distributed termination detection. Thus the complexity of the algorithm is $O(N^2)$. Here N is the number of the processes in the target system.

The deadlock detection procedure can be combined with the distributed termination detection procedure at the implementation phase. We separate them here only for clarity.

9.3.4 Missed Operations and Starvation

After the detection of deadlock and distributed termination, if there are still processes left in the waiting process set, we then check whether there is starvation or missed operations. Since monitoring cannot determine whether an event would occur in the future, we cannot determine whether there was a real starvation. Therefore we cannot determine whether there was a missed operation based on the collected history. For the following discussion we assume that the monitoring was long enough so that if the expected operations would occur, they would have been collected in the execution history. Thus missed operations should be interpreted as expected operations that did not execute within the expected period of time.

Missed operations could occur because of interprocess communication and semaphore synchronization. In interprocess communication, processes use send and receive calls to send or receive messages. We also model I/O operations as direct interprocess communication between the processes and the environment, which is represented as a dummy process. If a sender waits for an acknowledgment from the receiver and no receive call has been executed, there is a missed operation (receive). If a receiver waits for a message from a sender that has not sent the message, there is a missed operation (send). If a process waits for an input and the dummy process has not sent the input, there is a missed operation (input).

To detect the missed operations in the interprocess communication, a procedure similar to the deadlock detection procedure can be used. The difference from the deadlock detection is that if a waiting chain ends with a process that was waiting for a message and its partner was not in the waiting state and had not executed the requested operation, then we report that these processes in the waiting chain and the partner are involved in a missed operation situation. If a waiting chain ends with an input operation, then we report that the processes in the waiting chain and the dummy process, $P_{external}$, are in a missed operation situation.

In semaphore synchronization, both missed operations and starvation may occur. If a process did not execute a V operation before exiting the critical section, other processes could wait for the semaphore forever. This is the case of a *missed operation*. It is also possible that a process cannot get a semaphore and so waits forever because other processes with a higher priority continually accessed the semaphore. This is a case of the starvation. Because we cannot obtain an infinite event sequence, we cannot distinguish them. Thus, instead of reporting either missed operations or starvation, we provide the user with information and then the user can make the decision on the causes of the timing error. This algorithm is detailed as follows:

Suppose that a process waiting chain ends with process P_i which is waiting for semaphore S at time T. Instead of reporting starvation or a missed operation, we provide the user with information of the P and V operations that were performed on S after T. We report the processes that performed P and/or V operations on the semaphore and the frequency of the P and the V operations of each process. Determining whether it was a case of starvation or a missed operation is left to the user. For example, if the last process that occupied the semaphore had executed one or several pairs of P and V operations on the semaphore between time T and the time at which the monitoring ended, it is very possible there is starvation. If the last process did not execute any V operations, it is quite possible that there is a missed operation (V operation) in the last process.

Since interprocess communication only has missed operation errors and the detection algorithm for missed operations in this case is very similar to the deadlock detection algorithm discussed above, one can detect missed operations easily. Thus we assume that missed operations on interprocess communication have been detected and that the processes involved are excluded from W_STATE. Below, we describe an algorithm that reports information on missed operations and starvation for a given semaphore. This algorithm is executed to report if a process-waiting chain ends with a process P_k that was waiting for semaphore S. To simplify the discussion, we suppose that a procedure similar to deadlock detection searches the waiting chains and reports process P_k and semaphore S.

Algorithm SEMAPHORE:

/* This algorithm reports the processes that access semaphore S after process P_k has executed the P operation, and it reports the frequency of the P and V operations executed by each process. The PVOS is used in the algorithm. $Number[i][1]$ and $Number[i][2]$ contains the frequency of P and V operations of process P_i for $i = 0$ to $N - 1$, where N is the number of the processes in the target system.*/

ST1: Initialize Number[i][j] to zero for all i and j.
ST2: Find the node in which P_k executed the P operation on S.
ST2: Repeat until the end of the PVOS;
    IF (NODE(operation)="P") and (sema-ID=S) THEN
        Number[N(Process-Id)][1]=Number[N(Process-Id)][1]+1;
    ELSE
        Number[N(Process-Id)][2]=Number[N(Process-Id)][2]+1;
    ENDIF
    Last-node=NODE;
    NODE=NODE(Next).
ST3: Report the frequency of the P and V operations for each process;
    Report Last-node(Process-Id) as the last process Pm;
    IF Number[m][2]=0 THEN

> Suggest the missed operation;
> ELSE
> > Suggest the starvation.
> ENDIF

END of Algorithm.

9.3.5 Lost Messages and Communication Deadlocks

As discussed in Section 9.3.1, in most cases of lost messages and communication deadlocks, the partner (receiver/sender) has executed the requested operation (send/receive) on a different node. With synchronous communication, both the sender and the receiver would be waiting for an acknowledgment and the message. With asynchronous communication, the receiver is in the waiting state. Since it is impossible to tell the difference between lost messages and communication deadlocks based on the collected data, we can only provide the information about the involved processes. It is up to the user to make a decision using knowledge of the program and the communication network of the target system.

To detect loss of messages and communication deadlocks, a procedure similar to the deadlock detection procedure can be used. When a process waiting chain ends with a process that was waiting for the interprocess communication and if its partner is on a different node and has executed the requested operation, then we report that the error is caused by a lost message and/or communication deadlock.

9.4 Computation and Scheduling Causes

As mentioned at the beginning of this chapter, if the ending event of a timing constraint occurred and was observed, synchronization would not be the cause of the timing error. Since a process spends its time in three states (running, ready, and waiting), then computation and/or scheduling must be responsible for the timing error if synchronization is not the cause. In other words, if the relevant processes of the timing constraint have spent longer time on computation than allowed by the timing constraint, then the timing constraint is violated. If the relevant processes cannot obtain enough CPU time, the timing constraint cannot be satisfied either. In this section we show how to identify the computation and scheduling causes using the DCPIG and the PG.

9.4.1 Timing Analysis Using the PG

The timing analysis for computation and scheduling is divided into two cases. The first case occurs when, no matter how many processors are available, the program violates the timing constraint. In other words, the timing constraint is violated if the program needs more time under the process interaction pattern in the execution trace than the timing constraint has allowed. To determine if computation is the cause, the program graph (PG) is used. With the PG we define the node with no incoming edges and the node with no outgoing edges as the starting node, PG_{sn}, and the ending node, PG_{en}, respectively. The PG_{sn} and PG_{en} correspond to the TC_{st} and TC_{et}, respectively. A path, $Path$, is defined as a connected edge sequence from PG_{sn} to PG_{en}. The execution time of a path, $Path_{exec}$, is the sum of the execution times of all edges on the path. The $Path_{process}$ of a path denotes the union of the processes of all the edges on the path. A critical path, $PG_{critical}$, is a path with the maximum execution time. From the PG, we have Theorems 9.2 and 9.3:

Theorem 9.2 *For the PG of a given timing constraint TC, if $Path_{exec}$ of $PG_{critical}$ is larger than TC_{time}, then computation is a cause of the violation of the timing constraint.*

Theorem 9.3 *For the PG of a given timing constraint TC, if $Path_{exec}$ of a path is longer than TC_{time}, then the processes in $Path_{process}$ are responsible for the timing error.*

Proof: Since the PG is derived from the DCPIG, the PG reflects the program's execution time under the process interaction pattern in the execution trace. Each node of the PG denotes the synchronization of the two processes of the incoming edges; each edge denotes the time that the process spends on computation from the starting node to the ending node of the edge. For the given process interaction pattern, $Path_{exec}$ of $Path_{critical}$ is the time that the program needs to reach the ending point from the starting point on the $Path_{critical}$. If it is larger than TC_{time}, the $Path_{critical}$ will always need more time than TC_{time} to reach the ending event, no matter what environment is provided. If $Path_{exec}$ of a path from the TC_{sn} to the TC_{en} is larger than TC_{time}, the path will cause a violation of the timing constraint. The processes $Path_{process}$ that appear on such a path must be modified to reduce computation time in order to satisfy the timing constraint. ∎

9.4.2   Timing Analysis Using the DCPIG

The second case is that the timing constraint is violated under a given hardware environment, such as a limited number of processors or significant communication delays between processors. Since the number of processors available is limited, processes have to share the processors, so the total time to carry out the task increases. A timing constraint can be violated if its relevant processes are not allocated enough CPU time. A timing constraint can also be violated if the delivery of messages between the relevant nodes takes too long. The DCPIG can be used to detect these timing errors.

Timing Analysis for Computation and Scheduling

A *basic time interval* in a DCPIG is defined as a time interval that starts with one event and ends with another event, with no events existing between the two events. We re-define relevant processes of a timing constraint in terms of basic time intervals. A process is a *relevant process* of a basic time interval if one of its edges appeared in the DCPIG during the time interval. We say that a set of processes is in the running state during a basic time interval if at least one of the processes is in the running state during the interval; a set of processes is in the ready state during a basic time interval if at least one of the processes is in the ready state and none of them is in the running state during the basic time interval. A set of processes is in the waiting state during a basic time interval if all of the processes are in the waiting state during the interval.

The *global total waiting time* (TC_{gwt}) is defined as the sum of the basic time intervals during which all of the relevant processes are in the waiting state. The *global total ready time* (TC_{grt}) is defined as the sum of the basic time intervals during which all of the relevant processes are in the ready state. The *local total execution time* of a relevant node, n_i $(TC_{let}(n_i))$, is defined as the sum of the basic time intervals during which the relevant processes on the node are in the running state. The *local total waiting time* of a relevant node, n_i $(TC_{lwt}(n_i))$, is the sum of the basic time intervals during which the relevant processes on the node are in the waiting state, and the *absolute local waiting time* of a relevant node, n_i $(TC_{lwt-gwt}(n_i))$, is defined as $(TC_{lwt}(n_i))$, excluding the basic time intervals that have been counted in the global total waiting time. The *local total ready time* of a relevant node, n_i $(TC_{lrt}(n_i))$, is defined as the sum of the basic time intervals during which the relevant processes on the node are in the ready state, and the *absolute local ready time* of a relevant node, n_i $(TC_{lrt-grt}(n_i))$, is defined as $(TC_{lrt}(n_i))$, excluding the basic time intervals that have been counted in the global total ready time.

The *total execution time*, TC_{exec}, total waiting time, TC_{wait}, and *total ready time*, TC_{ready}, for a given timing constraint are computed as follows:

$$TC_{exec} = TC_{et} - TC_{st} - TC_{gwt} - TC_{grt}$$
$$- \min_{n_i \in TC_{rn}} (TC_{lwt-gwt}(n_i) + TC_{lrt-grt}(n_i)) \qquad (9.1)$$

$$TC_{wait} = TC_{gwt} + \min_{n_i \in TC_{rn}} (TC_{lwt-gwt}(n_i)) \qquad (9.2)$$

$$TC_{ready} = TC_{grt} + \min_{n_i \in TC_{rn}} (TC_{lrt-grt}(n_i)) \qquad (9.3)$$

The total execution time TC_{exec} is the time needed for the program to reach the ending point if the CPUs had not been allocated to nonrelevant processes and the relevant processes had not waited for I/O or messages. The total waiting time TC_{wait} is how much earlier the ending point would have been reached if the relevant processes had not waited for I/O or messages. The total ready time TC_{ready} is how much earlier the ending point would have been reached if the CPUs had not been allocated to nonrelevant processes.

In what follows we use the example in Section 9.2 to clarify the above definitions. We first compute the total execution, waiting, and ready times for the two timing constraints. Then we examine what they represent. For timing constraint 1, referring to Fig. 9.5, we have

$$
\begin{aligned}
TC_{rn} &= [node_i, node_j] \\
TC_{gwt} &= (t20 - t19) + (t33 - t32) \\
TC_{grt} &= (t10 - t9) + (t29 - t28) \\
TC_{let}(node_i) &= (t9 - t3) + (t19 - t10) + (t27 - t22) \\
&\quad + (t32 - t29) + (t35 - t33) \\
TC_{lwt-gwt}(node_i) &= (t22 - t20) \\
TC_{lrt-grt}(node_i) &= (t28 - t27) \\
TC_{lwt}(node_i) &= (t22 - t19) + (t33 - t32) \\
TC_{lrt}(node_i) &= (t10 - t9) + (t29 - t27) \\
TC_{let}(node_j) &= (t18 - t12) + (t23 - t20) + (t25 - t24) + (t28 - t26) \\
TC_{lwt-gwt}(node_j) &= (t19 - t18) + (t24 - t23) \\
TC_{lrt-grt}(node_j) &= (t26 - t25) \\
TC_{lwt}(node_j) &= (t20 - t18) + (t24 - t23) \\
TC_{lrt}(node_j) &= (t26 - t25) \\
TC_{exec} &= (t9 - t3) + (t18 - t10) + (t23 - t20) + (t25 - t24) \\
&\quad + (t28 - t26) + (t32 - t29) + (t35 - t33) \\
TC_{wait} &= (t20 - t19)(t33 - t32) + (t19 - t18) + (t24 - t23) \\
TC_{ready} &= (t10 - t9) + (t29 - t28) + (t28 - t27)
\end{aligned}
$$

For timing constraint 2, referring to Fig. 9.6, we have

$$
\begin{aligned}
TC_{rn} &= [node_j] \\
TC_{gwt} &= (t24 - t23) \\
TC_{grt} &= (t26 - t25) \\
TC_{let}(node_j) &= (t23 - t20) + (t25 - t24) + (t28 - t26) \\
TC_{lwt-gwt}(node_j) &= 0 \\
TC_{lrt-grt}(node_j) &= 0 \\
TC_{lwt}(node_j) &= TC_{gwt} \\
TC_{lrt}(node_j) &= TC_{grt} \\
TC_{exec} &= TC_{let}(node_j) \\
TC_{wait} &= TC_{gwt}
\end{aligned}
$$

$$TC_{ready} = TC_{grt}$$

Here we assumed that for timing constraint 1, the sum of the absolute local waiting time and ready time of $node_j$ is smaller than that of $node_i$, that is,

$$TC_{lwt-gwt}(node_j) + TC_{lrt-grt}(node_j)$$

$$< TC_{lwt-gwt}(node_i) + TC_{lrt-grt}(node_i)$$

that the absolute local waiting time of $node_j$ is smaller than that of $node_i$, that is,

$$TC_{lwt-gwt}(node_j) < TC_{lwt-gwt}(node_i)$$

and that the absolute local ready time of $node_i$ is smaller than that of $node_j$, that is,

$$TC_{lrt-grt}(node_i) < TC_{lrt-grt}(node_j)$$

Referring to Fig. 9.5 for timing constraint 1, the ending event of the timing constraint could occur earlier by $(t10 - t9) + (t29 - t28) + (t20 - t19) + (t33 - t32)$ if the global ready and waiting basic intervals are removed. If all the local ready and waiting basic intervals are removed on both nodes, $(t28 - t27) + (t22 - t20)$ can be reduced on $node_i$, and $(t26 - t25) + (t19 - t218) + (t24 - t23)$ can be reduced on $node_j$. The ending event of the timing constraint could occur earlier only by the smallest of the sums of local ready and waiting intervals on the relevant nodes. That is, the ending event could occur earlier only by $(t26 - t25) + (t19 - t18) + (t24 - t23)$, since we have assumed that the sum of the local ready and waiting intervals of $node_j$ is smaller than that of $node_i$. Even though process P_1 could execute much earlier the *Receive* at t32 on $node_i$, it would have to wait for the message from P_4 on $node_j$.

It is important to recognize that the *total execution time* TC_{exec} of a timing constraint is not the monitored execution time (i.e., $TC_{et} - TC_{st}$) minus the total waiting time and total ready time:

$$TC_{exec} \neq (TC_{st} - TC_{et}) - (TC_{wait} + TC_{ready})$$

The reason is that

$$TC_{wait} + TC_{ready}$$

$$\neq TC_{gwt} + TC_{grt} + \min_{n_i \in TC_{rn}} (TC_{lwt-gwt}(n_i) + TC_{lrt-grt}(n_i))$$

By removing global ready and waiting times from both sides, this inequality becomes

$$\min_{n_i \in TC_{rn}} (TC_{lwt-gwt}(n_i) + TC_{lrt-grt}(n_i))$$

$$\neq \min_{n_i \in TC_{rn}} (TC_{lwt-gwt}(n_i)) + \min_{n_i \in TC_{rn}} (TC_{lrt-grt}(n_i))$$

From the above example for timing constraint 1, it can be seen that the smallest sum of local ready and waiting times $((t26 - t25) + (t19 - t18) + (t24 - t23))$ which was on $node_j$ is not equal to the sum of the smallest local ready time $(t28 - t27)$ which was on $node_i$ and the smallest local waiting time $(t19 - t18) + (t24 - t23)$ which was on $node_j$.

From the above discussion we have the following theorems. The length of the timing constraint is represented as TC_{time}.

Theorem 9.4 *If TC_{exec} is larger than TC_{time}, then computation is an immediate cause of the timing error.*

Proof: According to definition 9.1, TC_{exec} is the time that the program needs to reach the ending event from the starting event under the given process synchronization and system-scheduling pattern. If the total execution time is larger than the timing constraint, the program will spend more time than the timing constraint even if there are no communication delays and I/O delays and all the relevant processes have the highest priority. To satisfy the timing constraint, the computation time of the program must be reduced. ∎

Theorem 9.5 *If TC_{ready} is larger than TC_{time}, then the scheduling of the operating system is an immediate cause of the timing error.*

Proof: From definition 9.3, the TC_{ready} is the total ready time of the target program for the given timing constraint. If the relevant processes wait for the CPU longer than TC_{time}, the system scheduling must be responsible for the timing error, or the priorities of the processes are not high enough to obtain the CPU. To satisfy the timing constraint, the relevant processes should be assigned higher priorities. ∎

Corollary 1 *For a relevant node n_i, if $TC_{let}(n_i)$ is larger than TC_{time}, the relevant processes on the node are responsible for the timing error.*

Corollary 2 *For a relevant node n_i, if $TC_{lrt}(n_i)$ is larger than TC_{time}, the scheduling on the node is responsible for the timing error, or the priorities of the relevant processes are not high enough.*

The converse of the two theorems is not always true. Neither does the computation cause imply that TC_{exec} is larger than the timing constraint, nor does the scheduling cause imply that TC_{ready} is larger than the timing constraint. If neither TC_{ready} nor TC_{exec} is larger than the timing constraint, we cannot determine if computation or scheduling is the immediate cause of the timing error. For this case we have the following theorem:

Theorem 9.6 *If $TC_{exec} + TC_{ready}$ is larger than TC_{time}, then the combination of computation and scheduling is an immediate cause of the timing error.*

To satisfy the TC, either the computation time must be reduced or the processes must be re-scheduled. The TC may not be satisfied by simply reducing the computation time or raising the priorities of the relevant processes. To help the user make the decision on reducing the computation time and/or promoting processes' priority, TC_{ready} and TC_{exec} should be reported.

Timing Analysis for Input and Communication Delays

For the time intervals during which the relevant processes (excluding dummy processes, $P_{external}$'s) are in the waiting state, we give the following two theorems:

Theorem 9.7 *If all relevant processes during a basic time interval are in the waiting state, they must wait for either external I/O interrupts or messages transmitted among the relevant nodes.*

Proof: From Theorem 9.1, if the ending event of the timing constraint is observed, the relevant processes of a timing constraint are not involved in any of the six synchronization causes. In other words, none of the relevant processes would be in the waiting state forever. Because all of the relevant processes are in the waiting state during the interval, none of the process waiting chains should end with a process in the running or ready state. There are four reasons for a process to enter the waiting state: (1) waiting for a semaphore, (2) waiting for the termination of a child, (3) waiting for a message, and (4) waiting for an I/O interrupt. Here we first prove that if a process-waiting chain of the timing constraint does not end with a process waiting for the termination of a child or an I/O interrupt, the waiting chain must end with a process that was waiting for the previous process in the waiting chain.

To illustrate this, let us assume that a waiting chain ended with a process P that was not waiting for a previous process in the waiting chain. Since all the relevant processes were in the waiting state during the basic interval in question, process P must be neither the running nor the ready state. That implies that process P must in the waiting state because a process can be only in one of these three states at a time during its lifetime. If process P is in the waiting state, it must be waiting for another process. This implies that the waiting chain did not end with process P, which contradicts the assumption. Thus each waiting chain must end with a process that was waiting for its previous process in the waiting chain.

There are three possible ways for two processes to wait for each other. The first way is that each of the two processes is waiting for a semaphore that is held by the other process. In this case the two processes will wait for each other forever in a deadlock, and the ending event would never occur. The second way is that each of the two process is waiting for the other process, meaning that both processes have executed a receive call to receive a message from each other. This is also a deadlock, and the ending event will not occur either. The last way is that one process is waiting for a message from the other, and the other process is waiting for an acknowledgment from the first. In other words, one process has sent a message to the other and is waiting for an acknowledgment, and the other process has executed a receive call to receive the message from the first process. If the two processes are on the same node, it is assumed that the communication will be completed with no delay, so the two processes will not be in the waiting state for a basic interval. If the two processes are on two different nodes, the two process will wait (in the waiting state) for each other until the message arrives. Thus we know that if a waiting chain does not wait for the termination of a child or an I/O interrupt, it must end with a process that is waiting for the previous process in the waiting chain. It is easy to see that the relevant processes involved in this kind of waiting chain are waiting for messages.

Another reason for a process to wait is for the termination of a child. If the child is on the same node, the parent will enter either the ready or running state when the termination event occurs. During the basic interval right before the termination event, the child is a relevant process, and it must be in the running state. Thus, during the interval before the termination event, the relevant processes are not in the waiting state. During the basic interval after the termination event, the child is not a relevant process. But the parent must be in either the ready or running state during the interval. Thus the relevant processes during the interval after the termination event are not in the waiting state either. In sum, if the child is on the same node as the waiting parent, the relevant processes will not be in the waiting state.

In a distributed real-time system, a child could be allocated at a different node from its parent's. If the child that the parent is waiting for is on a different node, the parent would not change into either the ready or running state at the time the termination event occurs. The kernel of the node at which the child is allocated must inform the parent of the termination by sending a message to the parent, and the parent would not change into either the ready or running state until the message is received. Due to communication delays, the message may not arrive at the parent immediately. Since the child is not a relevant process during the basic interval after it terminates, the processes on the waiting chain with the parent are relevant processes, and they would be in the waiting state until the message is received.

The last reason a process waits is for an I/O interrupt. If a waiting chain ends with a process waiting for an input, all the processes in the waiting chain would be in the waiting state until the input is received. It implies that the sooner the environment provides the input, the shorter the processes in the waiting chain would wait.

From the above discussion we can see that when the ending event of a timing constraint is observed, the relevant processes of the timing constraint must wait for either messages (regular interprocess communication messages and process termination messages) or I/O interrupts during waiting basic intervals. ∎

For example, during the time interval t19 to t20 in Fig. 9.5, the DCPIG for timing constraint 1, P_1 is waiting for the semaphore that has been occupied by P_3. P_3 is waiting for an acknowledgment from P_4, which is waiting for Msg2 from P_3. P_5 is waiting for Msg3 from P_4. So the relevant processes are waiting for the message Msg2. During timing interval t32 to t33 in the same figure, the only relevant process, P_1, is waiting for Msg5 from P4.

Theorem 9.8 *If TC_{wait} is larger than TC, the interprocessor communication delays and/or the delay of inputs are responsible for the timing error.*

Proof: According to Theorem 9.7, if all the relevant processes are in the waiting state, then they must wait for messages from nodes or I/O interrupts. TC_{wait} is the total time that the relevant processes are in the waiting state. Thus, if TC_{wait} is larger than the timing constraint, the communication delays and I/O operations must take longer than the timing constraint. ∎

Corollary 3 *For a relevant node n_i, if $TC_{lwt}(n_i)$ is larger than TC_{time}, the communication delay between n_i and others or the inputs to n_i are responsible for the timing error.*

For intraprocessor timing constraints, we give the following two theorems:

Theorem 9.9 *For a intraprocessor timing constraint, if all the relevant processes during a basic time interval are in the waiting state, they must wait for input interrupts from the environment.*

Proof: In intraprocessor timing constraints, all the relevant processes of the timing constraint are located on the same node. Therefore there is no interprocess messages or process termination messages from other nodes. Thus the relevant processes can only wait for I/O interrupts during the interval. ∎

Take, for example, the timing constraint 2 in the example (Section 9.2 is an intraprocessor timing constraint; its DCPIG is shown in Fig. 9.6). During basic interval t23 to t24, the relevant process P4 is waiting for its partner P5 for Msg4, and P5 is waiting for an *input* from the environment.

Theorem 9.10 *For a intraprocessor timing constraint, if TC_{gwt} is larger than the timing constraint, the environment is responsible for the timing error.*

Proof: According to Theorem 9.9, TC_{gwt} is the time that the relevant processes wait for I/O interrupts. If TC_{gwt} is larger than TC_{time}, the environment must not provide input in time. ∎

To be consistent with the definition of the three basic causes of timing errors, we have implied that the environment is modeled as a dummy process,

$P_{external}$. When a process is waiting for an input, we consider $P_{external}$ to be in the "running" state, or in "computation." For communication delays we assume that there is a dummy process, $P_{communication}$, running between the computer nodes, and we consider $P_{communication}$ to be in the "running" state during any communication delays. With these assumptions we can consider that "computation" is the cause of the timing errors caused by input and communication delays.

9.5   Summary

In a distributed real-time system the correctness of the system not only depends on the logical results of the computation but also on the times at which the results are produced. So the definition of the timing concept is very important. In this chapter we first defined the basic concepts of timing constraints and their associated processes. A timing constraint is a time restriction on processes occurring between a starting event and an ending event. The processes affected by a timing constraint are defined as the set of processes that interact with the starting process or the ending process of the timing constraint directly or indirectly via a communication mechanism. We then discussed the running, ready, and waiting state in a distributed real-time system, and identified three causes of timing errors, namely relating to computation, scheduling, and synchronization. Computation can cause a violation of a timing constraint if the processes spend more than the expected on computation. Scheduling can cause a timing error if a process is not allocated enough execution time. Synchronization can cause a timing error if relevant processes wait for an event that never occurs or is never received. The causes of timing errors can also be a combination of these three causes. Mentioned here is a fourth immediate cause of a timing error due to the combined effects of computation and scheduling mishaps.

Then, various graphical representations of timing behavior were discussed. Among them, colored process interaction graphs can be constructed to show the interaction among processes and the states and the state durations of processes. A dedicated colored process interaction graph is constructed in studying the behavior of individual timing constraints.

Last, we examined the six possible reasons for a set of processes to be in an indefinite waiting state during the timing analysis for the synchronization cause. The six reasons suggested are deadlock, distributed termination, missed operation, starvation, loss of message, and communication deadlock.

We identified two cases for the timing analysis of computation and scheduling causes. The first occurs when the program violates the timing constraints no matter how many processes are available. The second is that the timing constraint is violated when there is a hardware limitation or a communication delay. Formulas and theorems were derived in the analysis of these timing error causes.

Exercises

1. Describe the various timing constraints that are used in a distributed real-time system.

2. The timing behavior of a distributed real-time system can be represented by the relationship between events and the times at which the events occurred. Give an example to represent the timing behavior of a distributed real-time system using other notations.

3. What is the starting event and ending event in the second timing constraints example in Section 9.2.

4. Based on the example in Fig. 9.3, give the third timing constraints example, and draw its corresponding DCPIG and PG.

5. Prove Theorem 9.1.

6. Prove Theorem 9.2.

7. Section 9.1 specifies a taxonomy of timing errors that can help the designer understand how to handle errors. It is based on the states a process can be in. Can you think of a different way of organizing the errors that occur?

Chapter 10

Visualization and Debugging

Using computer graphics in disciplines such as algorithm simulation, program debugging, data structure visualization, and performance measurement has become widespread in the past few years. Much research [52, 194, 217, 224, 238, 264, 330, 433, 442] has been carried out, and much encouraging progress can be found in this area. In this chapter we will briefly review some of the research efforts in visualization for algorithm simulation, program debugging, data structure visualization, and performance measurement. We then discuss VDS, a visualization and debugging system that graphically displays program information.

Moher's PROVIDE is a source-level process visualization and debugging environment for illustrating a program's execution [264]. It allows users to control and observe program execution at various levels of abstraction. Reiss's PECAN provides users with multiple views of program code and data structures [330]. It can graphically display the data structures of objects, which allows the user to watch the generation of new values and the behavior of the manipulated objects. Yan and Lundstrom's AXE is a process-level performance visualizer for multiprocessor systems [433]. It can graphically display the system load (both hardware and software), communication cost, and process states to facilitate the studies of concurrent systems with respect to the areas of resource management strategies, concurrent programming formalization, hardware architectures, and operating system algorithms. Brown and Sedgewick's BALSA is an algorithm simulator that emulates the execution of algorithms by displaying graphical views of procedure calls forward or backward to help the user understand and evaluate the correctness of algorithms [52]. Malony and Reed's HyperView is a visualization tool that displays the architecture and system activities of distributed memory parallel processors with a hypercube architecture [238]. HyperView performs its visualization using three steps. Event traces are first generated from simulation or the program execution. The partial order of these event traces are then reconciled and saved for later correlation of the distributed events.

Finally, certain system aspects are displayed via different views such as network topology, message value, message count, and message waiting queues.
Similarly Zernik and Rudolph's animation system can animate a causality
graph from the information collected using MAD monitoring system [442].
The animation uses the time and work load of an execution to display views
of the workload and processing element race conditions. By examining the
execution from different views, the system performance bugs can be found
more easily. Kilpatrick and Schwan's ChaosMON is a system for monitoring
a program's execution and displaying its performance information for parallel and distributed systems [194]. It has a view language to specify what to
monitor and protocols to specify how the performance views are mapped and
displayed. Through the visualization of performance information, guidance
for performance analysis is also provided.

In practice, most of the research efforts in visualization for algorithm
simulation, program debugging, data structure visualization, and performance measurement are dedicated to display the ongoing changes of the objects rather than the interobject relationships. The objects could be computing nodes, programs, algorithms, processes, events, or data structures,
while the ongoing changes could be object's value or the states of computation. However, interprocess communication and synchronization make distributed real-time systems different from conventional sequential software.
These factors introduce bugs that are very difficult to isolate. Thus a visualization system that can display interprocess relationships is essential for the
understanding and analysis of distributed real-time systems. We will examine
such a system in the remainder of this chapter.

10.1 A Visualization and Debugging System

Sequential software lends itself to a single thread of execution that can be
easily displayed using a textual description. However, a distributed real-time
software has multiple threads of interaction among processes that cannot
be easily described using text. Thus the motivation behind visualization
is to graphically illustrate the execution behavior of a target system. Our
visualization system is designed to form an environment that allows users to
view and display the execution of a program at the process level of abstraction.

VDS [392, 393] is an X windows based colored graphical user interface
environment. The graphical user interface consists of three types of windows:
the display window, the control panel window, and the dialog boxes. The
display windows present graphs, animations and other debugging information. The control panel windows provide the user with menus for choosing
a variety of functions for visualizing and debugging the programs. Dialog
boxes pop out when VDS needs information from the user. Since VDS runs
under OpenWindows, all other tools under the OpenWindows can work properly with VDS. Users can issue UNIX shell commands for other jobs without

exiting VDS. The advantage of running VDS under a window environment is that the user can edit programs with her favorite editing tools and then debug her program using VDS, once she is done editing and compiling the program.

VDS is implemented as an off-line system, so it can be integrated into any monitoring system or be treated as a stand-alone system with execution traces as its input. As shown in Fig. 10.1, the execution traces are interpreted by the trace interpreter to eliminate all irrelevant data. The filtered data from various trace files are then reorganized into a single execution log (EL). This step reduces the huge volume of event data contained in each local trace file and stores them in a single global data repository. The event data in the EL is then correlated by the event correlator according to the desired level of abstraction (process level, function level, or source level). This step provides users the option of choosing levels of program abstraction tailored to their needs. Since VDS features process-level analysis, the event data in the EL is correlated according to their interprocess relationships and saved in the process-level execution log (PLEL) for visualization and debugging. In the PLEL the relevant process-level event data are organized in such a way that the higher levels of logical views containing the timing behavior and the causes of timing constraint violations can be easily derived. Since the data interpretation methods used by the trace interpreter and the data correlation method used by the event correlator are subject to the formats of recorded execution traces, they may have to be modified if the configuration of the monitor is changed.

Once the PLEL has been constructed, the timing analyzer reads data from the PLEL in order to compute the system-related time information, such as total execution time, total ready time, and total waiting time as discussed before. The PLEL is also interpreted and reorganized by the visualization interpreter into visualization templates that contain the data for displaying the graphs. The graph controller is used to control the display of various static graphs to reveal different views of the target system's behavior, while the animation controller is used to provide the VCR-like functions that allow users to control the playing of program evolution forward and backward. The trace back controller is used to control the mapping between graphs and the program code. Once an event in a graph has been selected by clicking a mouse, its corresponding program code will be mapped and shown automatically on a screen.

10.2 Foundation of Graphical Representation

Various graphical representations of program execution have been constructed as the foundation of our visualization system. The graphical representation can be displayed as static graphs or dynamic animations. With static graphs, different graphs reveal different views of a target program's timing behavior,

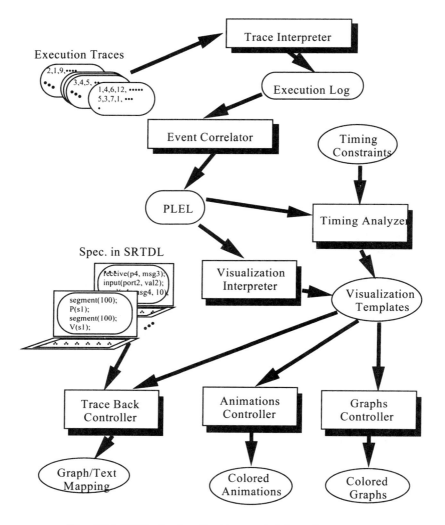

Fig. 10.1 VDS: A visualization and debugging system.

and it is the quickest way for understanding the target program as a whole. With dynamic animations the states of a target program are displayed one by one over the passage of time to illustrate its evolving execution. Animation is useful for observing the target program over a specific period of time. As time advances, the display changes and such changes can be presented in sequence to give the sense of an animated movie. Along with other information obtained from the timing analysis method (which will be presented in the next section), the visualization system aids the user in the time-consuming tasks of program understanding and debugging.

The static graphs and dynamic animations are displayed in different windows as needed. The multiple display windows allow different graphs and animations to be displayed at the same time. For small systems, the size of graphs can be scaled to fit into the display windows. However, for large systems, the entire graph may not fit into the display windows. Therefore in our system the display windows are designed to be scrollable and have zoom-in and zoom-out capabilities that allow the user to focus in on an area of interest.

Various static graphs are presented to help the understanding and debugging of distributed real-time systems. The colored process interaction graph (CPIG) is the major graph that depicts the interrelationship among processes. It also provides the entire detailed logical/timing information about the execution of the target system. The dedicated colored process interaction graph (DCPIG) is derived from the CPIG by imposing timing constraints on it. The DCPIG is used to reduce the complexity of the CPIG and focus the visualization and analysis on the imposed timing constraints. The filtered colored process interaction graph (FCPIG) is also derived from the CPIG. By filtering the CPIG, the user has the ability to display only events of interest on the FCPIG. The program status graph (PSG), showing the creating/created relationship of processes and their final states, is used to decide which processes are in a permanent waiting state. The semaphore allocation matrix (SAM) and the semaphore allocation graph (SAG), showing the allocating/waiting relationship between processes and semaphores, are used to detect the timing errors caused by the improper allocation of semaphores. The message-passing matrix (MPM) and the message-passing graph (MPG), showing the sending/receiving relationship among processes, are used to detect the timing errors caused by improper messages passing among processes. Each of these static graphs with its construction algorithm is discussed in turn in the following paragraphs. At the end of this chapter we present a debugging algorithm.

10.2.1   Colored Process Interaction Graphs

The CPIG is a two-dimensional graph that depicts the interaction of processes in a target program by showing the occurrence of events and the transition of process states. As shown in Fig. 9.4, labels are used to provide information about the processes, such as node identification, process identification, event type, and the time when the event occurred. In the CPIG, each node indicates a different computer in the target system. A node can have one or more processes existing at the same time. The life of a process can be treated as a sequence of events and state transitions. A colored vertical bar is used to indicate a process's state and how long it lasted. Three colors are chosen to denote the three possible states, running, ready, and waiting. The length of the colored vertical bar represents the time that a process remained in a particular state. For example, in Fig. 9.4, during time t_{16} to time t_{20}, process P_4 remained in the waiting state for a message from P_3. Once P_4 received the message, its state changed from waiting to running. With this colored representation, the changes of the process state can easily be detected. The interprocess communication and synchronization are denoted by directed edges. A directed edge links two different events which occur on two different processes, indicating the interaction between the two processes and the ordering of the two corresponding events. The direction of the directed edge denotes the precedence relationship between the two involved events; that is, the two events must be properly sequenced so that their corresponding processes can interact properly. On the other hand, if a directed edge is not displayed between two events, no precedence or ordering relationship exists between them, so the two events can occur simultaneously. For example, in Fig. 9.4, the directed edge from time t_{17} on P_3 to time t_{20} on P_4 depicts the direction P_3 to P_4, the process interaction types, message passing, and the precedence relationship; the send event on P_3 happens before the receive event on P_4. Note that a process will receive a message only if the message has arrived. If a receive event exists on a process but a message has not arrived, then the process has to wait for the message. In Fig. 9.4 we can see that process P_3 has a send event occurring at time t_{17}, while P_4 has a receive event occurring at time t_{16}, and P_4 does not receive a message from P_3 until time t_{20}. Once P_4 receives the message, an acknowledgment will be sent to P_3. Due to communication delays, we can see from the CPIG that P_3 does not get the acknowledgment until time t_{22}. Also the difference between the two time values $(t_{22} - t_{20})$ of the directed edge denotes the duration of the communication delay. With this graphical representation the multiple threads of process interaction and the information about when and how the interactions have occurred can be easily perceived. To construct the CPIG for each process, P_i, in the system, we draw an event-flow graph (EFG), as shown in Fig. 10.2, by connecting the sequence of events and state transitions of P_i. After the EFG for each process has been constructed, we merge all EFGs into a single graph, the CPIG, by connecting two associated events with a directed edge to represent the process interaction. A directed edge from the event E_i on the process P_i to the event E_j on the process P_j, is drawn if the two events represent one of the following:

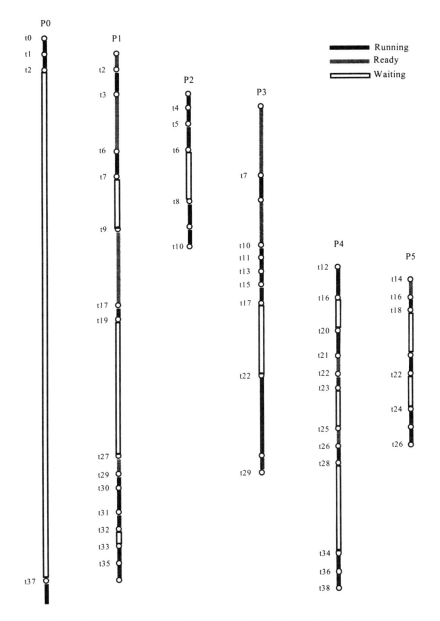

Fig. 10.2 EFG for each process P_i, $i = 0, 1, 2, 3, 4, 5$.

1. *Process creation.* E_i and E_j represent a spawn process command and process spawned pair.

2. *Process termination.* E_i is the termination event of a child (P_i), and E_j is a state transition event in which the parent (P_j) of the child P_i is awakened by the termination of child P_i (i.e., P_j changes its state from waiting to ready).

3. *Message passing.* E_i and E_j represent a message send/receive pair.

4. *Acknowledgment.* E_i and E_j represent a send/receive pair of acknowledgment.

5. *Wake-up state transition.* E_i is an interrupt/trap event, and E_j is a state transition event in which P_j is awakened by event E_i.

6. *Semaphore released.* E_i represents a release of a semaphore (S) (i.e., a V operation on S by P_i). P_j was waiting for semaphore S, and E_j is the event in which P_j is awakened by the release of semaphore S by P_i.

From these conditions we design an algorithm to construct the CPIG:

Algorithm CONSTRUCT-CPIG.

/* This algorithm uses the conditions listed above to construct a colored process interaction graph */

WHILE more processes in PEL;
      IF process is marked /* relevant process */
            WHILE more events in this process
                  IF event is marked /* relevant event */
                        Draw event's corresponding info.
                Get next event.
Get next process
WHILE more processes in STL /* Time Edge loop */
      Get first marked state
      current state (CS) = marked state
      current state time (CST) = time CS occurred
      WHILE more states in process
            Get next state, NS, and it's time of occurrence, NST.
            Draw an edge with a length of (NST - CST),
                  and a color corresponding to CS.
Get next process.
WHILE more processes in PIL /* Interaction Edge loop */
      IF process P_i is marked
            WHILE more interaction events E_i in process P_i

/* see text preceding this for case description */
IF one of the following cases exists
    (1) Process creation.
    (2) Process termination.
    (3) Message passing.
    (4) Acknowledgment.
    (5) Wake-up state transition.
    (6) Semaphore released.
THEN Draw the interaction edge between the two
    processes with the appropriate direction.
Get the next interaction event.
Get next process.

END of Algorithm CONSTRUCT-CPIG.

10.2.2   Dedicated Colored Process Interaction Graphs

Unlike the CPIG, which displays the entire execution behavior of a target program, the DCPIG reduces the debugging complexity by displaying only information relevant to the timing constraints. For illustration, let two timing constraints, TC_1 and TC_2, be imposed by the user. Following the construction method of the DCPIG, which will be shown later, we have Fig. 9.5 and Fig. 9.6 for the DCPIGs for TC_1 and TC_2, respectively. TC_1 and TC_2 are specified as follows:

TC_1 is the maximum amount of time that may elapse between the events create and output. The create event at (t_3, P_1) shows that P_1 creates P_2, and the output event at (t_{35}, P_1) shows that P_1 outputs a result to its external environment.

TC_2 is the maximum amount of time that may elapse between the events receive and send. The receive event at (t_{20}, P_4) shows that P_4 is receiving a message from P_3, and the send event at (t_{28}, P_4) shows that P_4 sends a message to P_1.

In Fig. 9.5, TC_1 is an interprocessor timing constraint with $node_i$ and $node_j$ as its relevant nodes. In Fig. 9.6, TC_2 is an intraprocessor timing constraint, and all of the relevant processes are on $node_j$. In the DCPIG a time interval denotes that during a particular period of time, all relevant processes remained in the same state. Two types of time intervals, the waiting time interval and the ready time interval, are displayed in the DCPIG. Both types have their own local and global time intervals represented by different colors. For example, in Fig. 9.5 various time intervals are displayed across the relevant processes of TC_1, such as the local waiting time interval across processes P_4 and P_5 between time t_{23} and time t_{24}. The method for constructing a

DCPIG is crucial because it decides what information will be shown in the DCPIG. A DCPIG only consists of information related to starting events and ending events of timing constraints. We can summarize the construction of the DCPIG as follows:

1. Cut off all of the events, vertical bars, and directed edges shown in CPIG that occurred before the starting event or after the ending event. If the starting event is at the middle of a vertical bar in a process, add a dummy event to it as the first event of that process.

2. Put the ending event into the DCPIG, and check the information from the ending event back to the starting event. If a vertical bar is connected to an event that is in the DCPIG, then add this vertical bar and the event on the other end into the DCPIG. If a directed edge is connected to an event that is in the DCPIG, then include this directed edge and the event on the other end of the edge into the DCPIG. If a directed edge is connected from the event which is in the DCPIG and the process of the event on the other end of the edge is already in the DCPIG, then add this directed edge and the event on the other end into the DCPIG. Repeat this step until all the events, vertical bars, and directed edges connected to the starting and ending events are included in the DCPIG.

3. Construct the system-related time intervals with the methods that will be presented in the next section.

4. Label the DCPIG with the information such as node identifications, process identifications, events, and time stamps.

10.2.3   Animations of CPIG and DCPIG

Animation of a program's execution is important both in tracing execution and detecting anomalies in a program. It can help users understand the current state of a program at a particular point in time and to be aware of how a state is transformed. During animation the interprocess relationship, event ordering, and process states can be visualized dynamically. Our visualization system provides VCR-like functions that allow users to control the playing of a program's execution forward or backward. With forward playing, users experience how a program is executed, and this interaction will allow users a better understanding of the program's behavior. If an anomaly is detected, backward playing can reverse the program evolution and help users find the causes of the detected anomaly. During forward or backward playing, users are free to pause the playing and get a snapshot of the current program evolution. Once an erroneous event causing the anomaly is found, a trace back technique is implemented to pinpoint the corresponding program code. To trace back, users first move the mouse to click on the erroneous event shown in the display window; then an editor window will pop out with the mapped program code highlighted. Users can edit the code directly in the editor window without leaving the visualization system.

10.2.4 Filtered Colored Processes Interaction Graphs

Sometimes it is too complicated to display the entire the CPIG, especially when the user is only interested in few events. Thus the motivation behind the FCPIG allows the user to focus on selected events. For example, in Fig. 10.3 only the events related to message passing are displayed. This makes the threads of message passing among processes quite clear and enables the user to easily understand and analyze the message passing behavior. All the information shown in the FCPIG is the same as that shown in the CPIG; the FCPIG simply has less information.

What follows is the algorithm used for constructing the FCPIG. The algorithm starts the construction of the FCPIG by first popping up a dialog box which asks the user which events should be displayed, the user makes choice by clicking the appropriate buttons. The drawing system then marks the chosen events and the corresponding information and draws the FCPIG using the same drawing procedure the CPIG uses.

Algorithm CONSTRUCT-FCPIG.

Pop up a dialog box to get events of interest
Get the requested types of events
WHILE more processes in PEL
      Mark all events of requested types
WHILE more processes in STL
      Mark all events of requested types
WHILE more processes in PIL
      Mark all events of requested types
Call Construction_of_CPIG /* Draw all the marked information */

END of Algorithm CONSTRUCT-FCPIG.

10.2.5 Program Status Graphs

The program status graph depicts the parent-child relationship between the creating and created processes. This parent-child relationship is represented by a directed edge, and those processes involved are denoted by circles. Besides indicating the relationship of creation, the PSG also identifies whether or not processes have terminated. The nonterminated processes will be highlighted to indicate the existence of errors. If one or more processes have not

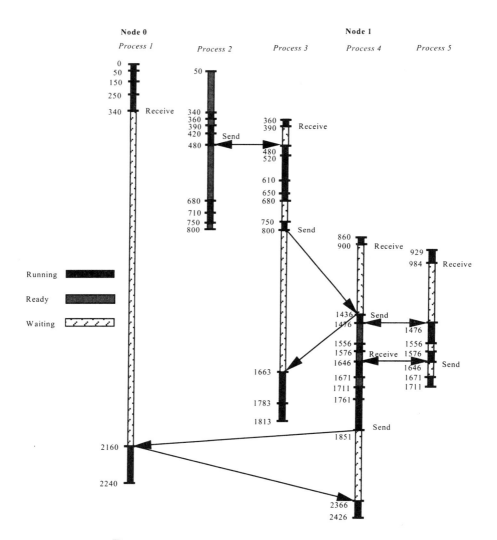

Fig. 10.3 Message passing displayed in FCPIG.

terminated, then the target system must have committed at least one of the six unlimited waiting errors. For example, the PSG in Fig. 10.4 shows that processes P_1, P_4, and P_5 are still waiting for some events to occur. Clearly these processes have unlimited waiting errors. What follows is the algorithm used for constructing the PSG.

Algorithm CONSTRUCT-PSG.

WHILE more processes in PIL
      WHILE more entries within this process
          with Edge_Type == CREATING
          IF process Head_Pid has not yet been drawn
          Draw a circle with Head_Pid inside.
          Draw a circle with Tail_Pid inside
          Draw an edge from circle Head_Pid to Tail_Pid
WHILE more processes in STL
      IF the last state of process is not equal to terminate
          Indicate the process by highlighting that circle

END of Algorithm CONSTRUCT-PSG.

10.2.6 Message-Passing Matrices and Graphs

The message passing matrix, MPM, is a two-dimensional table constructed from the process interaction list (PIL). The MPM is a debugging aid used to detect the target system's final status of message passing by denoting the events send/receive processes are waiting for. For example, as shown in the MPM in Fig. 10.4, a process in a column is the receiver, and a process in a row is the sender. A signed number in a particular row and column indicates that a message was passed between two processes. A positive sign means sending, while a negative sign means receiving. From Fig. 10.4 we can tell that process P_1 executes a receive event and is waiting for message M5 from process P_4. The message passing graph (MPG) shown in Fig. 10.4 is constructed from the PIL along with the construction of MPM. It complements the MPM by providing a graphical view of the MPM. In the MPG a process is denoted by a circle with a number inside. Directed edges are used to identify the type of event. A solid edge represents a sending event, and a dashed edge represents a receiving event. For normal message passing, a pair of solid and dashed edges should be displayed. In the MPG nonhighlighted circles connected with pairs of send and receive events are processes that have correct message passing events. The highlighted circles are processes that have communication errors.

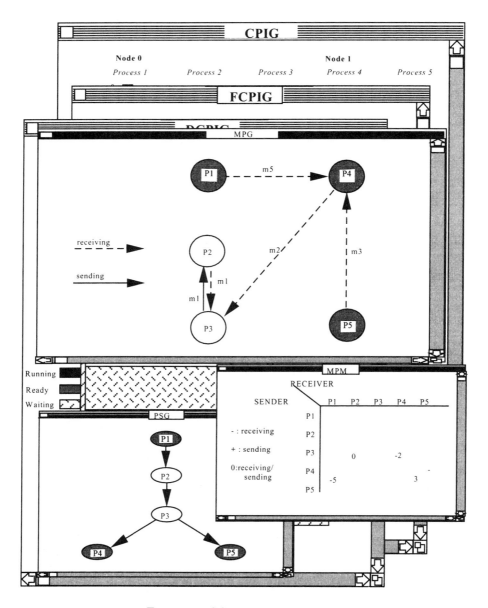

Fig. 10.4 PSG, MPM, and MPG.

For example, from the MPG in Fig. 10.4 we know that P_1, P_3, P_4, and P_5 have communication errors: P_4 is waiting for a send event from P_3, while P_1 and P_5 are waiting for a message from P_4. If only one of the two solid (sending) or dashed (receiving) edges is displayed in the MPG, then either a distributed termination error or a missing operation error has occurred between the two corresponding processes. If two processes have pairs of send/receive edges, but still are highlighted, then the message must be missing somewhere on the network, or a network deadlock has occurred. What follows is the algorithm used for constructing the MPM and MPG:

Algorithm CONSTRUCT-MPM-AND-MPG.

WHILE more processes in PIL
      WHILE more events in process_list
          IF Edge_type == SENDING
              Add msg_num to MPM[Head_pid][Tail_pid]
              Draw circle with Head_pid inside
                  if process has not been displayed yet
              Draw circle with Tail_pid inside
                  if process has not been displayed yet
              Draw a solid line with msg
                  from circle Head_pid to Tail_pid
          ELSE IF Edge_type == RECEIVING
              Subtract msg_num from MPM[Head_pid][Tail_pid]
              Draw circle with Head_pid inside
                  if process has not been displayed yet
              Draw circle with Tail_pid inside
                  if process has not been displayed yet
              Draw a dash line with msg-num
                  from circle Tail_pid to Head_pid
      WHILE more processes in STL
          IF the last state of process is not equal to terminate
          Highlight the process's circle

END of Algorithm CONSTRUCT-MPM-AND-MPG.

10.2.7   Semaphore Allocation Matrices and Graphs

The semaphore allocation matrix (SAM) is a two-dimensional table constructed from the semaphore waiting queue (SWQ). The SAM is another debugging aid that shows the target system's final allocation of semaphores to processes.

For example, as shown in the SAM in Fig. 10.5, processes and semaphores are annotated with numbers on columns and rows, respectively. A plus sign in row S_i and column P_j means that process P_j is holding semaphore S_i, while the minus sign in row S_i and column P_j means that process P_j is waiting for semaphore S_i. From Fig. 10.5 we can tell that process P_2 is holding semaphore S_1 and waiting for semaphore S_2, while P_3 is holding S_2 and waiting for S_1. The SAM can be further transformed to a semaphore allocation graph (SAG). The SAG, as shown in Fig. 10.5, complements the SAM by providing a graphical view of the final allocation between semaphores and processes. Processes that are involved in the violation of semaphore synchronization are denoted by circles with numbers inside. Directed edges are used to represent the relationship between processes and semaphores. For example, in Fig. 10.5 the directed edge between S_1 and P_2 means that S_1 is allocated to P_2, and the directed edge between P_2 and S_2 means that P_2 is waiting for S_2. This example shows a deadlock situation. For a semaphore synchronization, SAM and SAG should be empty if the target system terminated normally. If a cycle can be detected in the SAG, then there must be a deadlock. If no cycle is found, but still some processes and semaphores remain in the SMA and the SMG, then the error must be due to either distributed termination or a missed operation. What follows is the algorithm used for constructing the SAM and SAG:

Algorithm SWQ-TO-SAM.

WHILE more semaphores S_i in SWQ
    IF S_i's waiting_queue is not empty
        put '+' sign on SAM[S_i][Occ_pid]
WHILE more processes in waiting_queue
        put '-' sign on SAM[S_i][Wait_pid]

END of Algorithm SWQ-TO-SAM.

Algorithm CONSTRUCT-SAM-TO-SAG.

Define global variables s_num, p_num, top_s_num,
        top_p_num, node_cnt;
WHILE more semaphores have not been scanned;
/* Scan semaphore waiting matrix row by row; */
        Get the current semaphore number s_num;
        Set node_cnt to 0;
        Draw a node s_num;

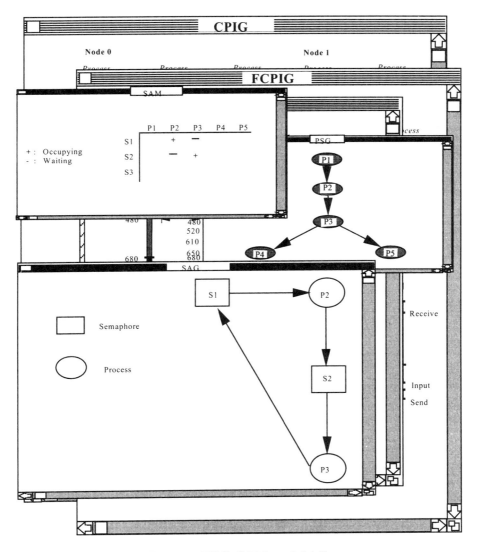

Fig. 10.5 PSG, SAM, and SAG.

node_cnt++;
Push BOS (bottom of stack) onto stack;
Call Construct_deadlock_cyclic_graph;
WHILE (return value is not 0)
      Call Construct_deadlock_cyclic_graph;
      IF (node_cnt $\leq$ 1) /* Only one node */
         remove s_num

END of Algorithm CONSTRUCT-SAM-TO-SAG.

The following algorithm is used by CONSTRUCT-SAM-TO-SAG.

Algorithm CONSTRUCT-DEADLOCK-CYCLIC-GRAPH.

IF (sema_existing_flag is No)
    /* Get p_num */
    Call FIND_PROCESS_OCCUPYING_SEMAPHORE;
ENDIF
IF s_num is unoccupied /* return value is 0, i.e., no '+' sign found */
    return 0;
ELSE
    IF (p_num already drawn)
        Draw an arc from s_num to p_num;
    ELSE
        Draw a node p_num;
        node_cnt++;
        Draw an arch from s_num to p_num;
    ENDIF
ENDIF
/* This function pushes all semaphores onto the stack */
Call P_WAITING_FOR_SEMAPHORE;
Set sema_existing_flag to No;
Pop the top of sp_stack and set it to (top_s_num,top_p_num);
IF ((top_s_num,top_p_num) == (BOS,BOS))
    return 0;
ELSE IF (top_s_num is already drawn)
    Draw an arc from top_p_num to top_s_num;
    Set sema_existing_flag to yes;
ELSE
    Draw a node on top_s_num;
    Draw an arc from top_p_num to top_s_num;
    node_cnt++;

Mark sam[top_s_num][top_p_num];
Set s_num to top_s_num;
ENDIF

END of Algorithm CONSTRUCT-DEADLOCK-CYCLIC-GRAPH.

These two functions are called by CONSTRUCT-DEADLOCK-CYCLIC-GRAPH.

Algorithm P_WAITING_FOR_SEMAPHORE.

For (p_num = 1; p_num $\leq$ TOT_P_num + 1; p_num++)
    IF (sam[s_num][p_num] == '-' and sam[s_num][p_num] unmarked)
        push (s_num, p_num) onto sp_stack;

END of Algorithm P_WAITING_FOR_SEMAPHORE.

Algorithm FIND_PROCESS_OCCUPYING_SEMAPHORE.

Set p_num = 1;
WHILE (p_num $\leq$ TOT_P_num)
    IF (sam[s_num][p_num] == '+'
        and sam[s_num][p_num] is unmarked)
        return s_num;
    ELSE
        increment p_num;
        return 0 /* no process is currently holding s_num */
    ENDIF

END of Algorithm FIND_PROCESS_OCCUPYING_SEMAPHORE.

What follows is the algorithm used for animation. The algorithm starts the animation right after it receives a PLAY command. It continues to animate until it receives a user-given PAUSE or STOP command. The PAUSE command toggles between pause or resume, allowing users to have a snapshot of the system states. The STOP command causes the system to stop the animation and exit.

Algorithm ANIMATION-CONSTRUCTION.

Set stop-flag to no.
WHILE stop-flag is no /* polling */
    Poll the expected PAUSE, STOP events.
    WHILE no PAUSE or STOP event occurs
        Rewind to the beginning of time table
        WHILE more time in the time table
            Clean previous frame.
            Draw current frame by calling Drawing Algorithm.
            Sleep for a while.
    IF the PAUSE event is polled
        Freeze screen and wait until another PAUSE event occurs.
    ELSE IF the STOP event is polled
        Set stop-flag to yes.
    ENDIF

END of Algorithm ANIMATION-CONSTRUCTION.

10.3   Debugging through Visualization

Besides program understanding, other major benefits of using visualization are program debugging and finding performance bottlenecks. Through the display of various graphs as shown above, erroneous program behavior can be easily detected and highlighted. In this section we conclude our discussion of graphs with a debugging algorithm that helps in finding the timing errors.

To debug the behavior of the target system's timing constraints, the CPIG is first displayed; then a timing constraint is requested from the user. If there are any processes that have not terminated because of synchronization errors, the routine Detect_Waiting_Errors will be called to determine the causes of the errors. If all processes are terminated, either normally or abnormally, then the debugging procedure computes the different timing intervals with respect to a given timing constraint (see Chapter 4 for details). With the various timing intervals, the timing behavior of programs can be displayed in the DCPIG. Timing statistics are also given to identify the possible causes of errors.

The detection of unlimited waiting errors can be classified into two categories. One category is the synchronization between semaphores and processes; the other is the synchronization of communication between senders and receivers. For semaphore synchronization, the SAM and the SAG are first constructed to show the final allocation of semaphores to processes. If any allocations are left at the end of program execution, some semaphore-related errors have occurred; otherwise, the algorithm checks for message passing errors. If cycles are found in the SAG, then a deadlock exists among the involved semaphores and processes. If no cycle is found and at least one process has terminated, a distributed termination has occurred; otherwise, one or more errors are due to a missing V operation. For synchronous message passing the MPM and the MPG are constructed to show how messages are passed among processes. If all send/receive pairs are matched, but some processes have not terminated, then a missed message or a communication deadlock must have occurred over the network; otherwise, the mismatched pairs indicate that the processes involved are not synchronized properly. For the mismatched send/receive pairs, if a cycle is found, then the processes are in a mutually waiting situation. If no cycles are found, but one process has terminated, then the terminated process must have missed a send or a receive event before its termination. If every process is in a waiting state and no cycles are found, then some send/receive operations must have been missed. Here is the outline of the debugging algorithm.

Algorithm DEBUGGING.

Display CPIG /* for the overview of target system */
Request timing constraint
Check if any waiting processes exist
/* Those processes with waiting states will be highlighted */
IF there are processes with waiting state
        /* Synchronization Errors */
        Call DETECT-WAITING-ERROR
ELSE /* Sync, Comp, Scheduling,
        or comb of Sync and Comp Errors */
        Call Construction_of_DCPIG
        Display DCPIG and timing statistics
        IF no timing errors found
                Provide this collected information for
                system performance improvement
        ELSE
                Highlight erroneous area
        ENDIF
ENDIF

END of Algorithm DEBUGGING.

Here are algorithms needed by DEBUGGING.

Algorithm DETECT-WAITING-ERROR.

/* Check for deadlock or distributed termination errors.
Call DETECT-SEMAPHORE-ERROR
IF error returned
      Correct errors and replay
ENDIF
      /* Check for distributed termination, mutual waiting,
      missed messages, or communication deadlocks */
Call DETECT-MESSAGE-PASSING-ERROR
IF error returned
      Correct errors and replay
ENDIF

END of Algorithm DETECT-WAITING-ERROR.

Algorithm DETECT-SEMAPHORE-ERROR.

Construct of SAM and SAG
Display SAM and SAG
IF any allocation left in SAG
      IF cycle is found on SAG /* Deadlock is found */
            Indicate the causes of deadlock, the involved
            processes, and semaphores
            Return error
      ELSE IF no cycle is found but one of the processes P_i
      left in SAG is terminated
            Indicate that the error is caused by the distributed
            termination of P_i, and display the involved processes
            and semaphores
            Return error
      ELSE /* no cycle is found
            and none of the processes is terminated */
            Indicate that one or more expected
            V events are missing among the processes involved
            Return error
      ENDIF
ELSE
      Return "no semaphore related errors have been found"
ENDIF

END of Algorithm DETECT-SEMAPHORE-ERROR.

Algorithm DETECT-MESSAGE-PASSING-ERROR.

Construct MPM and MPG
Display MPM and MPG
IF no processes with waiting state are found
      return ok
ENDIF
IF the involved edges between processes are not paired
      IF cycle is found
            Processes are mutually waiting for each other
            Return error
      ELSE
            IF one of the involved processes P_i is terminated
                  Error is caused by the distributed termination of P_i
                  Return error
            ELSE
                  There are missing operations
                  Return error
            ENDIF
      ENDIF
ELSE /* The edges are paired, but the processes
are still waiting for an event */
      Error is caused by missed message or communication deadlock
      Return error
ENDIF

END of Algorithm DETECT-MESSAGE-PASSING-ERROR.

In this chapter we have seen how interprocess communication and synchronization can be modeled graphically and thus be displayed visually to help the user debug a distributed system. Various static graphs can be used to display different relationships.

10.4   Summary

In this chapter we briefly reviewed how computer graphics have been used in algorithm simulation, data structure visualization, program debugging, and performance measurement. We then discussed the foundation of graphical representations. Graphical representations can be displayed as static graphs or dynamic animations. Static graphs can help the understanding and debugging of distributed real-time systems. Dynamic animations are useful for observing the run-time behavior of a target system over a specific period of time. Graphical representations discussed in this chapter include the colored process interaction graph, the dedicated colored process interaction graph, the filtered colored process interaction graph, the program status graph, the semaphore allocation matrix, the semaphore allocation graph, the message-passing matrix, and the message-passing graph. The colored process interaction graph is constructed to display the interrelationship among processes. The dedicated colored process interaction graph is derived from CPIG and is used to reduce the complexity of the CPIG during the visualization and debugging of a timing constraint. The filtered colored process interaction graph can display only events of interest to users. The program status graph shows the creating/created relationship of processes and their final state. The semaphore allocation matrix and the semaphore allocation graph display the allocation/waiting relationship between processes and semaphores. Users can detect the timing errors caused by the improper allocation of semaphores using SAM and SAG. The message-passing matrix and the message-passing graph show the sending/receiving relationship among processes. Improper messages passing among processes can be detected using the MPM and the MPG. We discussed the implementation of a visualization and debugging system, VDS. Detail algorithms were also developed to construct these graphical representations in VDS. Through the animation of these graphs, we can trace the program execution and detect anomalies in a distributed real-time system.

Exercises

1. The introduction lists several different projects for visualization (AXE, PECAN, PROVIDE, etc.). Which of these projects would be most helpful for debugging a DRTS?

2. What are algorithm simulation, scientific visualization, and program visualization? How can modern computer graphics technologies be used to implement these things?

3. How can program visualization help programmers debug programs?

4. What makes distributed real-time systems differ from conventional sequential systems? What characteristics of distributed real-time systems make them so difficult to debug, and how computer graphics can provide help in this regard?

5. How can static graphs and dynamic animation described in this chapter be used to debug programs?

6. What is the difference between source-level and process-level debugging? How does this affect the program visualization in terms of complexity and feasibility?

7. What are zoom in and zoom out? How can they be of help in program visualization at different levels of debugging?

8. Beside the mapping between source code and program execution, what other techniques used in hypertext and hypermedia can be used to help in this regard?

9. Dynamic animation consumes large amounts of memory and computing time if the animation is constructed frame by frame like motion pictures are made. What other techniques are available?

Chapter 11

A Petri Nets Based Timing Analysis

Besides the graphical representation, Petri nets have been popular for many years mainly because of their strong capability when modeling and analyzing concurrent systems. And it is well known that many system behavioral properties, such as *liveness* (deadlock-free) and *fairness* (starvation-free) can be modeled and analyzed with Petri nets. However, Petri nets alone cannot represent some temporal properties such as eventually. Thus, to solve the temporal problems, an extension of Petri nets is necessary. Our timing constraint Petri nets (TCPNs) [415] is one of the solutions. The objective of TCPNs is to provide a formal method for the modeling and analysis of distributed real-time systems from the *time* perspective. TCPNs are inspired by time and timed Petri nets. TCPNs extend Petri nets by adding durational timing constraints and minimum and maximum timing constraint pairs to places or transitions. For example, in Fig. 11.1 a transition t_2 has a timing constraint pair $(TC_{min}(t_2), TC_{max}(t_2))$ denoted as (0, 5) and its durational timing constraint $[FIRE_{dur}(t_2)]$ denoted as [6]. The major difference between TCPNs and time (timed) Petri nets is that TCPNs follow the weak firing mode and the analysis method is based on either the relative or absolute time mode. In contrast, time (timed) Petri nets follow the strong firing mode, and the analysis method is based on the relative time mode only. We will illustrate the advantage of using the weak firing mode and absolute time mode at the end of this chapter. TCPNs are most suitable for systems with conflict structures (priority, decision, and choice structures).

11.1 Definitions of TCPNs

A timing constraint Petri net is a 6-tuple $\langle P, T, F, C, D, M \rangle$ where, P is a set of places, $P = \{p_1, p_2, \ldots, p_m\}$; T is a set of transitions, i.e., $T = \{t_1, t_2, \ldots, t_n\}$; F is a set of arcs that connects places and transitions; C is a set of integer pairs, $(TC_{min}(pt_j), TC_{max}(pt_j))$, where pt_j is either a place or a transition; D is a set of firing durations, $[FIRE_{dur}(pt_j)]$; and M

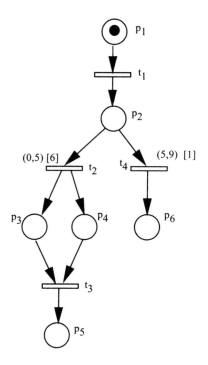

Fig. 11.1 A section of a Petri net with timing constraints.

is a set of markings with an m-vector, $\{M(p_1), \ldots, M(p_j), \ldots, M(p_m)\}$, where $M(p_j)$ denotes the number of tokens in place p_j. M_0 denotes the initial marking.

A transition t_j with a time pair $(TC_{min}(t_j), TC_{max}(t_j))$ is said to be *enabled* if each of its input places has at least one token. A transition t_j, which is enabled at time T_0 is said to be fireable during the time period from $T_0 + TC_{min}(t_j)$ to $T_0 + TC_{max}(t_j)$ in which $TC_{max}(t_j) \geq TC_{min}(t_j)$. A fireable transition can fire, but there is no guarantee that the firing will complete successfully because the firing of a transition takes a period of time $FIRE_{dur}(t_j)$. All the tokens used for enabling a transition t_j will be preserved during the t_j's firing, and the tokens can be used to enable other transitions if t_j fails to complete the firing. If all the transitions enabled by the tokens fail to complete their firing, then the tokens will be trapped in their corresponding places. A transition is said to be scheduleable if it is fireable and can complete its firing successfully. That is,

$$TC_{max}(t_j) - TC_{min}(t_j) \geq FIRE_{dur}(t_j)$$

A marking M_n is said to be reachable in Petri nets modeling if there is a firing sequence, $\sigma = (M_0, t_1, M_1, \ldots, t_j, M_j, \ldots, t_n, M_n)$ that transforms M_0 to

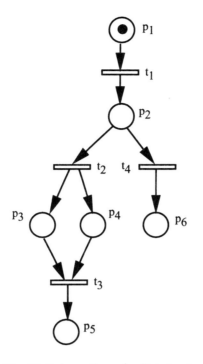

Fig. 11.2 A section of a Petri net.

M_n. The set of all possible markings reachable from M_0 is denoted by $R(M_0)$, and the set of all possible firing sequences from M_0 is denoted by $L(M_0)$ [279]. With the consideration of timing constraints, in TCPNs modeling, a marking M_n is said to be reachable if and only if all transitions in σ are proved to be scheduleable with respect to the timing constraints, $(TC_{max}$ (t_j) - TC_{min} $(t_j)) \geq FIRE_{dur}$ (t_j) In general, the time pairs associated with transitions are referred to as *transition time pairs*, and the time pairs associated with places are called *place time pairs*. Likewise duration times associated with transitions or places are called *transition durations* or *place durations*, respectively. For places and transitions that do not have explicit timing constraints associated with them, the default values of the time pair are (zero, infinity), and the default value of the duration is zero. These default values imply that the firing takes no time and can occur at any time.

Petri nets and TCPNs exhibit different behavior in reachability problems. A marking M_n that is reachable in Petri nets modeling is not necessarily reachable in TCPNs modeling because of the imposed timing constraints. In Petri nets modeling, a marking M_n is reachable if there exists at least one firing sequence σ that transforms M_0 to M_n after firing all transitions in σ at least once. However, due to the imposed timing constraints in TCPNs, such as $TC_{max}(t_j) \geq TC_{min}(t_j)$ and $(TC_{max}(t_j) - TC_{min}(t_j)) \geq FIRE_{dur}(t_j)$, transitions in σ may not be fireable or scheduleable according to the definitions of TCPNs modeling. If at least one transition in σ is non-fireable or nonscheduleable, then M_n is nonreachable. For example, for the Petri net in Fig. 11.2, let the initial marking $M_0 = (p_1)$, then we can derive markings $M_3 = (p5)$, and $M_4 = (p6)$. Both M_3 and M_4 are reachable after the firing sequence, $\exists \sigma_1 = (t_1 \ t_2 \ t_3)$ and $\sigma_2 = (t_1 \ t_4)$, respectively. Assuming that M_0, M_3, and M_4 remain the same, we can impose timing constraints onto t_2 and t_4 and form a TCPN, as shown in Fig. 11.1. In this case, based on the definition of a scheduleable transition, t_2 in σ_1 is nonscheduleable because the duration 6 is longer than the difference between the maximum and minimum timing constraint pair, (5 - 1) = 4. Whereas t_4 in σ_2 is scheduleable because the duration 1 is shorter than the difference between the maximum and minimum timing constraint pair, (9 - 5) = 4. From this we can conclude that M_3 is nonreachable, whereas M_4 is still reachable under the consideration of timing constraints.

To handle such differences of reachability problems in Petri nets and TCPNs modeling, a systematic method is required to determine whether M_n is reachable in TCPNs. In case M_n is nonreachable, then the method can be used to find the causes of non-reachability as well, that is, find the transitions that caused M_n to be nonreachable. In this chapter schedulability analysis is used to pinpoint transitions in σ that are not scheduleable when a marking in the TCPN is nonreachable.

11.2 Significance of TCPNs

The advantage of TCPNs over other time-related extensions of Petri nets is as follows: Time (timed) Petri nets conduct their analysis based on the relative time mode, which is only suitable for transition time pairs. In addition both time and timed Petri nets follow the strong firing mode, which not only violates the Petri nets firing mode but also prohibits them from representing conflict structures. TCPNs allow transition (place) time pairs to do an analysis based on either absolute or relative time modes. TCPNs follow the weak firing mode, which not only preserves the same firing mode used by Petri nets but also is capable of modeling and analyzing conflict structures.

Most of the time-related Petri nets are based on relative time. This will not cause any problems as long as the timing constraints can be modeled purely by transition time pairs. However, purely transition time pairs are not always sufficient. For example, [218] notes that two nets with either transition time pairs or place time pairs are isomorphic because they can be converted into each other without losing timing information. Unfortunately, this is true only when the token arrival times are not considered. We will use an example to demonstrate the need to know the token arrival time in order to perform certain timing analysis. In addition both time Petri nets and timed Petri nets use a strong firing mode that will cause problems when

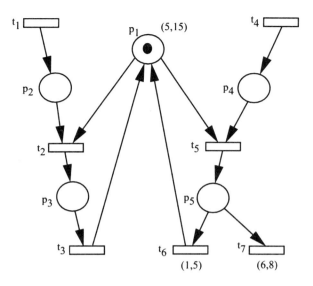

Fig. 11.3 A mutual exclusion example with place time pairs.

modeling conflict structures.

Fig. 11.3 gives a mutual exclusion example which models the use of an exclusive resource between two tasks A and B. Places and transitions are discussed as follows:

- If place p_1 has a token, then a resource is available.

- If place p_2 (p_4) has a token, then task A (B) is ready to acquire a resource.

- If place p_3 (p_5) has a token, then task A (B) is using a resource.

- If transition t_1 (t_4) fires, then task A (B) is requesting a resource.

- If transition t_2 (t_5) fires, then task A (B) is acquiring a resource.

- If transition t_3 (t_6) fires, then task A (B) is releasing a resource.

- If transition t_7 fires, then task B is destroying a resource.

Assume that once a resource is available, it can be acquired no sooner than 5 units of time and no later than 15 units of time. We attach a time pair $(5, 15)$ onto place p_1 as shown in Fig. 11.3 to represent these timing constraints on acquiring a resource. This example also shows that not all timing constraints can be modeled by transition time pairs. To demonstrate transition and place time pairs are not isomorphic unless the token arrival times are considered, we convert the net with place time pairs, as shown in Fig. 11.3, into a net

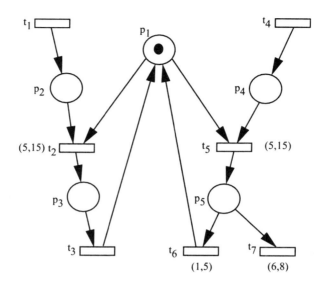

Fig. 11.4 A mutual exclusion example with transition time pairs.

with transition time pairs, as shown in Fig. 11.4, without considering token arrival times. Unfortunately, the meaning of timing constraints specified in Fig. 11.3 is distorted because the token arrival times in p_1, p_2, and p_4 are ignored. The timing constraint in Fig. 11.3 specifies that the token in place p_1 may be used to enable t_2 and t_5 only between 5 to 15 time units after the token arrived at p_1. However, the conversion shown in Fig. 11.4 implies that the token in p_1 can be used to enable t_2 and t_5 indefinitely if neither t_1 nor t_4 fire. As a result the conversion from place time pairs to transition time pairs is isomorphic only if one takes the token arrival time into consideration.

The conversion from transition time pairs to place time pairs with the consideration of token arrival times is done by computing the maximum of each input place's TC_{min} and the minimum of each input place's TC_{max}. In Fig. 11.3 let t_1 fire at time T_1, t_4 fire at time T_4, and a token arrive at p_1 at time T. A transition is enabled if and only if each of its input places have at least one token. Therefore in this example we have

t_2 enabled during $(\max\{T_1 + 0,\ T + 5\},\ \min\{T_1 + \infty,\ T + 15\})$,

and

t_5 enabled during $(\max\{T_4 + 0,\ T + 5\},\ \min\{T_4 + \infty, T + 15\})$

Since ∞ is always greater than $T + 15$, we have

t_2 enabled during $(\max\{T_1,\ T+5\},\ T+15)$,

and

t_5 enabled during $(\max\{T_4,\ T+5\},\ T+15)$

As we mentioned in the introduction, for a transition to be fireable, $TC_{min} \leq TC_{max}$. Therefore we have $\max\{T_1,\ T+5\} \leq T+15$, and $\max\{T_4,\ T+5\} \leq T+15$.

We can conclude that transitions t_2 and t_5 are fireable during the time intervals, $(\max\{T_1,\ T+5\},\ T+15)$ and $(\max\{T_4,\ T+5\},\ T+15)$, respectively. From this conclusion we can demonstrate another problem related to the strong firing mode. In Fig. 11.4, if both t_2 and t_5 do not fire by time $(T+15)$, then, by definition of the strong firing mode, then both t_2 and t_5 must fire at time $(T + 15)$. This contradicts the definition of conflict structures. Besides causing two conflict transitions to fire simultaneously, the strong firing mode may cause a transition not to fire at all. In other words, the strong firing mode is prone to cause dead transitions. For example, in Fig. 11.4 transition t_7 may never have a chance to fire if t_6 has a time pair $(1, 5)$ and t_7 has a time pair $(6, 8)$, because t_6 is forced to fire at time $T_5 + 5$ (assume that t_5 fires at T_5) if t_6 has not fired until $T_5 + 5$. Consequently t_7 will never fire and will become a dead transition.

Another advantage of the weak firing mode is in the modeling of lost tokens. In [218, 255] a failure transition and a fault condition are needed explicitly in order to model the loss of tokens from the use of the strong firing mode. This results in a number of shortcomings: (1) it violates the assumption of Petri nets that tokens never accidentally disappear, (2) designers have to explicitly model every possible location where tokens may be lost, and (3) extra transitions and places increase the complexity of both nets and reachability graphs. By using TCPNs (i.e., using the weak firing mode for modeling such failure-fault correlation), we do not need those extra failure transitions and fault conditions. In addition TCPNs modeling provides an intuitive representation of lost tokens without violating Petri nets modeling by utilizing the existence of trapped tokens to simulate the existence of lost tokens. If a transition t_j does not fire because of a lost token (fault), then one simply looks at all places prior to t_j in a firing sequence for any trapped tokens. If a trapped token can be found in place p, we know that the fault is caused by the output transitions of p failing to fire within its timing constraints (this is the failure that caused the fault). For example, in Fig. 11.3, if t_6 does not fire in time (a fault), then the cause of the fault (a failure) may be that a token was lost in place p_4, since transition t_5 failed to fire in time. This shows how timing constraint violations could result in the loss of tokens.

11.3   Schedulability Analysis Using TCPNs

In general, the analysis of a system specification can be done in two phases: the functional analysis and the timing analysis. The functional analysis is performed first to assert the correctness of the functionality. It can be performed using existing Petri nets analysis methods without considering timing constraints. The timing analysis is then performed to assert the correctness of the timing behavior. In general, valid timing behavior is assumed if the specification complies with the timing constraints. Since the functionality has been determined before the timing analysis begins, the functionality relationship among transitions is preserved with the newly attached timing constraints.

A real-time system is characterized by its timely response to external stimuli. In general, a response consists of a series of task executions, and a task execution is usually characterized by its start time, execution time, and deadline. For obtaining timely responses in a real-time system, a schedule of task executions must be specified, designed, and executed in a timely manner with respect to imposed timing constraints. The process of verifying that a schedule will meet the timing constraints is referred to as schedulability analysis [150, 375, 389]. Techniques proposed for schedulability analysis are usually considered from the design and run-time point of view. Stoyenko et al. present a set of language-independent schedulability analysis techniques [375] where they utilize the information about program organization and implementation and the hardware configuration to verify whether real-time software will meet its timing constraints. Haban and Shin [150] employ a real-time monitoring approach to analyze the monitored results, then feed the analyzed results back to the host operating system for dynamic scheduling and verification of the monitored tasks. Tokuda and Kotera in [389] use an interactive schedulability analyzer, *Scheduler 1-2-3*, for verifying at the design phase whether or not all tasks in a hard real-time system will be completed by their deadlines. Compared with the schedulability analysis presented in these three papers, which concentrate on the design and run-time phases, our focus is on the specification and analysis phases.

11.3.1   Basic Concepts

Usually we model a real-time system as a set of tasks. Each task is characterized by two events: the beginning event when a task begins its execution and the ending event when a task completes its execution. A task remains in execution between the two events. In addition tasks in real-time systems usually have timing constraints such as the ones defined in [96]. Dasarathy has classified the timing constraints. Three of them are (1) the maximum timing constraint, which is the maximum amount of time that may elapse between the occurrence of two events; (2) the minimum timing constraint, which is the minimum amount of time that must elapse between the occurrence of two events; and (3) the duration timing constraint, which is the maximum amount of time that a task can last.

In this chapter we present a schedulability analysis with an illustrated example featuring a real-time control system. We assume that the state where the system samples data is the initial marking M_0 and the state where the system provides its response is the final marking M_n. In TCPNs modeling, for a system specification to be valid, M_n must be reachable from M_0. For M_n to be reachable, all transitions in the firing sequences from M_0 to M_n must be strongly scheduleable. We will address how to determine if a transition is strongly scheduleable in a TCPN in this chapter.

Schedulability analysis is conducted in three steps: specification modeling, reachability simulation, and timing analysis. First, we model a real-time system by transforming its system specification along with its imposed timing constraints into a TCPN; we call this net N_s. Then we simulate the reachability graph of N_s to verify whether a marking M_n is reachable from an initial marking M_0. It is important to note that a reachable marking in Petri nets is not necessarily reachable in TCPNs due to the imposed timing constraints. Therefore, in the timing analysis step, a reachable marking M_n found in the reachability simulation step is analyzed to verify whether M_n is reachable under the consideration of timing constraints. M_n is said to be reachable in the TCPN if and only if we can find at least one firing sequence σ so that all transitions in σ are strongly scheduleable with respect to M_0 under the timing constraints. If M_n can be found, then we can assert that the specification is scheduleable under the imposed timing constraints; otherwise, the system specification needs to be modified or the timing constraints need to be relaxed.

11.3.2 Definitions

A marking M_n is said to be reachable if there is a firing sequence, $\sigma = (M_0 \ t_1 \ M_1 \ldots M_i \ t_i \ldots t_n \ M_n)$, or simply $(t_1 \ldots t_i \ldots t_n)$ that transforms M_0 to M_n. Due to the timing constraints, to prove M_n is reachable in TCPNs modeling, we have to prove that all the transitions in σ are strongly scheduleable with respect to M_0. In other words, let t_n be the final transition of σ from M_0 to M_n. M_n is reachable if and only if t_n and all the transitions that occurred prior to t_n are strongly scheduleable. In this section we present a method to determine whether a transition is strongly scheduleable under this definition. The firing sequence δ used in TCPNs is different from the firing sequence σ used in Petri nets. We define a $\delta_k(M_n)$ is a collection of places and transitions except the first transition in the kth firing sequence from M_0 to M_n, where n is the number of the final transition in $\delta_k(M_n)$.

For example, comparing δ and σ in Fig. 11.1,

$$\delta_1(M_3) = (p_2 \ t_2 \ p_3 \ t_3),$$

$$\delta_2(M_3) = (p_2\ t_2\ p_4\ t_3)$$
$$\delta_1(M_4) = (p_2\ t_4)$$

whereas

$$\sigma(M_3) = (t_1\ M_1\ t_2\ M_2\ t_3)$$
$$= (t_1\ p_2\ t_2\ p_3\ p_4\ t_3)$$
$$\sigma(M_4) = (t_1\ M_1\ t_4)$$
$$= (t_1\ p_2\ t_4)$$

Note that $\delta_k(M_n)$ is a by-product of finding σ in Petri nets, that is, $\delta_k(M_n)$ can be obtained from $L(M_0)$. Therefore no additional mechanism is needed to find $\delta_k(M_n)$, and the complexity of this schedulability analysis is the same as the reachability problem in Petri nets. The complexity is $O(mn)$ where m is the number of conflicting transitions (conditional flows) and n is the number of concurrent transitions. Terms are defined here to facilitate the following discussion.

Definition 11.1 $FIRE_{enabled}(t_j)$ is the time at which a transition t_j is enabled; $FIRE_{begin}(t_j)$ is the time at which a transition t_j begins the firing; $FIRE_{end}(t_j)$ is the time at which a transition t_j ends the firing; $FIRE_{dur}(t_j)$ is the period of time during which a transition t_j is firing.

From Definition 11.1 we have

$$FIRE_{dur}(t_j) = FIRE_{end}(t_j) - FIRE_{begin}(t_j) \tag{11.1}$$

$$FIRE_{enabled}(t_j) \leq FIRE_{begin}(t_j) \tag{11.2}$$

Definition 11.2 $IT(p_j)$ is a set of input transitions of p_j; $OT(p_j)$ is a set of output transitions of p_j; $IP(t_j)$ is a set of input places of t_j; $OP(t_j)$ is a set of output places of t_j.

Definition 11.3 $TC_{min}(p_j)$ and $TC_{max}(p_j)$ are the minimum and maximum elapsed time intervals between the token arrival time of p_j and the beginning and ending firing times of p_j's output transition. $TOKEN_{arr}(p_j)$ is the time at which a token arrives at a place p_j; $TOKEN_{rem}(p_j)$ is the time at which a token is removed from a place p_j.

From Definition 11.3 we have

$$TC_{min}(p_j) \leq FIRE_{begin}(t_i) - TOKEN_{arr}(p_j)$$

$$TC_{max}(p_j) \geq FIRE_{end}(t_i) - TOKEN_{arr}(p_j)$$

where $t_i \in OT(p_j)$

The movement of tokens from each input place to each output place of t_j uses no time. As a result the token removal time of place p_j is the same as the ending firing time of p_j's output transition. Similarly the token arrival time of p_j is the same as the ending firing time of p_j's input transition:

$$TOKEN_{rem}(p_j) = FIRE_{end}(t_i), \text{ where } t_i \in OT(p_j) \tag{11.3}$$

$$TOKEN_{arr}(p_j) = FIRE_{end}(t_i), \text{ where } t_i \in IT(p_j) \tag{11.4}$$

$$TOKEN_{rem}(p_j) \leq TOKEN_{arr}(p_j) + TC_{max}(p_j) \tag{11.5}$$

A place needs at least $TC_{min}(p_j)$ time units of delay to enable a transition, and it can hold a token only for at most $TC_{max}(p_j)$ after a token's arrival. Therefore a place can only enable its output transition during the time from $(TOKEN_{arr}(p_j) + TC_{min}(p_j))$ to $(TOKEN_{arr}(p_j) + TC_{max}(p_j))$. As a result the maximum enabling time needed by p_j to enable its output transition $OT(p_j)$ is $(TC_{max}(p_j) - TC_{min}(p_j))$. Since the firing of $OT(p_j)$ needs $FIRE_{dur}(OT(p_j))$ and has to be enabled before it can be fired, we have

$$FIRE_{dur}(t_i) \leq TC_{max}(p_j) - TC_{min}(p_j) \tag{11.6}$$
where $t_i \in OT(p_j)$; otherwise, t_i cannot be fired successfully.

11.3.3   Specification of a Real-Time Control System

A typical real-time system continuously samples and processes the data in a timely fashion. Fig. 11.5 is a TCPN transformed from the specifications listed below. The time pair of minimum and maximum timing constraints is denoted as (TC_{min}, TC_{max}) such as $(0, 45)$ in the figure, and the firing duration is denoted as $[FIRE_{dur}]$ such as $[25]$ in the figure. The system samples data (denoted as transition t_1) every 50 units of time (UT) from the external environment and provides either a normal response (denoted as transition t_6) or an emergency response (denoted as transition t_9) within 45 UT. If the system is not about to complete the normal response before its deadline due to some reason, then it tries to give the emergency response. Therefore we model the normal data input (denoted as transition t_2) with a higher priority than the emergency data input (denoted as transition t_7) by specifying t_2 with an earlier deadline. As we can see in Fig. 11.5, a conflict structure (p_2, t_2, and t_7) can be easily modeled with TCPNs. In contrast, time (timed) Petri nets do not have such capabilities. In TCPNs modeling, we assume that a token arrives at p_2 at time T, then t_7 may fire during $T + 10$ to $T + 30$ if t_2 does not fire at $T + 6$. In contrast, in time (timed) Petri nets modeling, t_7 will never fire because t_2 must fire at time $T + 6$. Therefore let the initial marking, M_0, be (p_1). We would like to use schedulability analysis to determine whether marking M_6, $(p_1 \ p_{12})$, which denotes the normal response, and marking M_9, $(p_1 \ p_{13})$, which denotes the emergency response are reachable. The following specifications are for a real-time control system.

- S_1. The system samples data from the external environment every 50 UT, and the system must respond with either a normal or an emergency response within 45 UT after the completion of sampling. The task of sampling takes 5 UT.

- S_2. Once the data is obtained, the system goes to the normal data input procedure (NDI) first, it goes to the emergency data input procedure (EDI) if the NDI failed.

- S_3. NDI must wait for 2 UT and complete within 6 UT after the completion of the sampling. The task of NDI takes 8 UT.

- S_4. EDI must wait for 10 UT and complete within 30 UT after the completion of the sampling. The task of EDI takes 2 UT.

- S_5. If the system executes the normal data input procedure, then the system must displays the sampled data on the screen before giving its normal response. The task of the normal response takes 10 UT.

- S_6. Displaying data is done by displaying the analyzed data on the background (the data must wait until both the background display and the data analysis are completed). The task of displaying data takes 15 UT.

- S_7. Displaying background can begin as soon as NDI is complete. The task of displaying background takes 5 UT.

- S_8. Due to the data transfer delay, analyzing data must wait for 5 UT after the completion of NDI. The task of analyzing data takes 25 UT.

- S_9. If the system goes to the emergency data input procedure, then the system only needs to analyze data and give the emergency responses (no data displaying is necessary). The task of emergency response takes 10 UT.

- S_{10}. Due to the data transfer delay, analyzing data must wait for 5 UT after the completion of EDI. The task of analyzing data takes 20 UT.

11.3.4   Analyzing Strongly Scheduleable Transitions

For a transition t_j to be fireable, it must be enabled by all its input places. Therefore we have Definition 11.4.

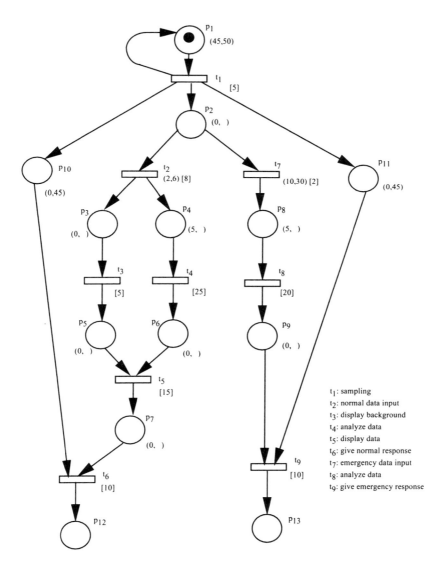

Fig. 11.5 A TCPN modeling of a real-time control system specification.

Definition 11.4 A transition t_j is said to be a weakly fireable transition and denoted as $WFT(t_j)$, if each of the input places of t_j currently has at least one token without considering the arrival times of tokens in each input place (or assuming that the arrival times of tokens are the same).

That is, given the time pair, $(ETBF(t_j), LTEF(t_j))$, which denotes the earliest time to begin firing and the latest time to end firing of t_j after t_j is enabled, then t_j is a WFT if and only if

$$ETBF(t_j) = \max\{TC_{min}(p_j)\} + TC_{min}(t_j)$$

$$LTEF(t_j) = \min\{TC_{max}(p_j), TC_{max}(t_j)\}$$

$$LTEF(t_j) - ETBF(t_j) \geq 0$$
where $p_j \in IP(t_j)$

Since the firing needs a duration time, it is not guaranteed that a fireable transition will complete its firing successfully. Therefore we have

Definition 11.5 transition t_j is a weakly scheduleable transition, and denoted as $WST(t_j)$, if t_j is a WFT and can be fired successfully without considering the arrival times of tokens in each input place.

That is, t_j's duration cannot be less than its fireable time so that

$$LTEF(t_j) - ETBF(t_j) \geq FIRE_{dur}(t_j)$$

For example, in Fig. 11.5, t_2 is not a WST because

$$\begin{aligned}
LTEF(t_2) - ETBF(t_2) &= \min\{TC_{max}(p_2), TC_{max}(t_2)\} \\
&\quad - (\max\{TC_{min}(p_2)\} + TC_{min}(t_2)) \\
&= 6 - 2 \\
&\leq 8 = FIRE_{dur}(t_2)
\end{aligned}$$

To make transition t_2 a WST, we relax the timing constraints by increasing $TC_{max}(t_2)$ from 6 to 10, so that

$$LTEF(t_2) - ETBF(t_2) = 10 - 2 = 8 = FIRE_{dur}(t_2)$$

Theorem 11.6 *A transition t_j is said to be a strongly fireable transition with respect to M_0, and denoted as $SFT(t_j)$, if t_j is a WFT and each of the input places of t_j has at least one token.*

That is, given the time pair, $(ETBF(t_j), LTEF(t_j))$, which denotes the earliest time to begin firing and the latest time to end firing of t_j after t_j is enabled, then t_j is a SFT if and only if

$$ETBF(t_j) = \max\{\min\{TOKEN_{arr}(p_j)\} + TC_{min}(p_j)\}$$
$$+TC_{min}(t_j)$$

$$LTEF(t_j) = \min\{\max\{TOKEN_{arr}(p_j)\}$$
$$+min\{TC_{max}(p_j), TCmax(t_j)\}\}$$

$$LTEF(t_j) - ETBF(t_j) \geq 0$$

or

$$ETBF(t_j) = \max\{FIRE_{end}(t_1) + \sum TC_{min}(pt_{mk}) + \sum FIRE_{dur}(t_{nk})\},$$
where $pt_{mk}, t_{nk} \in \delta_k(M_j)$

$$LTEF(t_j) = \min\{(FIRE_{end}(t_1) + \sum TC_{max}(pt_{mk}))\},$$
where $pt_{mk} \in \delta_k(M_j)$,

$$LTEF(t_j) - ETBF(t_j) \geq 0$$

Proof: t_j is fireable only if it is enabled by every input place of t_j simultaneously, and it will stop firing once one of its input places stops enabling it. To determine if t_j is fireable, we need to take into account the arrival time of all input places of t_j. Since $TC_{min}(p_j)$ and $TC_{max}(p_j)$ are fixed, we need only to find the lower bound and upper bound of $TOKEN_{arr}(p_j)$ in order to find $ETBF(t_j)$ and $LTEF(p_j)$. From (11-4), we know that $TOKEN_{arr}(p_j)$ is equal to $FIRE_{end}(IT(p_j))$. Therefore, we can find the bounds of $TOKEN_{arr}(p_j)$ by finding the bounds of $FIRE_{end}(IT(p_j))$ derived from $IP(p_j)$ back to the initial transition t_1. From Definition 11.3, we have

$$TOKEN_{arr}(p_j) + TC_{min}(p_j) + TC_{min}(t_j) \leq FIRE_{begin}(t_i) \qquad (11.7)$$
where $t_i \in OT(p_j)$.

$$FIRE_{end}(t_i) \leq TOKEN_{arr}(p_j) + TC_{max}(p_j) \qquad (11.8)$$
where $t_i \in OT(p_j)$.

From (11.1), we have

$$FIRE_{begin}(t_i) = FIRE_{end}(t_i) - FIRE_{dur}(t_i) \qquad (11-9)$$
where $t_i \in OT(p_j)$.

replacing $FIRE_{begin}(t_i)$ by (11-9) and applying it into (11-7), we have

$$TOKEN_{arr}(p_j) + TC_{min}(p_j) + TC_{min}(t_j)$$
$$\leq FIRE_{end}(t_i) - FIRE_{dur}(t_i)$$

where $t_i \in OT(p_j)$, or

$$TOKEN_{arr}(p_j) + TC_{min}(p_j) + TC_{min}(t_j) + FIRE_{dur}(t_i)$$
$$\leq FIRE_{end}(t_i) \tag{11-10}$$

where $t_i \in OT(p_j)$. From (11-8) and (11-10), we have

$$TOKEN_{arr}(p_j) + TC_{min}(p_j) + TC_{min}(t_j) + FIRE_{dur}(t_i)$$
$$\leq FIRE_{end}(t_i)$$
$$\leq TOKEN_{arr}(p_j) + TC_{max}(p_j) \tag{11-11}$$

where $t_i \in OT(p_j)$, or

$$FIRE_{end}(t_i) + TC_{min}(p_j) + TC_{min}(t_j) + FIRE_{dur}(t_i)$$
$$\leq FIRE_{end}(t_i)$$
$$\leq FIRE_{end}(t_i) + TC_{max}(p_j), \tag{11-12}$$

where $t_i \in OT(p_j)$. From $\delta_k(M_j)$ we know that

$$TOKEN_{arr}(p_j) = FIRE_{end}(t_{j-1})$$

which means that we can find $TOKEN_{arr}(p_j)$ by finding $FIRE_{end}(t_{j-1})$. Thus we have

$$TOKEN_{arr}(p_j) = FIRE_{end}(t_{j-1}) \tag{11-13}$$

We can determine the bounds of $TOKEN_{arr}(p_j)$ by deriving the bound of $FIRE_{end}(t_{j-1})$ as follows: From (11-12), we have

$$FIRE_{end}(t_{j-2}) + TC_{min}(p_{j-1}) + FIRE_{dur}(t_{j-1})$$
$$\leq FIRE_{end}(t_{j-1})$$
$$\leq FIRE_{end}(t_{j-2}) + TC_{max}(p_{j-1}) \tag{11-14}$$

Extending $FIRE_{end}(t_{j-2})$ by using (11-12), we have

$$FIRE_{end}(t_{j-3}) + TC_{min}(p_{j-2}) + FIRE_{dur}(t_{j-2})$$
$$\leq FIRE_{end}(t_{j-2})$$
$$\leq FIRE_{end}(t_{j-3}) + TC_{max}(p_{j-2}) \tag{11-15}$$

Combining (11-14) and (11-15), we have

$$FIRE_{end}(t_{j-3}) + TC_{min}(p_{j-2}) + TC_{min}(p_{j-1})$$
$$+ FIRE_{dur}(t_j - 2) + FIRE_{dur}(t_{j-1})$$
$$\leq FIRE_{end}(t_{j-1})$$

$$\leq FIRE_{end}(t_{j-3}) + TC_{max}(p_{j-2}) + TC_{max}(p_{j-1}) \quad (11\text{-}16)$$

We can continue deriving in the same way until $FIRE_{end}(t_1)$ is encountered, at which point we have

$$FIRE_{end}(t_1) + TC_{min}(p_2) + \ldots + TC_{min}(p_{j-1}) + TC_{min}(t_j)$$
$$+ FIRE_{dur}(t_2) + FIRE_{dur}(p_3) + \ldots + FIRE_{dur}(t_{j-1})$$
$$\leq FIRE_{end}(t_{j-1})$$
$$\leq FIRE_{end}(t_1) + TC_{max}(p_2) + \ldots + TC_{max}(p_{j-1}) \quad (11\text{-}17)$$

or

$$FIRE_{end}(t_1) + \sum TC_{min}(pt_{mk}) + TC_{min}(t_j) + \sum FIRE_{dur}(t_{nk})$$
$$\leq FIRE_{end}(t_{j-1})$$
$$\leq FIRE_{end}(t_1) + \sum TC_{max}(pt_{mk}) \quad (11\text{-}18)$$

where $pt_{mk}, t_{nk} \in \delta_k(M_j)$. Replacing $FIRE_{end}(t_j - 1)$ by $TOKEN_{arr}(p_j)$, we can determine the lower bound and upper bound of $TOKEN_{arr}(p_j)$ and get:

$$FIRE_{end}(t_1) + \sum TC_{min}(pt_{mk}) + TC_{min}(t_j) + \sum FIRE_{dur}(t_{nk})$$
$$\leq TOKEN_{arr}(p_j)$$
$$\leq FIRE_{end}(t_1) + \sum TC_{max}(pt_{mk}) \quad (11\text{-}19)$$

where $pt_{mk}, t_{nk} \in \delta_k(M_j)$. From (11-19), we get the lower bound and upper bound of $TOKEN_{arr}(p_j)$ and then

$$ETBF(t_j) = \max\{FIRE_{end}(t_1) + \sum TC_{min}(pt_{mk}) + \sum FIRE_{dur}(t_{nk})\}$$

where $pt_{mk} \in \delta_k(M_j)$ and $t_{nk} \in \delta_k(M_j)$.

$$LTEF(t_j) = \min\{(FIRE_{end}(t_1) + \sum TC_{max}(pt_{mk}))\}$$

where $pt_{mk} \in \delta_k(M_j)$. That is,

$ETBF(t_j) = $ The lower bound of t_j's enabled time of all paths from t_1 to t_j.

$LTEF(t_j) = $ The upper bound of t_j's end firing time of all paths from t_1 to t_j. ∎

For example, in Fig. 11.5, t_6 is not an SFT because
$\delta_1(M_6) = (p_2 \ t_2 \ p_3 \ t_3 \ p_5 \ t_5 \ p_7 \ t_6)$
$\delta_2(M_6) = (p_2 \ t_2 \ p_4 \ t_4 \ p_6 \ t_5 \ p_7 \ t_6)$
$\delta_3(M_6) = (p_{10} \ t_6)$

Let t_1 end its firing at T_0.

$$
\begin{aligned}
ETBF(t_6) &= \max\{[T_0 + (TC_{min}(p_2) + TC_{min}(t_2) + TC_{min}(p_3) \\
&\quad + TC_{min}(t_3) + TC_{min}(p_5) + TC_{min}(t_5) + TC_{min}(p_7)) \\
&\quad + (FIRE_{dur}(t_2) + FIRE_{dur}(t_3) + FIRE_{dur}(t_5))], \\
&\quad [T_0 + (TC_{min}(p_2) + TC_{min}(t_2) + TC_{min}(p_4) + TC_{min}(t_4) \\
&\quad + TC_{min}(p_6) + TC_{min}(t_5) + TC_{min}(p_7)) \\
&\quad + (FIRE_{dur}(t_2) + FIRE_{dur}(t_4) + FIRE_{dur}(t_5))], \\
&\quad [T_0 + TC_{min}(p_{10})]\} \\
&\quad + TC_{min}(t_6) \\
&= \max\{[T_0 + (0 + 2 + 0 + 0 + 0 + 0 + 0) + (8 + 5 + 15)], \\
&\quad [T_0 + (0 + 2 + 5 + 0 + 0 + 0 + 0) + (8 + 25 + 15)], \\
&\quad [T_0 + 0]\} \\
&\quad + 0 \\
&= T_0 + 53 \\
LTEF(t_6) &= \min\{[\min\{TC_{max}(p_7), TC_{max}(t_6)\} + T_0 \\
&\quad + (TC_{max}(p_2) + TC_{max}(t_2) + TC_{max}(p_3) + TC_{max}(t_3) \\
&\quad + TC_{max}(p_5) + TC_{max}(t_5)], \\
&\quad [\min\{TC_{max}(p_7), TC_{max}(t_6)\} \\
&\quad + T_0 + (TC_{max}(p_2) + TC_{max}(t_2) \\
&\quad + TC_{max}(p_4) + TC_{max}(t_4) + TC_{max}(p_6) + TC_{max}(t_5)], \\
&\quad [\min\{TC_{max}(p_{10}), TC_{max}(t_6)\} + T_0]\} \\
&= \min\{[\infty + T_0 + \infty + 6 + \infty + \infty + \infty + \infty)], \\
&\quad [\infty + T_0 + (\infty + 6 + \infty + \infty + \infty + \infty)], \\
&\quad [45 + T_0]\} \\
&= T_0 + 45
\end{aligned}
$$

$$
LTEF(t_6) - ETBF(t_6) = (T_0 + 45) - (T_0 + 53) = 45 - 53 < 0
$$

which contradicts Theorem 11.6. Therefore t_6 is not an SFT.

To make t_6 an SFT, we relax the timing constraints by increasing the $TC_{max}(p_{10})$ from 45 to 65 so that

$$
LTEF(t_6) = T_0 + 65
$$

$$
LTEF(t_6) - ETBF(t_6) = (T_0 + 65) - (T_0 + 53) = 12 > 0
$$

Theorem 11.7 *A transition t_j is said to be a strongly scheduleable transition with respect to M_0, and denoted as $SST(t_j)$, if t_j can be fired successfully under the consideration of the arrival time of a token in each input place.*

That is, given the time pair, $(ETBF(t_j), LTEF(t_j))$, which denotes the earliest time to begin firing and the latest time to end firing of t_j after t_j is enabled, then t_j is an SST if and only if

$$ETBF(t_j) = \max\{\min\{TOKEN_{arr}(p_j)\} + TC_{min}(p_j)\} + TC_{min}(t_j)$$

$$LTEF(t_j) = \min\{\max\{TOKEN_{arr}(p_j)\} \\ + \min\{TC_{max}(p_j), TCmax(t_j)\}\}$$

$$LTEF(t_j) - ETBF(t_j) \geq FIRE_{dur}(t_j)$$
where $p_j \in IP(t_j)$

or

$$ETBF(t_j) = \max\{FIRE_{end}(t_1) + \sum TC_{min}(pt_{mk}) + \sum FIRE_{dur}(t_{nk})\}$$
where $pt_{mk}, t_{nk} \in \delta_k(M_j)$,

$$LTEF(t_j) = \min\{(FIRE_{end}(t_1) + \sum TC_{max}(pt_{mk}))\}$$
where $pt_{mk} \in \delta_k(M_j)$,

$$LTEF(t_j) - ETBF(t_j) \geq FIRE_{dur}(t_j),$$
where $p_j \in IP(M_j)$.

Proof: The proof of this theorem is similar to the proof of Theorem 11.6. ■
For example, in Fig. 11.5, t_9 is not an SST because

$$\delta_1(M_9) = (p_2\ t_7\ p_8\ t_8\ p_9\ t_9)$$

$$\delta_2(M_9) = (p_{11}\ t_9)$$

Let t_1 end its firing at T_0. Then

$$
\begin{aligned}
ETBF(t_9) &= \max\{[T_0 + (TC_{min}(p_2) + TC_{min}(t_7) + TC_{min}(p_8) + \\
&\quad TC_{min}(t_8) + TC_{min}(p_9)) + FIRE_{dur}(t_7) + FIRE_{dur}(t_8)], \\
&\quad [T_0 + TC_{min}(p_{11})]\} \\
&\quad + TC_{min}(t_9) \\
&= \max\{[T_0 + (0 + 10 + 5 + 0 + 0) + (2 + 20)], [T_0 + 0]\} + 0 \\
&= T_0 + 37
\end{aligned}
$$

$$
\begin{aligned}
LTEF(t_9) &= \min\{[\min\{TC_{max}(p_9), TC_{max}(t_9)\} + T_0 \\
&\quad + TC_{max}(p_2) + TC_{max}(t_7) + TC_{max}(p_8) + TC_{max}(t_8)], \\
&\quad \min\{TC_{max}(p_{11}), TC_{max}(t_9)\} + T_0]\} \\
&= \min\{[\infty + T_0 + \infty + 30 + \infty + \infty], [45 + T_0]\} \\
&= T_0 + 45
\end{aligned}
$$

$$
\begin{aligned}
LTEF(t_9) - ETBF(t_9) &= (T_0 + 45) - (T_0 + 37) \\
&= 8 < FIRE_{dur}(t_9) = 10
\end{aligned}
$$

which contradicts Theorem 11.7. Therefore t_9 is not an SST.

To make t_9 an SST, we relax the timing constraints by reducing the $TC_{min}(p_8)$ from 5 to 1 so that we have

$$
\begin{aligned}
ETBF(t_9) &= max\{[T_0 + (0 + 10 + 1 + 0 + 0) + (2 + 20)], [T_0 + 0] + 0\} \\
&= T_0 + 33 \\
LTEF(t_9) &= T_0 + 45
\end{aligned}
$$

$$
\begin{aligned}
LTEF(t_9) - ETBF(t_9) &= (T_0 + 45) - (T_0 + 33) \\
&= 12 \\
&> FIRE_{dur}(t_9) = 10
\end{aligned}
$$

Theorem 11.8 *If at least one of the transitions in a TCPN is not strongly scheduleable with respect to the initial marking M_0, then this net is not a scheduleable net.*

Proof: For a transition t_j in a TCPN, it is fireable for only a limited period of time. In addition, the firing of a transition in a TCPN lasts for a duration of time. If the fireable time of t_j is less than its firing duration, then t_j cannot complete its firing successfully. In other words, t_j is not scheduleable under the imposed timing constraints. ∎

11.4   Run-Time Analysis Using TCPNs

Based on the collected run-time information collected via our monitoring system [397, 398, 413], we can perform the run-time analysis using the following theorems. If any non-safe place or nonscheduleable transition is detected, then the detected places and the transitions are the most likely cause of the timing constraint violations.

Theorem 11.9 *A transition that is live in Petri nets is not necessarily a weakly or strongly scheduleable transition in TCPNs. However, a transition that is dead in Petri nets is definitely a nonscheduleable transition in TCPNs.*

Proof: Due to the stringent firing rules of TCPNs, the firing of a transition with TC_{dur} can only be started and must be completed within the time pair (TC_{min}, TC_{max}), or the transition is disabled. Therefore a live transition in Petri nets could become dead because of the imposed timing constraints. ■

Theorem 11.10 *A place that is safe in Petri nets and time (timed) Petri nets is not necessary safe in TCPNs. However, a place that is safe in TCPNs is definitely safe in both Petri nets and time (timed) Petri nets.*

Proof: According to the strong firing mode of time Petri nets, a transition must fire and will consume one token from each of its input places if the maximum timing constraint is met. In contrast, in TCPNs, a nonscheduleable transition would not fire in this case, and so the net would not consume any tokens. This causes its input places to accumulate tokens and makes the net non-safe. ■

Theorem 11.11 *For a non-safe place p_j in TCPNs, the firing sequence that includes p_j is the bottleneck of performance, or the output transitions of p_j are too slow to meet the timing constraints.*

Proof: For a non-safe place p_j, a token is trapped because the firing sequence that includes p_j takes too much time to move a token into p_j. Thus p_j's output transitions do not have enough time to consume tokens. A bottleneck in the system performance has then been found. ■

For example, in Petri nets or time (timed) Petri nets modeling, all places shown in the net fragment in Fig. 11.6 are safe. However, this is not the case in TCPNs modeling and analysis because any place may be non-safe after a few runs of the specification if some of the transitions are too slow. Assuming that place P_0 is non-safe after a few runs of the specification, we can detect that transition t_1 (sampling) is too slow to collect enough data. To solve this, we can modify the specification by relaxing the timing constraints in certain places.

11.5   Synthesis With TCPNs

Real-time system specification and verification tries to find the most timely valid responses for the system. Most of the verification methods proposed nowadays are able to verify whether a timely response is valid with respect to the timing requirements, but not many of them can synthesize the approximate range of such timely responses. Besides proving that those timely responses are scheduleable to the specified timing requirements, the other objective of this schedulability analysis is to synthesize the best approximation of time range for the timely response. In this chapter the synthesis is conducted by computing the best approximation of the earliest time to begin firing (ETBF) and the latest time to end firing (LTEF) for each scheduleable transition. The

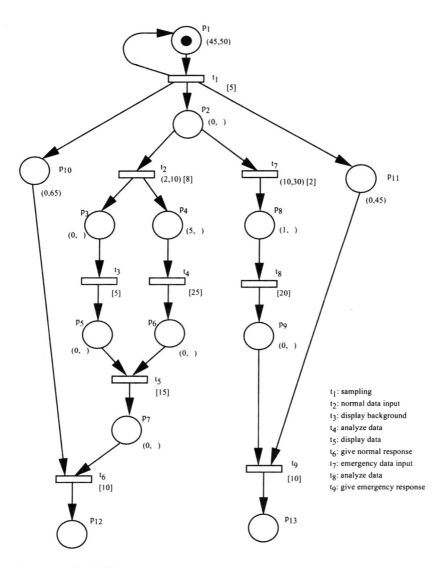

Fig. 11.6 A TCPN with strongly scheduleable TC_{min} and TC_{max} on each transition.

computation of synthesis consists of forward and backward computations. Forward computation is used to construct the best approximation of ETBF, and backward computation is used to construct the best approximation of LTEF.

11.5.1 Forward Computation

In general, the forward computation follows the schedulability analysis method (especially the Theorem 11.7) presented in the previous subsection. The forward computation converts the specified TC_{min} and TC_{max} time pairs into the ETBF and LTEF time pairs, then analyzes whether the ETBF and LTEF time pairs are strongly scheduleable or not. If they are not, then the ETBF and LTEF are refined by relaxing TC_{min} and TC_{max} until all transitions are strongly scheduleable. Note that the time mode used in TC_{min} and TC_{max} is referred to as the relative time between the two transitions' firing, whereas the time mode used in ETBF and LTEF is absolute time with respect to the time of the initial marking. In the following discussion we use forward computation to compute the ETBF and LTEF of each transition based on the refined TC_{min} and TC_{max} specifications in Fig. 11.6. The result of forward computation is shown in Fig. 11.7.

The ETBF and LTEF of t_6 and t_9, as shown in Fig. 11.7, have been obtained in a previous section, and they are both strongly scheduleable transitions to the time of the initial marking T_0, which is the time at which transition t_0 completes its firing.

$$LTEF(t_6) - ETBF(t_6) = (T_0 + 65) - (T_0 + 53) = 12$$
$$> FIRE_{dur}(t_6)$$

$$LTEF(t_9) - ETBF(t_9) = (T_0 + 45) - (T_0 + 33) = 12$$
$$> FIRE_{dur}(t_9)$$

Based on Theorem 11.7, we compute and analyze the remaining transitions in the net in Fig. 11.6 by finding their firing sequence, δ, and ETBF and LTEF as follows:

For transition t_2, whose $\delta(M_2) = (p_2 t_2)$, we have

$$
\begin{aligned}
ETBF(t_2) &= T_0 + TC_{min}(p_2) + TC_{min}(t_2) \\
&= T_0 + 0 + 2 = T_0 + 2 \\
LTEF(t_2) &= \min\{TC_{max}(p_2), TC_{max}(t_2)\} + T_0 \\
&= 10 + T_0
\end{aligned}
$$

$$LTEF(t_2) - ETBF(t_2) = T_0 + 10 - (T_0 + 2)$$

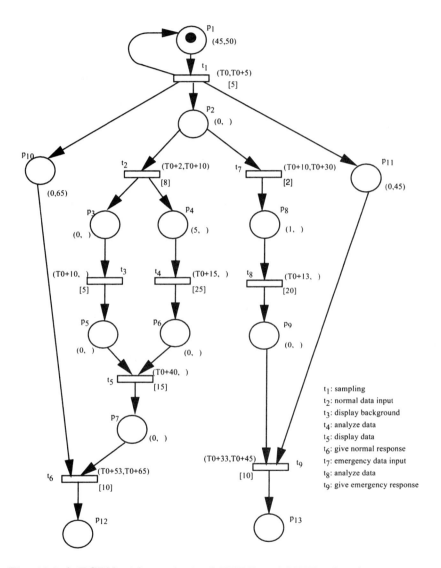

Fig. 11.7 A TCPN with synthesized ETBF and LTEF after forward computation.

$$= 8 = FIRE_{dur}(t_2)$$

Therefore t_2 is an SST.

For transition t_3, whose $\delta(M_3) = (p_2\ t_2\ p_3\ t_3)$, we have

$$
\begin{aligned}
ETBF(t_3) &= T_0 + TC_{min}(p_2) + TC_{min}(t_2) + TC_{min}(p_3) \\
&\quad + FIRE_{dur}(t_2) + TC_{min}(t_3) \\
&= T_0 + 0 + 2 + 0 + 8 + 0 \\
&= T_0 + 10 \\
LTEF(t_3) &= \min\{TC_{max}(p_3), TC_{max}(t_3)\} + T_0 \\
&\quad + TC_{max}(p_2) + TC_{max}(t_2) \\
&= \infty + T_0 + \infty + 10 \\
&= \infty
\end{aligned}
$$

$$
\begin{aligned}
LTEF(t_3) - ETBF(t_3) &= \infty - (T_0 + 10) \\
&= \infty \\
&> FIRE_{dur}(t_3) = 5
\end{aligned}
$$

Therefore t_3 is an SST.

For transition t_4, whose $\delta(M_4) = (p_2\ t_2\ p_4\ t_4)$, we have

$$
\begin{aligned}
ETBF(t_4) &= T_0 + TC_{min}(p_2) + TC_{min}(t_2) + TC_{min}(p_4) \\
&\quad + FIRE_{dur}(t_2) + TC_{min}(t_4) \\
&= T_0 + 0 + 2 + 5 + 8 + 0 \\
&= T_0 + 15 \\
LTEF(t_4) &= \min\{TC_{max}(p_4), TC_{max}(t_4)\} + T_0 \\
&\quad + TC_{max}(p_2) + TC_{max}(t_2) \\
&= \infty + T_0 + \infty + 10 \\
&= \infty
\end{aligned}
$$

$$
\begin{aligned}
LTEF(t_4) - ETBF(t_4) &= \infty - (T_0 + 15) \\
&= \infty > FIRE_{dur}(t_4) = 25
\end{aligned}
$$

Therefore, t_4 is an SST.

For transition t_5, whose

$$\delta_1(M5) = (p_2\ t_2\ p_3\ t_3\ p_5\ t_5)$$

$$\delta_2(M5) = (p_2 \ t_2 \ p_4 \ t_4 \ p_6 \ t_5)$$

we have

$$
\begin{aligned}
ETBF(t_5) &= \max\{[T_0 + TC_{min}(p_2) + TC_{min}(t_2) + TC_{min}(p_3)\\
&\quad + TC_{min}(t_3) + TC_{min}(p_5)\\
&\quad + (FIRE_{dur}(t_2) + FIRE_{dur}(t_3))],\\
&\quad [T_0 + TC_{min}(p_2) + TC_{min}(t_2) + TC_{min}(p_4)\\
&\quad + TC_{min}(t_4) + TC_{min}(p_6)\\
&\quad + (FIRE_{dur}(t_2) + FIRE_{dur}(t_4))]\} + TC_{min}(t_5)\\
&= \max\{[T_0 + (0 + 2 + 0 + 0 + 0) + (8 + 5)],\\
&\quad [T_0 + (0 + 2 + 5 + 0 + 0) + (8 + 25)]\} + 0\\
&= T_0 + 40\\
LTEF(t_5) &= \min\{[\min\{TC_{max}(p_5), TC_{max}(t_5)\} + T_0\\
&\quad + TC_{max}(p_2) + TC_{max}(t_2) + TC_{max}(p_3) + TC_{max}(t_3)],\\
&\quad [\min\{TC_{max}(p_6), TC_{max}(t_5)\} + T_0 + TC_{max}(p_2)\\
&\quad + TC_{max}(t_2) + TC_{max}(p_4) + TC_{max}(t_4)]\}\\
&= \min\{[\infty + T_0 + \infty + 10 + \infty + \infty],\\
&\quad [15 + T_0 + \infty + 10 + \infty + \infty]\}\\
&= \infty
\end{aligned}
$$

$$
\begin{aligned}
LTEF(t_5) - ETBF(t_5) &= \infty - (T_0 + 40)\\
&= \infty > FIRE_{dur}(t_5) = 15
\end{aligned}
$$

Therefore, t_5 is an SST.

For transition t_7, whose $\delta(M7) = (p_2 \ t_7)$, we have

$$
\begin{aligned}
ETBF(t_7) &= T_0 + TC_{min}(p_2) + TC_{min}(t_7)\\
&= T_0 + 0 + 10\\
&= T_0 + 10\\
LTEF(t_7) &= \min\{TC_{max}(p_2), TC_{max}(t_7)\} + T_0\\
&= 30 + T_0
\end{aligned}
$$

$$
\begin{aligned}
LTEF(t_7) - ETBF(t_7) &= T_0 + 30 - (T_0 + 10)\\
&= 20 > FIRE_{dur}(t_7) = 2
\end{aligned}
$$

Therefore t_7 is an SST.

For transition t_8, whose $\delta(M8) = (p_2 \ t_7 \ p_8 \ t_8)$, we have

$$
\begin{aligned}
ETBF(t_8) &= T_0 + TC_{min}(p_2) + TC_{min}(t_7) + TC_{min}(p_8) \\
&\quad + FIRE_{dur}(t_7) + TC_{min}(t_8) \\
&= T_0 + 0 + 10 + 1 + 2 + 0 \\
&= T_0 + 13 \\
LTEF(t_8) &= \min\{TC_{max}(p_8), TC_{max}(t_8)\} + T_0 \\
&\quad + TC_{max}(p_2) + TC_{max}(t_7) \\
&= \infty + T_0 + \infty + 30 = \infty
\end{aligned}
$$

$$
\begin{aligned}
LTEF(t_8) - ETBF(t_8) &= \infty - (T_0 + 13) \\
&= \infty > FIRE_{dur}(t_8) = 20
\end{aligned}
$$

Therefore t_8 is a SST.

11.5.2 Backward Computation

As shown in Fig. 11.7, we highlight those transitions whose $LTEF(t_i)$ are denoted as infinity because the default value of TC_{max} is infinity. In this subsection we use backward computation to refine infinity to a meaningful upper bound for each transition. The backward computation is based on the temporal order of a transition's firing within a firing sequence. If we can find a transition t_j whose $LTEF(t_j)$ is bounded, then we can find an upper bound of $LTEF(t_j)$ for all the transitions that fired before t_j. The back synthesis is conducted by computing the $LTEF(t_j)$ for each transition t_j, using the equation:

$$
LTEF(t_j) = \min\{LTEF(t_k) - FIRE_{dur}(t_k) - TC_{min}(p_k)\}
$$
where $p_k \in OP(t_j)$ and $p_k \in IP(t_k)$

The computation of $LTEF(t_j)$ for each transition t_j with infinity shown in Fig. 11.7, is as follows, and the result is highlighted in Fig. 11.8.

$$
\begin{aligned}
LTEF(t_5) &= LTEF(t_6) - FIRE_{dur}(t_6) - TC_{min}(p_6) \\
&= (T_0 + 65) - 10 - 0 \\
&= T_0 + 55 \\
LTEF(t_3) &= LTEF(t_5) - FIRE_{dur}(t_5) - TC_{min}(p_4) \\
&= (T_0 + 55) - 15 - 0 \\
&= T_0 + 40 \\
LTEF(t_4) &= LTEF(t_5) - FIRE_{dur}(t_5) - TC_{min}(p_5)
\end{aligned}
$$

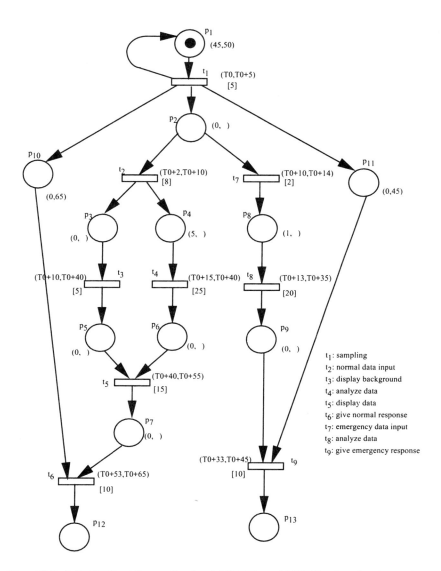

Fig. 11.8 A TCPN with synthesized ETBF and LTEF after backward computation.

$$
\begin{aligned}
&= (T_0 + 55) - 15 - 0 \\
&= T_0 + 40 \\
LTEF(t_2) &= \min\{[LTEF(t_3) - FIRE_{dur}(t_3) - TC_{min}(p_2)], \\
&\quad [LTEF(t_4) - FIRE_{dur}(t_4) - TC_{min}(p_3)\} \\
&= \min\{(T_0 + 40 - 5 - 0), (T_0 + 40 - 25 - 5)\} \\
&= T_0 + 10 \\
LTEF(t_8) &= LTEF(t_9) - FIRE_{dur}(t_9) - TC_{min}(p_8) \\
&= (T_0 + 45) - 10 - 0 \\
&= T_0 + 35 \\
LTEF(t_7) &= LTEF(t_8) - FIRE_{dur}(t_8) - TC_{min}(p_7) \\
&= (T_0 + 35) - 20 - 1 \\
&= T_0 + 14
\end{aligned}
$$

Combining forward and backward computation provides designers of real-time systems with a more meaningful timing specification.

11.6 Summary

In this chapter we introduced timing constraint Petri nets (TCPNs) and described how to use them to model a real-time system specification and determine if the specification is scheduleable with respect to imposed timing constraints. TCPNs are inspired by time and timed Petri nets. TCPNs extend Petri nets by adding durational timing constraints and minimum and maximum timing constraints pairs to places and transitions. The strength of TCPNs over other time-related Petri nets is in the modeling and analysis of conflict structures. We have shown how TCPNs can model maximum and minimum timing constraints in a real-time systems through formal definitions and examples. In terms of analysis, we normally can perform a functional or a timing analysis on a real-time software specification. A functional analysis asserts the correctness of system's functionality. However, it is more important for a real-time system to assert the correctness of its timing behavior. In this chapter we focused on the schedulability analysis of real-time systems using TCPNs. Schedulability analysis is conducted in three steps: specification modeling, reachability simulation, and Timing analysis. In the specification modeling step, we set up a real-time system by transforming its system specification and its imposed timing constraints into a TCPN. We then simulate the reachability of the TCPN to verify if a marking is reachable from an initial marking. It is important to know that a reachable marking in Petri nets is not necessarily reachable in TCPNs because of the imposed timing constraints. In the timing analysis step, a reachable marking found in the reachability simulation step is analyzed to verify whether a marking is reachable with the timing constraints. The presented schedulability analysis always computes the worst case of the scheduling of a system specification at the imposed timing constraints. Once all transitions in a firing sequence of a final marking in a TCPN are verified to be strongly scheduleable with respect to the initial marking, we say such a specification is asserted with respect to its timing requirements. Throughout the example of modeling and analyzing a real-time control system, we also successfully demonstrated that it is possible to perform the specification and the scheduling analysis using the same representation, the TCPNs.

Exercises

1. List the major differences between time Petri nets and timed Petri nets.

2. List the major differences between time Petri nets and timing constraint Petri nets.

3. Describe transition time pairs and place time pairs. Are two isomorphic nets still isomorphic if they were imposed with the same timing constraints but represented by transition and time pairs, respectively?

4. Describe weakly and strongly firing modes.

5. Is the reachability problems of TCPNs the same as the reachability problems of PNs? If not, describe the differences.

6. What are relative time and absolute time, and how are they represented in TCPNs?

7. What is a conflict structure? How do TCPNs model a conflict structure with timing constraints?

8. As far as the complexity of reachability problem is concerned, will TCPNs have a higher complexity than Petri nets? Why?

9. What are weakly and strongly fireable transitions?

10. What are weakly and strongly schedulable transitions?

11. Is a fireable transition in Petri nets always fireable in TCPNs?

12. What kinds of timing information should be collected in order to perform run-time schedulability analysis?

13. Fig. 11.3 shows a mutual exclusion example. Show how a third device could be added that also uses place p_1 to access the resource.

14. To make t_2 in Fig. 11.5 a *WST*, the timing constraint was relaxed. What allow us to relax the timing constraint?

15. Explain the difference between WST, WFT, SST and SFT.

16. Explain how synthesis with TCPNs is useful.

Bibliography

[1] M. Accetta, R. Baron, D. Golub, R. Rashid, A. Tevanian, and M. Young. Mach: A new kernel foundation for UNIX development. In *Proc. of Summer 1986 USENIX Conf.*, 1986.

[2] M. Ahuja, T. Carlson, A. Gahlot, and D. Shands. Timestamping events for interferring affects relation and potential casualty. In *Proc. of IEEE 15 Int.'l Computer Software and Applications Conf.*, Tokyo, pp. 606–611, September 1991.

[3] M. Alford. SREM at the age of eight. *IEEE Computer*, 18(4):36–46, April 1985.

[4] R. Alur, C. Courcoubetis, and D. L. Dill. Model checking for real-time systems. In *Proc. of IEEE 5th Symp. on Logic in Computer Science*, 1990.

[5] R. Alur and D. L. Dill. Automata for modeling real-time systems. In M. S. Paterson, ed., *ICALP '90, Automata, Languages and Programming, LNCS 443*, pp. 322–335. Springer-Verlag, New York, 1990.

[6] R. Alur and D. L. Dill. The theory of timed automata. In J. W. de Bakker, C. Huizing, W. P. de Roever, and G. Rozenberg, eds., *Real-Time: Theory in Practice, Proc. of REX Workshop, LNCS 600*, pp. 74–106. Springer-Verlag, Berlin, 1991.

[7] R. Alur and T. Henzinger. Real-time logic: Complexity and expressiveness. In *Proc. of IEEE 5th Symp. on Logic in Computer Science*, 1990.

[8] R. Alur and T. Henzinger. Logic and models of real-time: A survey. In J. W. de Bakker, C. Huizing, W. P. de Roever, and G. Rozenberg, eds., *Real-Time: Theory in Practice, Proc. of REX Workshop, LNCS 600*, pp. 74–106. Springer-Verlag, Berlin, 1991.

[9] R. Alur, T. Henzinger, and P.-H. Ho. Automatic symbolic verification of embedded systems. In *Proc. of IEEE 14th Real-Time System Symp.*, 1993.

[10] A. L. Ambler and M. M. Burnett. Influence of visual technology on the evolution of language environments. *IEEE Computer*, pp. 9–22, October 1989.

[11] G. R. Andrews. Paradigms for process interaction in distributed programs. *ACM Computing Surveys*, 23(1):49–90, March 1991.

[12] M. Annaratone et al. The Warp machine: Architecture, implementation and performance. *IEEE Trans. on Computers*, C-36(12):1523–1538, December 1987.

[13] B. Appelbe. Software tools for visualization of performance. In M. Simmons and R. Koskela, eds., *Performance Instrumentation and Visualization*, pp. 147–155. Addison-Wesley, Reading, MA, 1990.

[14] Z. Aral and I. Gertner. High-level debugging in parasight. In *Proc. of ACM Workshop on Parallel and Distributed Debugging*, Madison, WI, pp. 151–161, May 1988.

[15] Z. Aral and I. Gertner. Non-intrusive and interactive profiling in parasight. In *Proc. of ACM/SIGPLAN on Parallel Programming: Experience with Applications, Language and Systems*, New Haven, CT, pp. 21–30, July 1988.

[16] Z. Aral, I. Gertner, and G. Schaffer. Debugging primitives for multiprocessors. In *Proc. of 3d Int.'l Conf. on Architectural Support for Programming Languages and Operating Systems*, Boston, pp. 87–93, April 1989.

[17] Y. Artsy, H.-Y. Chang, and R. Finkel. Interprocess communication in Charlotte. *IEEE Software*, 4(1):22–28, January 1987.

[18] K. Arvind. A new probabilistic algorithm for clock synchronization. In *Proc. of IEEE 10th Real-Time Systems Symp.*, Santa Monica, CA, pp. 330–339, December 1989.

[19] J. M. Atlee and J. Gannon. State-based model checking of event-driven system requirements. *IEEE Trans. on Software Engineering*, 19(1):24–40, January 1993.

[20] B. Auernheimer and R. A. Kemmerer. RT-ASLAN: A specification language for real-time systems. *IEEE Trans. on Software Engineering*, SE-12(9):879–889, September 1986.

[21] G. S. Avrunin, L. K. Dillon, and J. C. Wileden. Experiments with automated constrained expression analysis of concurrent software systems. In *Proc. of ACM SIGSOFT 3d Symp. on Software Testing, Analysis, and Verification*, Key West, FL, pp. 124–13, December 1989.

[22] J. M. Ayache, J. P. Courtiat, and M. Diaz. REBUS, a fault-tolerant distributed system for industrial real-time control. *IEEE Trans. on Computers*, C-31(7):637–647, July 1982.

[23] D. F. Bacon and S. C. Goldstein. Hardware-assisted replay of muti-processor programs. In *Proc. of ACM/ONR Workshop on Parallel and Distributed Debugging*, Santa Cruz, CA, pp. 194–206, May 1991.

[24] J. C. M. Baeten and J. A. Bergstra. The state operator in real-time process algebra. In J. W. de Bakker, C. Huizing, W. P. de Roever, and G. Rozenberg, eds., *Real-Time: Theory in Practice, Proc. of REX Workship, LNCS 600*, pp. 107–123. Springer-Verlag, Berlin, 1991.

[25] F. Baiardi, N. De Francesco, and G. Vaglini. Development of a debugger for a concurrent language. *IEEE Trans. on Software Engineering*, SE-12(4):547–553, April 1986.

[26] M. L. Bailey, D. Socha, and D. Notkin. Debugging parallel programs using graphical views. *ICPP*, 2:46–49, 1988.

[27] S. Balaji et al. S-Nets: A Petri net based model for performance evaluation of real-time scheduling algorithms. *J. Parallel Distrib. Comput.*, 15:225–235, 1992.

[28] R. Baron, R. Rashid, E. Siegel, A. Tevanian, and M. Young. Mach-1: An operating environment for large-scale multiprocessor applications. *IEEE Software*, 2(7):65–67, July 1985.

[29] F. Baskett, J. H. Howard, and J. T. Montague. Task communication in Demos. In *Proc. of 6th ACM Symp. Op. Syst. Princ.*, ACM Press, New York, pp. 23–31, November 1977.

[30] P. Bates. Debugging heterogeneous distributed systems using event-based models of behavior. In *Proc. of ACM Workshop on Parallel and Distributed Debugging*, Madison, WI, pp. 11–22, May 1988.

[31] P. Bates. Distributed debugging tools for heterogeneous distributed systems. In *Proc. of 8th Int.'l Conf. on Distributed Computing Systems*, pp. 308–317, June 1988.

[32] P. Bates and J. Wileden. High level debugging of distributed systems: The behavioral abstraction. *J. Systs. Software*, 3:255–264, April 1983.

[33] M. Beaven, B. Elmore, D. C. Marinescu, and R. Stansifer. VERT – verification of real-time programs. In *Proc. of IEEE 15th Int.'l Computer Software and Applications Conf.*, Tokyo, pp. 618–625, September 1991.

[34] A. Beguelin, J. Dongarra, A. Geist, and V. Sundream. Visualization and debugging in heterogeneous environment. *IEEE Computer*, 26(6):88–95, June 1993.

[35] B. Beizer. *Software Testing Techniques*. Van Nostrand, Reinhold, Nwe York, 1990.

[36] A. Benveniste and P. LeGuernic. Hybrid dynmical systems theory and the Signal language. *Trans. Auto. Control*, 1990.

[37] G. Berry and L. Cosserat. The Esterel synchronous programming language and its mathematical semantics. In *Proc. of CMU Seminar on Concurrency, LNCS 197*. Springer-Verlag, 1985.

[38] O. Berry and D. Jefferson. Critical path analysis of distributed simulation. In *Proc. of Conf. on Distributed Simulation*, San Diego, CA, pp. 57–66, January 1985.

[39] D. Berstein, A. Bolmarcich, and K. So. Performance visualization of parallel programs on shared memory multiprocessor system. *ICPP*, pp. II.1–II.10, 1989.

[40] B. Berthomieu and M. Diaz. Modeling and verification of time dependent systems using Time Petri nets. *IEEE Trans. on Software Engineering*, SE-17(3):259–273, March 1991.

[41] D. Bhatt, A. Ghonami, and R. Ramanujan. An instrumented testbed for real-time distributed systems development. In *Proc. of IEEE 8th Real-Time Systems Symp.*, San Jose, CA, pp. 241–250, December 1987.

[42] Y. D. Bi and J. J.-P. Tsai. Integrating data collection, debugging, and visualization. In *Proc. of 7th Int.'l Conf. on Advanced Science and Technology*, Argonne, IL, pp. 267–279, March 1991.

[43] J. Billington, G. R. Wheeler, and M. C. Wilbur-Ham. PROTEAN: A high-level Petri net tool for the specification and verification of communication protocols. *IEEE Trans. on Software Engineering*, SE-14(3):301–316, March 1988.

[44] A. Black. Supporting distributed applications: Experience with Eden. In *Proc. of 10th ACM Symp. Operating Systems Principles*, pp. 181–193, December 1985.

[45] D. Black. Scheduling support for concurrency and parallelism in the Mach operating system. *IEEE Computer*, 23(5):35–43, May 1990.

[46] T. Bolognesi and F. Lucidi. From timed petri nets to timed LOTOS. In L. Logrippo, R. Probert, and H. Ural, eds., *10th IFIP Symp. on Protocol Specification, Testing, and Verification*, North-Holland, Amsterdam, pp. 377–406. 1990.

[47] T. Bolognesi and F. Lucidi. Timed process algebras with urgent interactions and a unique powerful binary operator. In J. W. de Bakker, C. Huizing, W. P. de Roever, and G. Rozenberg, eds., *Real-Time: Theory in Practice, Proc. of REX Workship, LNCS 600*, pp. 124–148. Springer-Verlag, Berlin, 1991.

[48] F. Boussinot and R. de Simone. The Esterel language. *Proc. of IEEE*, 79:1293–1304, September 1991.

[49] J. Boykin and A. Langerman. Mach/4.3 BSD: A conservative approach to parallelization. *Computer Systems*, 1990.

[50] W. C. Brantley, K. P. McAuliffe, and T. A. Ngo. RP3 performance monitoring hardware. In M. Simmons, R. Koskela, and I. Bucher, eds., *Instrumentation for Future Parallel Computing Systems*, pp. 35–45. Addison-Wesley, Reading, MA, 1989.

[51] M. H. Brown. Exploring algorithms using Balsa-II. *IEEE Computer*, 21(5):14–36, May 1988.

[52] M. H. Brown and R. Sedgewick. Techniques for algorithm animation. *IEEE Software*, 2(1):28–39, January 1985.

[53] T. F. Brown et al. The feature interaction problem in telecommunications systems. In *7th Int.'l Conf. on Software Engineering for Telecommunication Switching Systems*, Bournemouth, U.K., pp. 59–66, July 1989.

[54] B. Bruegge. A portable platform for distributed event environments. In *Proc. of ACM/ONR Workshop on Parallel and Distributed Debugging*, Santa Cruz, CA, pp. 184–193, May 1991.

[55] B. Bruegge and T. Gross. A program debugger for a systolic array. In *Proc. of ACM Workshop on Parallel and Distributed Debugging*, Madison, WI, pp. 174–182, May 1988.

[56] G. Bruno and G. Marchetto. Process-translatable Petri nets for the rapid prototyping of process control systems. *IEEE Trans. on Software Engineering*, SE-12(2):346–357, February 1986.

[57] F. J. Burkowski, G. V. Cormack, and G. D. P. Dueck. Architectural support for synchronous task communication. In *Proc. of 3d Int.'l Conf. on Architectural Support for Programming Languages and Operating Systems*, Boston, pp. 40–53, April 1989.

[58] A. Burns and A. Wellings. *Real-Time Systems and Their Programming Languages*. Addison-Wesley, Reading, MA, 1990.

[59] R. W. Butler and G. B. Finelli. The infeasiblity of quantifying the reliability of life-critical real-time software. *IEEE Trans. on Software Engineering*, 19(1):3–12, January 1993.

[60] M. Cain. Managing run-time interactions between call-processing features. *IEEE Communication Magazine*, pp. 44–50, February 1992.

[61] D. Callahan, K. Kennedy, and J. Subholk. Analysis of event synchronization in a parallel programming tool. In *Proc. of 2d ACM SIGPLAN Symp. on Principles and Practice of Parallel Programming*, Seattle, WA, pp. 21–30, March 1990.

[62] E. J. Cameron et al. Interaction benchmark for IN and Beyond. *IEEE Communication Magazine*, pp. 64–69, March 1993.

[63] E. J. Cameron and Y.-J. Lin. A real-time transition model for analysis behavioral compatibility of telecommunications services. In *Proc. of ACM/SIGSOFT '91 Conf. on Software for Critical Systems*, New Orleans, pp. 101–111, December 1991.

[64] E. J. Cameron and H. Velthuijsen. Feature interactions in telecommunications systems. *IEEE Communication Magazine*, pp. 18–23, August 1993.

[65] E. J. Camerson and D. M. Cohen. The IC* system for debugging parallel programs via interactive monitoring and control. In *Proc. of ACM Workshop on Parallel and Distributed Debugging*, Madison, WI, pp. 267–270, May 1988.

[66] T. A. Cargill and B. N. Locanthi. Cheap hardware support for software debugging and profiling. In *Proc. of 2d Int.'l Conf. on Architectural Support for Programming Languages and Operating Systems*, Palo Alto, CA, pp. 82–83, October 1987.

[67] R. H. Carver and K. C. Tai. Reproducible testing of concurrent programs based on shared variables. In *Proc. of 6th Int.'l Conf. on Distributed Computing Systems*, Washington, DC, pp. 428–433, October 1986.

[68] P. Caspi, N. Halbwachs, D. Pilaud, and J. Plaice. LUSTRE: A declarative language for programming synchronous systems. In *Proc. of 14th Symp. of Principles of Programming Languages*, January 1987.

[69] G. A. Champine, D. E. Geer Jr., and W. N. Ruh. Project Athena as a distributed computer system. *IEEE Computer*, 23(9):40–51, September 1990.

[70] K. M. Chandy and L. Lamport. Distributed snapshots: Determining global states of distributed systems. *ACM Trans. on Computing Systems*, 3(1):63–75, February 1985.

[71] K. M. Chandy, J. Misra, and L. M. Hass. Distributed deadlock detection. *ACM Trans. on Computing Systems*, pp. 144–156, May 1983.

[72] H. Y. Chen, J. J.-P. Tsai, and Y. Bi. An event-based real-time logic for the specification and analysis of real-time systems. *Int.'l J. Artificial Intelligence*, 2(1):71–91, January 1993.

[73] Y. Chen, W. T. Tsai, and D. Chao. Dependency analysis—a Petri net based technique for synthesizing large concurrent systems. *IEEE Trans. on Parallel and Distributed System*, 4(4):414–426, April 1993.

[74] D. R. Cheriton. The V kernel: A software base for distributed systems. *IEEE Software*, 1(2):19–24, April 1984.

[75] D. R. Cheriton. The V distributed system. *Comm. of ACM*, 31(3):314–333, March 1988.

[76] W. H. Cheung, J. P. Black, and E. Manning. A framework for distributed debugging. *IEEE Software*, pp. 106–115, January 1990.

[77] R. S. Chin and S. T. Chanson. Distributed object-based programming systems. *ACM Computing Surveys*, 23(1):91–124, March 1991.

[78] S. E. Chodrow, F. Jahanian, and M. Donner. Run-time monitoring of real-time systems. In *Proc. of IEEE 12th Real-Time Systems Symp.*, San Antonio, TX, pp. 74–83, December 1991.

[79] J. D. Choi and S. L. Min. Race frontier: Reproducing data race in parallel-program debugging. In *Proc. of 3d ACM SIGPLAN Symp. on Principles and Practice of Parallel Programming*, Williamsburg, VA, pp. 145–154, April 1991.

[80] J. D. Choi and J. M. Stone. Balancing run time and replay costs in a trace-and-replay system. In *Proc. of ACM/ONR Workshop on Parallel and Distributed Debugging*, Santa Cruz, CA, pp. 26–34, May 1991.

[81] A. L. Choudhary et al. A modified priority-based probe algorithm for distributed deadlock detection and resolution. *IEEE Trans. on Software Engineering*, 15(1):10–17, January 1989.

[82] W. W. Chu, C.-M. Sit, and K. K. Leung. Task response time for real-time distributed systems with resource contentions. *IEEE Trans. on Software Engineering*, 17(10):1077–1092, October 1991.

[83] I. Cidon et al. Local distributed deadlock detection by cycle detection and clustering. *IEEE Trans. on Software Engineering*, 13(1):3–14, January 1987.

[84] E. M. Clarke, E. A. Emerson, and A. P. Sistla. Automatic verification of finite state concurrent systems using temporal logic. *ACM Trans. on Programming Language Systems*, 8(2):244–263, April 1986.

[85] L. A. Clarke, D. J. Richardson, and S. J. Zeil. TEAM: A support environment for testing, evaluation, and analysis. In *Proc. of ACM SIG-SOFT/SIGPLAN Software Engineering Sympo. on Practical Software Development Environments*, Boston, pp. 153–162, November 1988.

[86] B. Cogswell and Z. Segall. MACS: A predicatable architecture for real-time systems. In *Proc. of IEEE 12th Real-Time Systems Symp.*, San Antonio, TX, pp. 296–305, December 1991.

[87] S. Cohen and D. Lehmann. Dynamic systems and their distributed termination. In *Proc. of 2d ACM Symp. on Distributed Computing*, pp. 29–33, 1982.

[88] R. Cohn. Source level debugging of automatically parallelized code. In *Proc. of ACM/ONR Workshop on Parallel and Distributed Debugging*, Santa Cruz, CA, pp. 132–143, May 1991.

[89] M. Consens, A. Mendelzon, and A. Ryman. Visualizing and querying software structures. In *IEEE Int.'l Conf. on Software Engineeing*, Melbourne, Australia, pp. 138–156, May 1992.

[90] R. Cooper. Pilgram: A debugger for distributed systems. In *Proc. of 7th Int.'l Conf. on Distributed Computing Systems*, pp. 458–465, 1987.

[91] P. Corsini and C. A. Reete. Multibug: Interactive debugging in distributed systems. *IEEE Micro*, 6(3):26–33, June 1986.

[92] J. P. Courtiat and M. Diaz. Time in state-based formal description techniques for distributed systems. In J. W. de Bakker, C. Huizing, W. P. de Roever, and G. Rozenberg, eds., *Real-Time: Theory in Practice, Proc. of REX Workshop, LNCS 600*, pp. 149–175. Springer-Verlag, Berlin, 1991.

[93] F. Cristian. Understanding fault tolerant distributed systems. *Comm. of ACM*, 34(2):56–78, February 1991.

[94] R. Curtis and L. Wittie. BugNet: A debugging system for parallel programming environments. In *Proc. of 3d Int.'l Conf. on Distributed Computing Systems*, Miami, FL, pp. 394–399, October 1982.

[95] R. Curtis and L. Wittie. Time management for debugging distributed systems. In *Proc. of 5th Int.'l Conf. on Distributed Computing Systems*, Denver, CO, pp. 545–550, May 1985.

[96] B. Dasarathy. Timing constraints of real-time systems: Constructs for expressing them, methods of validating them. *IEEE Trans. on Software Engineering*, SE-11(1):80–86, January 1985.

[97] M. Degl'Innocenti, G. L. Ferrari, G. Pacini, and F. Turini. RSF: A formalism for executable requirement specifications. *IEEE Trans. on Software Engineering*, SE-16(11):1235–1246, November 1990.

[98] R. A. DeMillo et al. *Software Testing and Evaluation*. Benjamin Cummings, Menlo Park, CA, 1987.

[99] R. A. DeMillo and F. G. Sayward. Program mutation: a new approach to program testing. In *Software Testing 2, Infotech International*, Berkshire, England, pp. 108–127, 1979.

[100] D. J. Dewitt, R. Finkel, and M. Solomon. The Crystal multicomputer: Design and implementation experience. *IEEE Trans. on Software Engineering*, SE-13(8):953–966, August 1987.

[101] E. W. Dijkstra. Guarded commands, nondeterminacy and formal derivation of programs. *Comm. ACM*, 18(8):453–457, August 1975.

[102] L. Dillon. Symbolic execution-based verification of ada tasking programs. In *Proc. of 3d Int.'l IEEE Conf. on Ada Applications and Environments*, pp. 3–13, May 1988.

[103] L. K. Dillon, G. Kutty, L. E. Moser, P. M. Melliar-Smith, and Y. S. Ramakrishna. Graphical specification for concurrent software systems. In *IEEE Int.'l Conf. on Software Engineering*, Melbourne, Australia, pp. 213–224, May 1992.

[104] A. Dinning and E. Schonberg. An empirical comparison of monitoring algorithms for access anomaly detection. In *Proc. of 2d ACM SIGPLAN Symp. on Principles and Practice of Parallel Programming*, Seattle, WA, pp. 1–10, March 1990.

[105] P. S. Dodd and C. V. Ravishankar. Monitoring and debugging distributed real-time programs. *Software-Practice and Experience*, 22(10):863–877, October 1992.

[106] F. Douglis, J. K. Ousterhout, M. F. Kaashoek, and A. S. Tanenbaum. A comparison of two distributed systems: Amoeba and Sprite. *Computing Systems*, 1991.

[107] T. Duncan and W. H. Huen. Software structure of No. 5 ESS–A distributed telephone switching system. *IEEE Trans. on Communications*, COM-30(6):1379–1385, June 1982.

[108] M. Eisenstada et al. Visual knowledge engineering. *IEEE Trans. on Software Engineering*, SE-16(10):1164–1177, October 1990.

[109] A. K. Elmagarmid, N. Soundararajan, and M. T. Liu. A distributed deadlock detection and resolution algorithms and its correctness. *IEEE Trans. on Software Engineering*, 14(10):1443–1452, October 1988.

[110] I. J. P. Elshoff. A distributed debugger for Amoeba. In *Proc. of ACM Workshop on Parallel and Distributed Debugging*, Madison, WI, pp. 1–10, May 1988.

[111] E. A. Emerson. Temporal and modal logic. In J. van Leeuwen, ed., *Handbook of Theoretical Computer Science*, vol. B, pp. 995–1072. Elsevier Science, North Holland, 1990.

[112] E. A. Emerson and E. M. Clarke. Using branching time logic to synthesize synchronization skeletons. *Science of Computer Programming*, 1982.

[113] E. A. Emerson, A. K. Mok, S. P. Sistla, and J. Srinivasan. Quantitative temporal reasoning. *Real-Time Systs. J.*, 4(4):331–352, April 1992.

[114] R. Fairley. *Software Engineering Concepts*. McGraw-Hill, New York, 1985.

[115] S. R. Faulk and D. L. Parnas. On synchronization in hard-real-time systems. *Comm. of ACM*, 31, March 1988.

[116] A. A. Faustini and E. B. Lewis. Toward a real-time dataflow language. *IEEE Software*, 3(1):29–35, January 1986.

[117] M. Felder, D. Mandrioli, and A. Morzenti. Proving properties of real-time systems through logical specifications and Petri net models. *IEEE Trans. on Software Engineering*, 20(2):127–141, February 1994.

[118] S. I. Feldman and C. B. Brown. IGOR: A system for program debugging via reversible execution. In *Proc. ACM SIGPLAN and SIGOPS Workshop on Paralleland Distributed Debugging*, Madison, WI, pp. 112–123, May 1988.

[119] D. Ferrari. Consideration on the insularity of performance perturbation. *IEEE Trans. on Software Engineering*, SE-16(6):6787–683, June 1986.

[120] C. Fidge. Logical time in distributed computing systems. *IEEE Computer*, 24(8):28–33, August 1991.

[121] C. J. Fidge. Partial orders for parallel debugging. In *Proc. of ACM Workshop on Parallel and Distributed Debugging*, Madison, WI, pp. 183–194, May 1988.

[122] S. A. Fineberg, T. L. Casavant, T. Schwederski, and H. J. Siegel. Nondeterministic instruction time experiment on the PASM system prototype. In *Proc. of 1988 Int.'l Conf. on Parallel Processing*, University Park, pp. 444–451, August 1988.

[123] F. W. Fong and S. M. Shatz. Derivation of Petri net models of ada tasking constructs involving time. In *Proc. of IEEE 13th Int.'l Computer Software and Applications Conf.*, Orlando, FL, pp. 24–31, September 1989.

[124] A. Forin. Debugging of heterogeneous parallel systems. In *Proc. of ACM Workshop on Parallel and Distributed Debugging*, Madison, WI, pp. 130–140, May 1988.

[125] R. J. Fowler, T. J. Leblanc, and J. M. Mellor-Crummey. An integrated approach to parallel program debugging performanceanalysis on large-scale multiprocessors. In *Proc. of SIGPLAN/SIGOPS Workshop on Parallel and Distributed Debugging*, Madison, WI, pp. 163–173, May 1988.

[126] M. K. Franklin and A. Gabrielian. A transformational method for verifying safety properties in real-time systems. In *Proc. of IEEE 10th Real-Time Systems Symp.*, Santa Monica, CA, pp. 112–123, December 1989.

[127] D. Gabbay, A. Pnueli, S. Shelah, and J. Stavi. On the temporal analysis of fairness. In *Proc. of 7th Annual Symp. on Principles of Programming Languages*, 1980.

[128] A. Gabrielian and M. K. Franklin. State-based specification of complex real-time systems. In *Proc. of 9th Real-Time Systems Symp.*, pp. 2–11, 1988.

[129] A. Gabrielian and M. K. Franklin. Multilevel specification of real-time systems. *Comm. of ACM*, 34(5):51–60, May 1991.

[130] H. Garcia-Molina, F. Germano, Jr., and W. H. Kohler. Debugging a distributed computing system. *IEEE Trans. on Software Engineering*, SE-10(2):210–219, March 1984.

[131] R. Gerber and I. Lee. Communicating shared resources: A model for distributed real-time systems. In *Proc. of IEEE 10th Real-Time Systems Symp.*, Santa Monica, CA, pp. 68–78, December 1989.

[132] R. Gerber and I. Lee. A proof system for communicating shared resources. In *Proc. of IEEE 11th Real-Time Systems Symp.*, Lake Buena Vista, FL, pp. 288–299, December 1990.

[133] R. Gerber and I. Lee. A layered approach to automating the verification of real-time systems. *IEEE Trans. on Software Engineering*, 18(9):768–784, September 1992.

[134] S. L. Gerhart. A broad spectrum toolset for upstream testing, verification, and analysis. In *Proc. of ACM SIGSOFT 2d Workshop on Software Testing, Verification, and Analysis*, Banff, Canada, pp. 4–12, July 1988.

[135] S. M. German. Monitoring for deadlock and blocking in Ada tasking. *IEEE Trans. on Software Engineering*, SE-10(6):764–777, November 1984.

[136] C. Ghezzi, D. Mandrioli, S. Morasca, and M. Pezze. A unified high-level Petri net formalism for time-critical systems. *IEEE Trans. on Software Engineering*, SE-17(2):106–171, February 1991.

[137] C. Ghezzi, D. Mandrioli, and A. Morzenti. TRIO, a logic language for executable specification of real-time systems and software. *J. Syst. and Software*, 12(2):107–123, May 1990.

[138] A. Goldberg et al. Restoring consistent global states of distributed computations. In *Proc. of ACM/ONR Workshop on Parallel and Distributed Debugging*, Santa Cruz, CA, pp. 144–154, May 1991.

[139] G. S. Goldszmidt, S. Katz, and S. A. Yemini. High level language debugging for concurrent programs. *ACM Trans. on Computer Systems*, 8(4), November 1990.

[140] A. J. Gordon and R. A. Finkel. TAP: A tool to find timing errors in distributed programs. In *Proc. of Workshop on Software Testing*, Banff, Canada, pp. 154–163, July 1986.

[141] A. J. Gordon and R. A. Finkel. Handling timing errors in distributed programs. *IEEE Trans. on Software Engineering*, SE-14(10):1525–1535, October 1988.

[142] M. M. Gorlick. The flight recorder: An architectural aid for system monitoring. In *Proc. of ACM/ONR Workshop on Parallel and Distributed Debugging*, Santa Cruz, CA, pp. 175–183, May 1991.

[143] M. Graf. A visual environment for the design of distributed systems. In *Proc. of 1987 Workshop on Visual Languages*, pp. 330–344, 1987.

[144] J. Griffin. Parallel debugging system user's guide. In *Tech. Report, Los Alamos National Laboratory,* Los Alamos, NM, 1988.

[145] V. J. Griswold. Core algorithms for autonomous monitoring of distributed systems. In *Proc. of ACM/ONR Workshop on Parallel and Distributed Debugging,* Santa Cruz, CA, pp. 36–45, May 1991.

[146] N. K. Gupta and R. E. Seviora. An expert system approach to real-time system debugging. In *Proc. of 1st Conf. on Artificial Intelligence Applications,* Denver, CO, pp. 336–343, 1984.

[147] N. K. Gupta and R. E. Seviora. Knowledge based message trace analyzer. In *Proc. of Real-time System Symp.,* Los Alamitos, CA, pp. 39–48, December 1984.

[148] R. Gusella and S. Zatti. The accuracy of the clock synchronization achieved by TEMPO in Berkeley UNIX 4.3BSD. *IEEE Trans. on Software Engineering,* SE-15(7):847–853, July 1989.

[149] D. Haban. DTM—A method for testing distributed systems. In *Proc. of 6th Symp. on Reliability in Distributed Software and Database Systems,* Williamsburg, VA, pp. 66–73, 1987.

[150] D. Haban and K. G. Shin. Application of real-time monitoring to scheduling tasks with random execution times. *IEEE Trans. on Software Engineering,* SE-16(12):1374–1389, December 1990.

[151] D. Haban and W. Weigel. Global events and global breakpoints in distributed systems. In *Proc. of 21nd Hawaii Int.'l Conf. on System Sciences,* pp. 166–175, 1988.

[152] D. Haban and D. Wybranietz. A hybrid monitor for behavior and performance analysis of distributed systems. *IEEE Trans. on Software Engineering,* SE-16(2):197–211, February 1990.

[153] W. A. Halang. Real-time systems: Another perspective. *Systs. Software,* 18(1):101–108, April 1992.

[154] N. Halbwachs, P. Caspi, P. Raymond, and D. Pilaud. The synchronous programming language LUSTRE. *Proc. of IEEE,* 79:1305–1320, September 1991.

[155] N. Halbwachs, F. Lagnier, and C. Ratel. Programming and verifying real-time systems by means of the synchronous data-flow language LUSTRE. *IEEE Trans. on Software Engineering,* SE-18(9):785–793, September 1992.

[156] N. Halbwachs and F. Rocheteau. Implementing reactive programs on circuits: A hardware implementation of LUSTRE. In J. W. de Bakker, C. Huizing, W. P. de Roever, and G. Rozenberg, eds., *Real-Time: Theory in Practice, Proc. of REX Workship, LNCS 600*, pp. 195–208. Springer-Verlag, Berlin, 1991.

[157] H. Hansson and B. Jonsson. A framework for reasoning about time and reliability. In *Proc. of IEEE 10th Real-Time Systems Symp.*, Santa Monica, CA, pp. 102–111, December 1989.

[158] D. Harel. Statecharts: A visual formalism for complex system. *Science of Computer Porgramming*, 1987.

[159] D. Harel, H. Lachover, A. Naamad, A. Pnueli, M. Poloti, R. Sherman, A. Shtull-Trauring, and M. Trakhtenbrot. STATEMATE: A working environment for the development of complex reactive systems. *IEEE Trans. on Software Engineering*, SE-16(4):403–414, April 1990.

[160] D. Harel, O. Lichtenstein, and A. Pnueli. Explicit clock temporal logic. In *Proc. of 5th Annual IEEE Symp. on Logic in Computer Science*, Philadelphia, pp. 401–413, June 1990.

[161] M. Heath and J. Ethridge. Visualizing the performance of parallel programs. *IEEE Software*, 8(5):29–39, September 1991.

[162] D. Helmbold and D. Luckham. Debugging Ada tasking programs. *IEEE Software*, 2(3):47–57, March 1985.

[163] T. A. Henzinger, Z. Manna, and A. Pnueli. Timed transition systems. In J. W. de Bakker, C. Huizing, W. P. de Roever, and G. Rozenberg, eds., *Real-Time: Theory in Practice, Proc. of REX Workship, LNCS 600*, pp. 226–251. Springer-Verlag, Berlin, 1991.

[164] U. Herchsen, R. Klar, W. Kleinoder, and F. Kneibl. Measuring simultaneous events in a multiprocessor systems. *Performance Evaluation Review*, 11(4):77–88, April 1982.

[165] C. A. R. Hoare. Communicating sequential processes. *Comm. of ACM*, 21(8):666–677, August 1978.

[166] C. A. R. Hoare. *Communicating Sequential Processes*. Prentice-Hall, Englewood Cliffs, NJ, 1985.

[167] M. A. Holliday and M. K. Vernon. A generalized timed Petri net model for performance analysis. *IEEE Trans. on Software Engineering*, SE-13(12):1297–1310, December 1987.

[168] J. K. Hollingsworth, R. B. Irvin, and B. P. Miller. The integration of application and system based metrics in a parallel program performance tool. In *Proc. of 3d ACM SIGPLAN Symp. on Principles and Practice of Parallel Programming*, Williamsburg, VA, pp. 189–200, April 1991.

[169] C. J. Hou and K. G. Shin. Allocation of periodic task modules with precedence and deadline constraints in distributed real-time systems. In *Proc. of IEEE 13th Real-Time Systems Symp.*, Phoenix, AZ, pp. 146–155, December 1992.

[170] A. A. Hough and J. E. Cuny. Perspective views: A technique for enhancing parallel program visualization. In *Proc. of 1990 Int.'l Conf. on Parallel Processing*, pp. II.124–II.132, August 1990.

[171] A. A. Houng and J. E. Cuny. Belvedere: Prototype of a pattern-oriented debugger for highly parallel computation. In *Proc. of 1987 Int.'l Conf. on Parallel Processing, St.* Charles IL, pp. 735–738, August 1987.

[172] C. S. Hsieh. Timing analysis of cyclic concurrent programs. In *Proc. of 1989 Software Engineering Conf.*, Pittsburgh, pp. 312–318, May 1989.

[173] C. Huizing and R. Gerth. Semantics of reactive systems in abstract time. In J. W. de Bakker, C. Huizing, W. P. de Roever, and G. Rozenberg, eds., *Real-Time: Theory in Practice, Proc. of REX Workshop, LNCS 600*, pp. 291–314. Springer-Verlag, Berlin, 1991.

[174] R. J. K. Jacob. A state transition diagram language for visual programming. *IEEE Computer*, pp. 51–59, August 1985.

[175] M. S. Jaffe, N. G. Leveson, M. P. E. Heimdahl, and B. E. Melhart. Software requirements analysis for real-time process control systems. *IEEE Trans. on Software Engineering*, SE-17:241–258, 1991.

[176] F. Jahanian. Verifying properties of systems with variable timing constraints. In *Proc. of IEEE 10th Real-Time Systems Symp.*, Santa Monica, CA, pp. 319–328, December 1989.

[177] F. Jahanian and A. Goyal. A formalism for monitoring real-time constraints at run-time. In *Proc. of 1990 Fault Tolerance Symp.*, Ann Arbor, pp. 148–155, May 1990.

[178] F. Jahanian, R. Lee, and A. K. Mok. Semantics of modechart in real-time logic. In *Proc. of 21nd Hawaii Int.'l Conf. on System Sciences*, pp. 479–498, 1988.

[179] F. Jahanian and A. K. Mok. Safety analysis of timing properties in real-time systems. *IEEE Trans. on Software Engineering*, SE-12(9):890–904, September 1986.

[180] F. Jahanian and A. K. Mok. A graph-theoretic approach for timing analysis and its implementation. *IEEE Trans on Computers*, C-36(8):961–975, August 1987.

[181] F. Jahanian and R. Rajkumar. An integrated approach to monitoring and scheduling in real-time systems. In *IEEE Workshop on Real-Time Operating Systems and Software*, May 1991.

[182] F. Jahanian and D. A. Stuart. A method for verifying properties of modechart specifications. In *Proc. of IEEE 9th Real-Time Systems Symp.*, Huntsville, AL, pp. 12–21, December 1988.

[183] J. Joyce, G. Lomow, K. Slind, and B. Unger. Monitoring distributed systems. *ACM Trans. on Computer Systems*, 5(2):121–150, May 1987.

[184] J. E. Coolahan Jr. and N. Roussopoulos. Timing requirements for time driven systems using augmented Petri nets. *IEEE Trans. on Software Engineering*, SE-9(5):603–616, September 1983.

[185] J. E. Lumpp Jr., R. K. Shultz, and T. L. Casavant. Design of a system for software testing and debugging for multiprocessor avionics systems. In *Proc. of IEEE 15 Int.'l Computer Software and Applications Conf.*, Tokyo, pp. 261–268, September 1991.

[186] J. E. Lumpp Jr., H. J. Siegel, D. C. Marinescu, and T. L. Casavant. Specification and identification of events for debugging and performance monitoring of distributed multiprocessor systems. In *Proc. of 10th Int.'l Conf. on Distributed Computing Systems*, Paris, pp. 477–483, May 1990.

[187] P. K. Harter Jr. Response times in level-structured systems. *ACM Trans. on Computer Systems*, 5(3):232–248, August 1987.

[188] P. K. Harter Jr. Response times in level-structured systems. *ACM Trans. on Computer Systems*, 5(3):232–248, August 1987.

[189] P. K. Harter Jr., D. M. Heimbigner, and R. King. IDD: An interactive distributed debugger. In *Proc. of 5th Int'l Conf. on Distributed Computing Systems*, Denver, CO, pp. 498–506, 1985.

[190] M. F. Kaashoek and A. S. Tanenbaum. Group communication in the Amoeba distributed operating systems. In *Proc. of 11th IEEE Conf. on Distributed Computing Systems*, 1991.

[191] J. H. Kepecs and M. H. Solomon. Soda: A simplified operating system. *Operating System Rev.*, 19(4):45–56, October 1985.

[192] Y. Kesten and A. Pnueli. Timed and hybrid Statecharts and their textural representation. In *Proc. of Formal Techniques in Real-Time and Fault-Tolerant Systems,* Nijmegen, Netherlands, January 1992.

[193] R. M. Kieckhafer et al. The MAFT architecture for distributed fault tolerance. *IEEE Trans. on Computers,* C-37(4):398–405, April 1988.

[194] C. Kilpatrick and K. Schwan. ChaosMON—application-specific monitoring and display of performance information for parallel and distributed systems. In *Proc. of ACM/ONR Workshop on Parallel and Distributed Debugging,* Santa Cruz, CA, pp. 57–67, May 1991.

[195] D. B. Kirk. SMART (strategic memory allocation for real-time cache design. In *Proc. of IEEE 10th Real-Time Systems Symp.,* Santa Monica, CA, pp. 229–237, December 1989.

[196] E. Kligerman and A. D. Stoyenko. Real-time Euclid: A language for reliable real-time systems. *IEEE Trans. on Software Engineering,* 12(9):941–949, September 1986.

[197] A. S. Klusener. Abstraction in real-time process algebra. In J. W. de Bakker, C. Huizing, W. P. de Roever, and G. Rozenberg, eds., *Real-Time: Theory in Practice, Proc. of REX Workshop, LNCS 600,* pp. 325–352. Springer-Verlag, Berlin, 1991.

[198] E. Knapp. Deadlock detection in distributed database systems. *ACM Computing Surveys,* pp. 303–328, 1987.

[199] H. Kopetz et al. Distributed fault-tolerant real-time systems: The MARS approach. *IEEE Micro,* 9(1):25–40, February 1989.

[200] H. Kopetz and W. Merker. The architecture of MARS. In *Proc. of 15th int.'l Symp. on Fault-tolerant Computing,* Ann Arbor, pp. 274–279, October 1985.

[201] H. Kopetz and W. Ochsenreiter. Clock synchronization in distributed real-time systems. *IEEE Trans. on Computers,* C-36(8):933–940, August 1987.

[202] R. Koymans. Specifying real-time properties with metric temporal logic. *Real-Time Systems J.,* 1990.

[203] R. Koymans. Real time: A philosophical perspective. In J. W. de Bakker, C. Huizing, W. P. de Roever, and G. Rozenberg, eds., *Real-Time: Theory in Practice, Proc. of REX Workshop, LNCS 600,* pp. 353–370. Springer-Verlag, Berlin, 1991.

[204] J. Kramer et al. Graphical configuration programming. *IEEE Computer,* pp. 53–64, October 1989.

[205] A. D. Kshemkalyani and M. Singhal. Invariant-based verification of a distributed deadlock detection algorithm. *IEEE Trans. on Software Engineering*, SE-17(8):789–799, August 1991.

[206] R. Kurki-Suonio. Stepwise design of real-time systems. *IEEE Trans. on Software Engineering*, SE-19(1):56–69, January 1993.

[207] L. Lamport. Time, clock, and the ordering of events in a distributed system. *Comm. of ACM*, 21:558–565, July 1978.

[208] L. Lamport. Using time instead of timeout for fault-tolerant distributed systems. *ACM Trans. Programming Languages and Systems*, 6:254–280, April 1984.

[209] L. Lamport and P. M. Melliar-Smith. Synchronizing clocks in the presence of faults. *J. ACM*, 32:52–78, January 1985.

[210] M. V. LaPolla. Towards a theory of abstraction and visualization for debugging massively parallel programs. In *Proc. of 25th Hawaii Int.'l Conf. on System Sciences*, Kauai, HI, pp. 184–195, January 1992.

[211] R. J. LeBlanc and A. D. Robbins. Event-driven monitoring of distributed programs. In *Proc. of 5th Int.'l Conf. on Distributed Computing Systems*, pp. 515–522, 1985.

[212] T. J. LeBlanc and J. M. Mellor-Crummey. Debugging parallel programs with instant replay. *IEEE Trans. on Computers*, C-36(4):471–482, April 1987.

[213] T. J. LeBlanc, J. M. Mellor-Crummey, and R. J. Fowler. Analyzing parallel program executions using multiple views. *J. Parallel and Distrib. Comput.*, 9:203–217, June 1990.

[214] C. H. LeDoux and D. S. Parker. Saving traces for Ada debugging. In *Proc. of Ada Int.'l Conf.*, Paris, pp. 97–108, 1985.

[215] I. Lee, P. Brémond-Grégorie, and R. Gerber. A process algebraic approach to the specification and analysis of resource-bounded real-time system. *Proc. of IEEE*, 82(1):158–171, January 1994.

[216] P. LeGuernic, T. Gautier, M. LeBorgne, and C. LeMarine. Programming real-time application with Signal. *Proc. of IEEE*, 79:1321–1336, September 1991.

[217] T. Lehr et al. Visualizing performance debugging. *IEEE Computer*, 22(10):38–51, October 1989.

[218] N. G. Leveson and J. L. Stolzy. Safety analysis using Petri nets. *IEEE Trans. Software Engineering*, SE-13(3):386–397, March 1987.

[219] J. Li, I. Suzuki, and M. Yamashita. A new structural induction theorem for rings of temporal Petri nets. *IEEE Trans. on Software Engineering*, 20(2):115–126, February 1994.

[220] K. Li, J. F. Naughton, and J. S. Plank. Real-time, concurrent checkpoints for parallel programs. In *Proc. of 2d ACM SIGPLAN Symp. on Principles and Practice of Parallel Programming*, Seattle, WA, pp. 79–88, March 1990.

[221] B. H. Liebowitz and J. H. Carson. *Multiple Processor Systems for Real-time Applications*. Prentice–Hall, Englewood Cliffs, NJ, 1985.

[222] C. C. Lin and R. J. LeBlanc. Event-based debugging of object/action programs. In *Proc. of ACM Workshop on Parallel and Distributed Debugging*, Madison, WI, pp. 23–34, May 1988.

[223] K.-J. Lin and S. Natarajan. Expressing and maintaining timing constraints in FLEX. In *Proc. of IEEE 9th Real-Time Systems Symp.*, Huntsville, AL, pp. 96–105, December 1988.

[224] L. B. Linden. Parallel program visualization using ParVis. In M. Simmons and R. Koskela, eds., *Performance Instrumentation and Visualization*, pp. 157–187. Addison-Wesley, Reading, MA, 1990.

[225] L. B. Linden. Parallel program visualization using ParVis. In M. Simmons and R. Koskela, eds., *Performance Instrumentation and Visualization*, pp. 157–187. Addison-Wesley, Reading, MA, 1990.

[226] A.-C. Liu and R. Parthasarathi. Hardware monitoring of a multiprocessor systems. *IEEE Micro*, pp. 44–51, October 1989.

[227] R. L. London and R. A. Duisberg. Animating programs using Smalltalk. *IEEE Computer*, pp. 61–71, August 1985.

[228] D. L. Long and L. A. Clarke. Task interaction graphs for concurrence analysis. In *Proc. of Int.'l Conf. on Software Engineering*, pp. 44–52, May 1989.

[229] N. Lopez-Benitez. Dependability modeling and analysis of distributed programs. *IEEE Trans. on Software Engineering*, 20(5):345–352, May 1994.

[230] B. Lozzerini, C. A. Prete, and L. Lopriore. A programmable debugging aid for real-time software development. *IEEE Micro*, 6(3):34–42, June 1986.

[231] R. R. Lutz and J. S. K. Wong. Detecting unsafe error recovery schedules. *IEEE Trans. on Software Engineering*, SE-18(8):749–760, August 1992.

[232] D. Lyttle and R. Ford. A symbolic debugger for real-time embedded Ada software. *Software-Practice and Experience*, 20(5):499–514, May 1990.

[233] B. P. Mahony and I. J. Hayes. A case-study in timed refinement: A mine pump. *IEEE Trans. on Software Engineering*, SE-18(9):817–825, September 1992.

[234] O. Maler, Z. Manna, and A. Pnueli. From timed to hybrid systems. In J. W. de Bakker, C. Huizing, W. P. de Roever, and G. Rozenberg, eds., *Real-Time: Theory in Practice, Proc. of REX Workshop, LNCS 600*, pp. 447–484. Springer-Verlag, Berlin, 1991.

[235] A. D. Malony. Multiprocessor instrumentation: Approach for Cedar. In M. Simmons, R. Koskela, and I. Bucher, eds., *Instrumentation for Future Parallel Computing Systems*, pp. 1–33. Addison-Wesley, Reading, MA, 1989.

[236] A. D. Malony. JED: Just an event display. In M. Simmons and R. Koskela, eds., *Performance Instrumentation and Visualization*, pp. 99–115. Addison-Wesley, Reading, MA, 1990.

[237] A. D. Malony. Event-based performance perturbation: A case study. In *Proc. of 3d ACM SIGPLAN Symp. on Principles and Practice of Parallel Programming*, Williamsburg, VA, pp. 201–212, April 1991.

[238] A. D. Malony and D. A. Reed. Visualizing parallel computer system performance. In M. Simmons, R. Koskela, and I. Bucher, eds., *Instrumentation for Future Parallel Computing Systems*, pp. 59–89. Addison-Wesley, Reading, MA, 1989.

[239] A. D. Malony and D. A. Reed. Models for performance perturbation analysis. In *Proc. of ACM/ONR Workshop on Parallel and Distributed Debugging*, Santa Cruz, CA, pp. 15–25, May 1991.

[240] A. D. Malony, D. A. Reed, and H. A. G. Wijshoff. Performance measurement intrusion and perturbation analysis. *IEEE Trans. on Parallel and Distributed Systems*, 3(4):433–450, July 1992.

[241] Y. Manabe and M. Imase. Global conditions in debugging distributed programs. *J. Parallel Dist. Comput.*, 15(1):62–69, May 1992.

[242] Z. Manna and A. Pnueli. *The Temporal Logic of Reactive and Concurrent Systems*. Springer-Verlag, New York, 1992.

[243] C. R. Manning. Traveler: The application observatory. In *Proc. of European Conf. on Object Oriented Programming*, Paris, pp. 97–105, June 1987.

[244] C. Maples. Analyzing software performance in a multiprocessor environment. *IEEE Software*, pp. 50–63, July 1985.

[245] D. C. Marinescu, J. E. Lumpp Jr., T. L. Casavant, and H. J. Siegel. A model for monitoring and debugging parallel and distributed software. In *Proc. of 13th IEEE Int. 'l Computer Software and Applications Conf.*, Kissimmee, FL, pp. 81–88, September 1989.

[246] D. C. Marinescu, J. E. Lumpp Jr., T. L. Casavant, and H. J. Siegel. Models for monitoring and debugging tools for parallel and distributed software. *J. Parallel Dist. Comput.*, pp. 171–184, June 1990.

[247] K. E. Martersteck et al. The 5ESS switching system. *AT&T Technical Manual*, 64(6):1305–1564, July 1985.

[248] B. Martin et al. An object-based taxonomy for distributed computing systems. *IEEE Computer*, 24(8):17–27, August 1991.

[249] K. Marzullo. Maintaining the time in a distributed system. *Operating System Rev.*, 19(4):44–54, October 1985.

[250] C. E. McDowell and D. P. Helmbold. Debugging concurrent programs. *ACM Computing Surveys*, 21(4):593–622, December 1989.

[251] B. Melamed and R. J. T. Morris. Visual simulation: The performance analysis workstation. *IEEE Computer*, pp. 87–94, August 1985.

[252] P. M. Melliar-Smith and R. L. Schwartz. Formal specification and mechanical verification of SIFT: A fault-tolerant flight control system. *IEEE Trans. on Computers*, C-31(7):616–630, July 1982.

[253] J. M. Mellor-Crummey and T. J. LeBlanc. A software instruction counter. In *Proc. of 3d Int. 'l Conf. on Architectural Support for Programming Languages and Operating Systems*, Boston, pp. 78–86, April 1989.

[254] C. W. Mercer and H. Tokuda. The ARTS real-time object model. In *Proc. of IEEE 11th Real-Time Systems Symp.*, Lake Buena Vista, FL, pp. 2–10, December 1990.

[255] P. M. Merlin and D. J. Farber. Recoverability of communication protocols implications of a theoretical study. *IEEE Trans. on Communications*, COM-24(9):1036–1043, September 1976.

[256] B. P. Miller. DPM: Measurement system for distributed programs. *IEEE Trans. on Computers*, C-37(2):243–248, February 1988.

[257] B. P. Miller and J.-D. Choi. Breakpoints and halting in distributed programs. In *Proc. of 8th Int. 'l Conf. on Distributed Computing Systems*, San Jose, CA, pp. 316–321, June 1988.

[258] B. P. Miller and J.-D. Choi. A mechanism for efficient debugging of parallel programs. In *Proc. of ACM SIGPLAN '88 Conf. on Programming Language Design and Implementation*, Atlanta, GA, pp. 135–144, June 1988.

[259] B. P. Miller et al. IPS-2: the second generation of a parallel program measurement system. *IEEE Trans. on Parallel and Distributed Systems*, 1(2):206–217, April 1990.

[260] B. P. Miller, C. Macrander, and S. Sechrest. A distributed programs monitor for Berkeley UNIX. *Software Practice and Experience*, 16(2):183–200, February 1986.

[261] R. Milner. In *Communication and Concurrency*. Prentice-Hall, Englewood Cliffs NJ, 1989.

[262] A. Mink, R. Carpenter, G. Nacht, and J. Roberts. Multiprocessor performance measurement instrumentation. *IEEE Computer*, 23(9):63–75, September 1990.

[263] A. Mink and G. Nacht. Performance measurement of a shared-memory multiprocessor using hardware instrumentation. In *Proc. of 22nd Hawaii Int.'l Conf. on System Sciences*, Kailua-Kona, HI, pp. 267–276, January 1989.

[264] T. G. Moher. PROVIDE: A process visualization and debugging environment. *IEEE Trans. on Software Engineering*, 14(6):849–857, June 1988.

[265] A. K. Mok. Formal analysis of real-time equations rule-based systems. In *Proc. of IEEE 10th Real-Time Systems Symp.*, Santa Monica, CA, pp. 308–318, December 1989.

[266] A. K. Mok. Coping with implementation dependencies in real-time system verification. In J. W. de Bakker, C. Huizing, W. P. de Roever, and G. Rozenberg, eds., *Real-Time: Theory in Practice, Proc. of REX Workship, LNCS 600*, pp. 485–501. Springer-Verlag, Berlin, 1991.

[267] A. K. Mok. Toward mechanization of real-time system design. In *Foundations of Real-Time Computing: Formal Specifications and Methods*. Kluwer Press, Norwell, MA, 1991.

[268] A. K. Mok et al. Synthesis of a real-time message processing system with data-driven timing constraints. In *Proc. of IEEE 8th Real-Time Systems Symp.*, San Jose, CA, pp. 133–143, December 1987.

[269] F. Moller and C. Tofts. A temporal calculus of communicating systems. In *Proc. of CONCUR'90, LNCS 458*, pp. 401–415. Springer-Verlag, North-Holland, 1990.

[270] E. T. Morgan and R. R. Razouk. Interactive state-space analysis of concurrent systems. *IEEE Trans. on Software Engineering*, 1987.

[271] M. Moriconi and D. F. Hare. Visualizing program designs through PegsSys. *IEEE Computer*, pp. 72–85, August 1985.

[272] A. Morzenti. Validating real-time systems by executing logic specifications. In J. W. de Bakker, C. Huizing, W. P. de Roever, and G. Rozenberg, eds., *Real-Time: Theory in Practice, Proc. of REX Workshop, LNCS 600*, pp. 485–501. Springer-Verlag, Berlin, 1991.

[273] A. Morzenti and P. S. Pietro. Object-oriented logical specification of time-critical systems. *ACM Trans. on Software Engineering and Methodology*, 3(1):56–98, January 1994.

[274] L. E. Moser and P. M. Melliar-Smith. Formal verification of safety-critical systems. *Software Practice and Experience*, 20(8):799–821, August 1990.

[275] B. Moszkowski. A temporal logic for multilevel reasoning about hardware. *IEEE Computer*, 18(2):10–19, February 1985.

[276] S. J. Mullender, G. Van Rossum, A. S. Tanenbaum, R. Van Renesse, and H. Van Staveren. Amoeba: A distributed operating system for the 1990s. *IEEE Computer*, 23(5):44–53, May 1990.

[277] S. J. Mullender and A. S. Tanenbaum. The design of a capability-based distributed operating system. *Computer J.*, 24(4):289–300, March 1986.

[278] J. K. Muppala, S. P. Woolet, and K. S. Trivedi. Real-time systems performance in the presence of failure. *IEEE Computer*, 24(5):37–47, May 1991.

[279] T. Murata. Petri nets: Properties, analysis and application. *Proc. of IEEE*, 77(4):541–580, April 1989.

[280] T. Murata and C. Lin. Applications of Petri nets to non-monotonic logic. In *Proc. of Joint Technical Conf. on Circuit-Systems, Computer and Communications*, Cheju, Korea, December 1990.

[281] T. Murata, V. S. Subrahmanian, and T. Wakayama. A Petri net model for reasoning in the presence of inconsistency. *IEEE Trans. on Knowledge and Data Engineering*, 3(3):281–292, September 1991.

[282] T. Murata and D. Zhang. A predicate-transition net model fo parallel interpretation of logic programs. *IEEE Trans. on Software Engineering*, 14(4):481–497, April 1988.

[283] D. J. Musliner, E. H. Durfee, and K. G. Shin. Execution monitoring and recovery planning with time. In *IEEE 7th Conf. on Artificial Intelligence Applications*, pp. 385–388.

[284] G. J. Myers. *The Art of Software Testing*. Wiley-Interscience, New York, 1979.

[285] K. T. Narayana and A. A. Aaby. Specification of real-time systems in real-time temporal interval logic. In *Proc. of IEEE 9th Real-Time Systems Symp.*, Huntsville, AL, pp. 86–95, December 1988.

[286] N. Natarajan. A distributed scheme for detecting communication deadlocks. *IEEE Trans. on Software Engineering*, 12(4):531–537, April 1986.

[287] J. Nehmer, D. Haban, F. Mattern, D. Wybranietz, and H. D. Rombach. Key concepts of the INCAS multicomputer project. *IEEE Trans. on Software Engineering*, SE-13(8):913–923, August 1987.

[288] V. P. Nelson. Fault-tolerant computing: Fundamnetal concepts. *IEEE Computer*, 23(7):19–25, July 1990.

[289] R. H. B. Netzer and B. P. Miller. Improving the accuracy of data race detection. In *Proc. of 3d ACM SIGPLAN Symp. on Principles and Practice of Parallel Programming*, Williamsburg, VA, pp. 133–144, April 1991.

[290] X. Nicollin and J. Sifakis. An overview and synthesis on timed process algebraa. In J. W. de Bakker, C. Huizing, W. P. de Roever, and G. Rozenberg, eds., *Real-Time: Theory in Practice, Proc. of REX Workshop, LNCS 600*, pp. 526–548. Springer-Verlag, Berlin, 1991.

[291] X. Nicollin, J. Sifakis, and S. Yovine. From ATP to timed graphs and hybrid systems. In J. W. de Bakker, C. Huizing, W. P. de Roever, and G. Rozenberg, eds., *Real-Time: Theory in Practice, Proc. of REX Workshop, LNCS 600*, pp. 549–572. Springer-Verlag, Berlin, 1991.

[292] D. Notkin et al. Interconnecting heterogeneous computer systems. *Comm. of ACM*, 31(3):258–273, March 1988.

[293] M. Notomi and T. Murata. Hierarchical reachability graph of bounded Petri nets for concurrent-software analysis. *IEEE Trans. on Software Engineering*, 20(5):325–336, May 1994.

[294] D. M. Ogle, K. Schwan, and R. Snodgrass. Application-dependent dynamic monitoring of distributed and parallel systems. *IEEE Trans. on Parallel and Distributed Systems*, 4(7):764–778, July 1993.

[295] J. S. Ostroff. Modelling, specification and verifying real-time embedded computer systems. In *Proc. of IEEE 8th Real-Time Systems Symp.*, San Jose, CA, pp. 124–132, December 1987.

[296] J. S. Ostroff. Real-time temporal logic decision procedures. In *Proc. of IEEE 10th Real-Time Systems Symp.*, Santa Monica, CA, pp. 92–101, December 1989.

[297] J. S. Ostroff. *Temporal Logic for Real-Time Systems.* Research Studies Press, England, 1989.

[298] J. S. Ostroff. Deciding properties of timed transition models. *IEEE Trans on Parallel and Distributed Systems*, 1(2):170–183, April 1990.

[299] J. S. Ostroff. Verification of safety critical systems using TIM/RTTL. In J. W. de Bakker, C. Huizing, W. P. de Roever, and G. Rozenberg, eds., *Real-Time: Theory in Practice, Proc. of REX Workship, LNCS 600*, pp. 573–602. Springer-Verlag, Berlin, 1991.

[300] J. S. Ostroff. Formal methods for the specification and design of real-time safety critical systems. *Journal Systems Software*, 18(1):33–60, April 1992.

[301] J. K. Ousterhout et al. The Sprite network operating systems. *IEEE Computer*, 21(2):23–36, February 1988.

[302] D. Z. Pan and M. A. Linton. Supporting reverse execution of parallel programs. In *Proc. of ACM Workshop on Parallel and Distributed Debugging*, Madison, WI, pp. 124–129, May 1988.

[303] Y. E. Papelis and T. L. Casavant. Specification and analysis of parallel/distributed software and systems by Petri nets with transition enabling functions. *IEEE Trans. on Software Engineering*, SE-18(3):252–261, March 1992.

[304] N. Parrington and M. Roper. *Understanding Software Testing.* Ellis Horwood, West Sussex, England, 1989.

[305] D. Pease et al. PAWS: A performance evaluation tool for parallel computing systems. *IEEE Computer*, 24(1):18–29, January 1991.

[306] D. Peng and K. G. Shin. Modeling of concurrent task execution in a distributed system for real-time control. *IEEE Trans. on Computers*, C-36(4):500–516, April 1987.

[307] J. L. Peterson and A. Silberschatz. *Operating System Concepts.* Addison-Wesley, Reading, MA, 1987.

[308] B. Plattner. Real-time execution monitoring. *IEEE Trans. on Software Engineering*, SE-10(6):756–764, November 1984.

[309] A. Pnueli and E. Harel. Application of temporal logic to the specification of real-time systems. In M. Joseph, ed., *Proc. of Formal Techniques in Real-Time and Fault-Tolerant Systems, LNCS 331*, pp. 94–98. Springer-Verlag, Heidelberg, 1988.

[310] A. Podgursk and L. A. Clarke. The implications of program dependencies for software testing, debugging, and maintenance. In *Proc. of ACM SIGSOFT 3d Symp. on Software Testing, Analysis, and Verification*, Key West, FL, pp. 168–178, December 1989.

[311] A. Podgursk and L. A. Clarke. A formal model of program dependencies and its implications for software testing, debugging, and maintenance. *IEEE Trans. on Software Engineering*, SE-16(9):965–979, September 1990.

[312] M. L. Powell and B. P. Miller. Process migration in Demos/MP. In *Proc. 9th ACM Symp. Op. Syst. Princ.*, ACM Press, New York, pp. 110–118, October 1983.

[313] V. Pratt. Modelling concurrency with partial orders. *Int.'l J. Parallel Programming*, 15(1), January 1986.

[314] P. Puschner and C. Koza. Calculating the maximum execution time of real-time programs. *J. Real Time Systems*, 1, September 1989.

[315] G. Raeder. A survey of current graphical programming techniques. *IEEE Computer*, pp. 11–25, August 1985.

[316] S. C. V. Raju, R. Rajkumar, and F. Jahanian. Monitoring timing constraints in distributed real-time systems. In *Proc. of IEEE 13th Real-Time Systems Symp.*, Phoenix, AZ, pp. 57–67, December 1992.

[317] Y. S. Ramakrishna, L. E. Moser, P. M. Melliar-Smith, L. K. Dillon, and G. Kutty. Really visual temporal reasoning. In *Proc. of IEEE Real-Time Symp.*, Raleigh-Durham, NC, pp. 262–273, December 1993.

[318] C. V. Ramamoorthy and G. S. Ho. Performance evaluation of asynchronous concurrent systems using Petri nets. *IEEE Trans. Software Engineering*, SE-6(9):440–449, September 1980.

[319] P. Ramanathan, D. D. Kandlur, and K. G. Shin. Hardware-assistant software clock synchronization for homogeneous distributed systems. *IEEE Trans. on Computers*, C-39(4):514–524, April 1990.

[320] P. Ramanathan, K. G. Shin, and R. W. Butler. Fault-tolerant clock synchronization in distributed systems. *IEEE Computer*, pp. 33–42, October 1990.

[321] C. Ramchandani. Analysis of asynchronous concurrent systems by Petri nets. In *Project MAC, TR-120, MIT,* Cambridge, MA, February 1974.

[322] S. Rangarajan and S. K. Tripathi. Efficient synchronization of clocks in a distributed system. In *Proc. of IEEE 12th Real-Time Systems Symp.,* San Antonio, TX, pp. 22–31, December 1991.

[323] R. F. Rashid. From RIG to Accent to Mach: The evolution of a network operating system. In *Fall Joint Computer Conf., AFIPS,* pp. 1128–1137, September 1986.

[324] R. F. Rasid and G. G. Robertson. Accent: A communication–oriented network operating system kernel. In *Proc. 8th ACM Symp. Op. Syst. Princ.,* ACM Press, New York, pp. 64–75, December 1981.

[325] A. P. Ravn, H. Rischel, and K. M. Hansen. Specifying and verifying requirements of real-time systems. *IEEE Trans. on Software Engineering,* 19(1):41–55, January 1993.

[326] M. Raynal. *Distributed Algorithms and Protocols,* Jack Howlett, *trans.* Wiley, New York, 1988.

[327] R. R. Razouk and M. M. Gorlick. A real-time interval logic for reasoning about execution of real-time programs. *Proc. of ACM SIFSOFT 3d Symp. on Software Testing, Analysis, and Verification,* 14(8):10–19, December 1989.

[328] R. R. Razouk and C. V. Phelps. Performance analysis using time Petri nets. In Y. Yemini et al., eds., *Proc. of 4th IFIP Protocol Specification, Testing and Verification.* North-Holland, Amsterdam, 1985.

[329] M. Reilly. Instrumentation for application performance tuning: The M31 system. In M. Simmons, R. Koskela, and I. Bucher, eds., *Instrumentation for Future Parallel Computing Systems,* pp. 143–158. Addison-Wesley, Reading, MA, 1989.

[330] S. P. Reiss. PECAN: Program development systems that support multiple views. *IEEE Trans. on Software Engineering,* 13(3):276–285, March 1985.

[331] M. Roesler and W. A. Burkhard. Resolution of deadlocks in object-oriented distributed systems. *IEEE Trans. on Computers,* pp. 1212–1224, August 1989.

[332] G. C. Roman and K. C. Cox. A declarative approach to visualizing concurrent computations. *IEEE Computer*, 22:25–37, October 1989.

[333] G. C. Roman and K. C. Cox. Program visualization: The art of mapping programs to pictures. In *IEEE Int.'l Conf. on Software Engineeing*, Melbourne, Australia, pp. 412–420, May 1992.

[334] P. K. Rowe and B. Pagurek. Remedy: A real-time, multiprocessor, system level debugger. In *Proc. of IEEE 8th Real-Time Systems Symp.*, San Jose, CA, pp. 230–240, December 1987.

[335] J. Rushby and F. Henke. Formal verification of algorithms for critical systems. In *Proc. of ACM/SIGSOFT 91 Conf. on Software for Critical Systems*, New Orleans, pp. 1–15, December 1991.

[336] J. M. Rushby and F. Henke. Formal verification of algorithms for critical systems. *IEEE Trans. on Software Engineering*, 19(1):13–23, January 1993.

[337] R. D. Sansom, D. P. Julin, and R. F. Rashid. Extending a capability based system into a network environment. In *Proc. of SIGCOMM ACM*, 1986.

[338] R. W. Scheifler and J. Gettys. The X window system. *ACM Trans. Graph*, 5(2), April 1986.

[339] S. Schneider, J. Davies, D. M. Jackson, G. M. Reed, and J. N. Reed. Timed CSP: Theory and practice. In J. W. de Bakker, C. Huizing, W. P. de Roever, and G. Rozenberg, eds., *Real-Time: Theory in Practice, Proc. of REX Workshop, LNCS 600*, pp. 640–675. Springer-Verlag, Berlin, 1991.

[340] J. D. Schoeffler. Distributed computer systems for industrial process control. *IEEE Computer*, 17(2):11–18, February 1984.

[341] J. D. Schoeffler. A real-time programming event monitor. *IEEE Trans. on Education*, 31(4):245–250, November 1988.

[342] K. Schwan and H. Zhou. Dynamic scheduling of hard real-time tasks and real-time threads. *IEEE Trans. on Software Engineering*, 18(8):736–747, August 1992.

[343] R. E. Seviora. Knowledge-based program debugging systems. *IEEE Software*, 4(3):20–32, May 1987.

[344] J. Sharp. *An Introduction to Distributed and Parallel Processing*. Blackwell Scientific, Oxford, 1987.

[345] S. E. Shatz and J.-P. Wang. Introduction to distributed software engineering. *IEEE Computer*, pp. 23–31, October 1987.

[346] A. C. Shaw. Reasoning about time in higher-level language software. *IEEE Trans. on Software Engineering*, 15(7):875–889, July 1989.

[347] A. C. Shaw. Communicating real-time state machines. *IEEE Trans. on Software Engineering*, 18(9):805–816, September 1992.

[348] T. Shimomura and S. Isoda. CHASE: A bug-locating assistant system. In *Proc. of IEEE 15 Int.'l Computer Software and Applications Conf.*, Tokyo, pp. 412–417, September 1991.

[349] K. G. Shin. HARTS: A distributed real-time architecture. *IEEE Computer*, 24(5):25–35, May 1991.

[350] K. G. Shin and P. Ramanathan. Transmission delays in hardware clock synchronization. *IEEE Trans. on Computers*, C-37(11):1465–1467, November 1988.

[351] B. Shneiderman et al. Display strategies for program browsing: Concepts and experiment. *IEEE Software*, pp. 7–15, May 1986.

[352] H. J. Siegel, L. J. Siegel, F. C. Kemmerer, D. T. Mueller, H. E. Smalley, and S. D. Smith. PASM: A partitionable simd/mimd system for image processing and pattern recognition. *IEEE Trans. on Computers*, C-30(12):934–947, December 1981.

[353] M. Singhal. Deadlock detection in distributed systems. *IEEE Computer*, 18(11):37–48, November 1989.

[354] M. Singhal. Deadlock detection in distributed systems. *IEEE Computer*, 18(11):37–48, November 1989.

[355] M. Singhal and T. L. Casavant. Distributed computing systems. *IEEE Computer*, 24(8):12–15, August 1991.

[356] M. K. Sinha and N. Natarajan. A priority-based distributed deadlock detection algorithm. *IEEE Trans. on Software Engineering*, 11(1):67–80, January 1985.

[357] P. K. Sinha et al. The Galaxy distributed operating system. *IEEE Computer*, 24(8):34–41, August 1991.

[358] A. P. Sistla and E. M. Clarke. Complexity of propositional linear temporal logics. *J. ACM*, 32(3):733–749, July 1985.

[359] D. Skillcorn and J. Glasgow. Real time specification using Lucid. *IEEE Trans. on Software Engineering*, 15(2):221–229, February 1989.

[360] M. Sloman and J. Kramer. *Distributed Systems and Computer Networks*. Prentice-Hall, London, 1987.

[361] E. T. Smith. Debugging tools for message-based, communicating processes. In *Proc. of 4th Int.'l Conf. on Distributed Computing Systems*, pp. 303–310, 1984.

[362] E. T. Smith. A debugger for message-based processes. *Software Practice and Experience*, 15(11):1073–1086, November 1985.

[363] R. Snodgrass. A relational approach to monitoring complex systems. *ACM Trans. on Computer Systems*, 6(2):157–196, May 1988.

[364] D. Socha, M. L. Bailey, and D. Notkin. Voyeur: Graphical views of parallel programs. In *Proc. of ACM Workshop on Parallel and Distributed Debugging*, Madison, WI, pp. 206–215, May 1988.

[365] N. A. Speirs and P. A. Barrett. Using passive replicates in Delta-4 to provide dependable distributed computing. In *Proc. of 9th Int.'l Symp. on Fault-Tolerant Computing*, Chicago, pp. 184–190, November 1989.

[366] J. A. Stankovic. A perspective on distributed computer systems. *IEEE Trans. on Computers*, C-33(12):1102–1114, December 1984.

[367] J. A. Stankovic. Misconceptions about real-time computing: A serious problem for next-generation systems. *IEEE Computer*, 21(10):10–19, October 1988.

[368] J. A. Stankovic and K. Ramamritham. The design of the Spring kernel. In *Proc. of IEEE 8th Real-Time Systems Symp.*, San Jose, CA, pp. 146–157, December 1987.

[369] J. A. Stankovic and K. Ramamritham. *Tutorial: Hard Real-time Systems*. Computer Society Press, Washington, DC, 1988.

[370] J. A. Stankovic, K. Ramamritham, and S. Cheng. Evaluation of a flexible task scheduling algorithm for distributed hard real-time systems. *IEEE Trans. on Computers*, 34(12):1130–1143, December 1985.

[371] J. T. Stasko. Tango: A framework and system for algorithm animation. *IEEE Computer*, 23(9):28–39, September 1990.

[372] J. M. Stone. Debugging concurrent process: A case study. In *Proc. of ACM SIGPLAN '88 Conf. on Programming Language Design and Implementation*, Atlanta, GA, pp. 145–153, June 1988.

[373] J. M. Stone. A graphical representation of concurrent processes. In *Proc. of ACM Workshop on Parallel and Distributed Debugging*, Madison, WI, pp. 226–235, May 1988.

[374] A. D. Stoyenko. The evaluation and state-of-the-art of real-time languages. *J. Systems Software*, pp. 61–83, 1992.

[375] A. D. Stoyenko, C. Hamacher, and R. C. Holt. Analyzing hard-real-time programs for guaranteed schedulability. *IEEE Trans. on Software Engineering*, SE-17(8):737–750, August 1991.

[376] I. Suzuki. Formal analysis of the alternating bit protocol by temporal Petri nets. *IEEE Trans. on Software Engineering*, 16(11):1273–1281, November 1990.

[377] I. Suzuki and H Lu. Temporal Petri nets and their application to modeling and analysis of a handshake daisy chain arbiter. *IEEE Trans. on Computers*, C-38(5):696–704, May 1989.

[378] K. C. Tai. On testing concurrent programs. In *Proc. COMPSAC*, pp. 310–317, 1985.

[379] K. C. Tai. Condition-based software testing strategies. In *Proc. COMPSAC*, pp. 564–569, 1990.

[380] K. C. Tai, R. H. Carver, and E. E. Obaid. Deterministic execution debugging of concurrent Ada programs. In *Proc. of IEEE 13th Int.'l Computer Software and Applications Conf.*, Orlando, FL, pp. 102–109, September 1989.

[381] T. C. Tai and R. H. Carver. Testing and debugging ofconcurrent software by deterministic execution. In *Technical Report TR-87-19. Dept. of Computer Science, North Carolina State University*, Raleigh, 1988.

[382] T. C. Tai, R. H. Carver, and E. E. Obaid. Debugging of concurrent Ada programs by deterministic execution. *IEEE Trans. on Software Engineering*, SE-17(1):45–63, January 1991.

[383] A. S. Tanenbaum. *Morden Operating Systems*. Prentice-Hall, Englewood Cliffs, NJ, 1992.

[384] A. S. Tanenbaum, R. Van Renesse, H. Van Staveren, G. J. Van Sharp, S. J. Mullender, S. J. Jansen, and G. Van Rossum. Experience with the Amoeba distributed operating system. *Comm. of ACM*, 33(2):46–63, December 1990.

[385] R. N. Taylor. A general-purpose algorithms for analyzing concurrent programs. *Communications of ACM*, 26(5):362–376, May 1983.

[386] P. Thambidurai and K. S. Trivedi. Transient overload in fault-tolerant real-time systems. In *Proc. of IEEE 10th Real-Time Systems Symp.*, Santa Monica, CA, pp. 126–133, December 1989.

[387] H. Tokuda. Towards predictable and reliable distributed real-time systems. In *Proc. of IEEE 13th Int.'l Computer Software and Applications Conf.*, Orlando, FL, pp. 437–438, September 1989.

[388] H. Tokuda and M. Kotera. A real-time tool set for the ARTS kernel. In *Proc. of IEEE 9th Real-Time Systems Symp.*, Huntsville, AL, pp. 289–299, December 1988.

[389] H. Tokuda and M. Kotera. Scheduler 1-2-3: An interactive schedulability analyzer for real-time systems. In *Proc. of IEEE 12th Int.'l Computer Software and Applications Conf.*, Chicago, pp. 211–219, October 1988.

[390] H. Tokuda, M. Kotera, and C. W. Mercer. A real-time monitor for a distributed real-time operating system. In *Proc. of ACM Workshop on Parallel and Distributed Debugging*, Madison, WI, pp. 68–77, May 1988.

[391] J. J.-P. Tsai. A knowledge-based approach to software design. *IEEE J. on Selected Areas in Communications*, 6(5):828–841, June 1988.

[392] J. J.-P. Tsai, Y. Bi, and S. J. H. Yang. VDS: A system for debugging distributed real-time systems with monitoring support. *Int.'l J. Software Engineering and Knowledge Engineering*, 1996.

[393] J. J.-P. Tsai, Y. Bi, and S. J. H. Yang. Visualising and debugging timing violations for distributed real-time software systems. *IEEE Software*, 1996.

[394] J. J.-P. Tsai and Y. D. Bi. On real-time software testing and debugging. In *Proc. of 1990 Int.'l Computer Software and Applications Conf.*, Chicago, pp. 512–518, October 1990.

[395] J. J.-P. Tsai and Y. D. Bi. Timing errors in real-time systems and their detection. In *Proc. of IEEE Int.'l Symp. on Software Reliability Engineering*, Austin, TX, pp. 116–123, May 1991.

[396] J. J.-P. Tsai, K. Y. Fang, and H. Y. Chen. A knowledge-based debugger for real-time software systems based on a non-interference testing architecture. In *Proc. 13th IEEE Int.'l Computer Software and Applications Conf.*, Kissimmee, FL, pp. 642–649, September 1989.

[397] J. J.-P. Tsai, K. Y. Fang, and H. Y. Chen. A noninvasive architecture to monitoring real-time distributed systems. *IEEE Computer*, 23(3):11–23, March 1990.

[398] J. J.-P. Tsai, K. Y. Fang, H. Y. Chen, and Y. D. Bi. A non-interference monitoring and replay mechanism for real-time software testing and

debugging. *IEEE Trans. on Software Engineering*, SE-16(8):897–916, August 1990.

[399] J. J.-P. Tsai and H. C. Jang. A knowledge-based approach for the specification and analysis of real-time software systems. *Int.l J. Artificial Intelligence Tools*, 1(1), 1992.

[400] J. J.-P. Tsai, H. C. Jang, and K. Schellinger. RT-FRORL: A formal requirements specification language for specifying and analyzing real-time systems. In *Proc. of 14th IEEE Computer Software and Applications Conf.*, Tokyo, September 1991.

[401] J. J.-P. Tsai and A. Liu. A knowledge-based system for rapid prototyping. *J. Knowledge-Based Systems*, 2(4):239–248, December 1989.

[402] J. J.-P. Tsai and R. Sheu. A distributed cooperative agents architecture for software development. In *IJCAI Int.'l Workshop on Intelligent Cooperative Information Systems, IJCAI'91*, Sydney, Australia, pp. 51–76, August 1991.

[403] J. J.-P. Tsai, S. T. Tsai, and A. Liu. A frame and rule based system to support software development using an integrated software engineering paradigm. *IEEE Tools for Artificial Intelligence Workshop*, Fairfax, VA, pp. 282–289, October 1989.

[404] J. J.-P. Tsai and T. Weigert. Exploratory prototyping through the use of frame and production systems. In *Proc. of IEEE Computer Software and Applications Conf.*, Orlando, FL, pp. 445–462, September 1989.

[405] J. J.-P. Tsai and T. Weigert. A knowledge-based approach for checking software information using a non-monotonic reasoning system. *J. Knowledge-Based Systems*, 3(3):131–138, September 1990.

[406] J. J.-P. Tsai and T. Weigert. HCLIE: A logic-based requirements language for new software engineering paradigms. *IEEE Software Engineering J.*, 6(4):137–151, July 1991.

[407] J. J.-P. Tsai, T. Weigert, and M. Aoyama. A declarative approach to software requirements specification language. In *Proc. of 1988 IEEE Computer Languages Conf.*, Miami Beach, FL, pp. 414–421, October 1988.

[408] J. J.-P. Tsai, T. Weigert, and H. C. Jang. A hybrid knowledge representation for requirements specification and reasoning. In *Proc. of IEEE Conf. on Tools for Artificial Intelligence*, Fairfax, VA, pp. 70–76, November 1990.

[409] J. J.-P. Tsai, T. Weigert, and H. C. Jang. Non-monotonic logic as a basis for requirements specification and analysis. In *Int. 'l Symp. on Artificial Intelligence*, pp. 13–15, November 1991.

[410] J. J.-P. Tsai, T. Weigert, and H. C. Jang. A hybrid knowledge representation as a basis of requirement specification and specification analysis. *IEEE Trans. on Software Engineering*, 18(12):1076–1110, December 1992.

[411] J. J.-P. Tsai and T. J. Weigert. *Knowledge-Based Software Development for Real-Time Distributed System.* World Scientific, Singapore, 1993.

[412] J. J.-P. Tsai, S. Yang, and Y. Bi. Visualization and debugging of distributed real-time software systems. In *Proc. of 1992 IEEE Int. 'l Conf. on Automation, Robotics, and Computer Vision*, pp. inv–5.6.1–inv–5.6.5, September 1992.

[413] J. J.-P. Tsai and S. J. H. Yang. *Monitoring and Debugging of Distributed Real-Time Systems.* IEEE Computer Society Press, *Los Alamitos, CA*, 1995.

[414] J. J.-P. Tsai, S. J. H. Yang, and Y. H. Chang. Schedulability analysis of real-time systems using timing constraint Petri nets. In *IEEE 7th European Computer Science Conf.*, pp. 375–388, June 1993.

[415] J. J.-P. Tsai, S. J. H. Yang, and Y. H. Chang. Timing constraint Petri nets and their application to schedulability analysis of real-time systems specification. *IEEE Trans. on Software Engineering*, 21(1):32–49, January 1995.

[416] S. Tsuruta, K. Fukuoka, S. Miyamoto, and S. Mitsumori. A debugging tool for real-time software: The non-repeated runs approach. In *Proc. IFAC/IFIP Real-time Programming*, Kyoto, pp. 49–56, 1981.

[417] A. Tuchman et al. Run-time visualization of program data. In *Proc. of 1991 IEEE Visualization*, San Diego, CA, pp. 255–251, October 1991.

[418] R. A. Volz and T. N. Mudge. Timing issues in the distributed execution of Ada programs. *IEEE Trans. on Computers*, C-36(4):449–459, April 1987.

[419] G. Vossen and S. S. Wang. Toward efficient algorithms for deadlock detection and resolution in distributed systems. In *Proc. of 5th Int. 'l Conf. on Data Engineering*, pp. 287–295, 1989.

[420] N. J. Wahl and S. R. Schach. A methodology and distributed tool for debugging dataflow program. In *Proc. of ACM SIGSOFT 2d Workshop*

on Software Testing, Verification, and Analysis, Banff, Canada, pp. 98–105, July 1988.

[421] Y. Wakahara et al. A method for detecting service interactions. *IEEE Communication Magazine,* pp. 32–37, August 1993.

[422] C.-H. Wang et al. Automated analysis of bounded response time for two NASA expert systems. In *Proc. of ACM/SIGSOFT '91 Conf. on Software for Critical S ystems,* New Orleans, pp. 147–161, 1991.

[423] F. Wang, A. Mok, and E. A. Emerson. Formal specification of asynchronous distributed real-time systems by APTL. In *IEEE Int.'l Conf. on Software Engineering,* Melbourne, Australia, pp. 188–198, May 1992.

[424] F. Wang, A. Mok, and E. A. Emerson. Distributed real-time system specification and verification in APTL. *ACM Trans. on Software Engineering and Methodology,* 2(4):346–378, October 1993.

[425] C. B. Weinstock. SIF: system design and implementation. In *Proc. of 10th int. Symp. on Fault-tolerant Computing,* New York, pp. 75–77, October 1980.

[426] J. H. Wensley, L. Lamport, J. Goldberg, M. W. Green, K. N. Levitt, P. M. Melliar-Smith, R. E. Shostak, and C. B. Weinstock. SIFT: Design and analysis of a fault-tolerant computer for aircraft control. *Proc. of IEEE,* 66(11):1240–1245, October 1978.

[427] C. A. Witschorik. The real-time debugging monitor for the Bell system 1A processor. *Software-Practice and Experience,* 13:727–743, 1983.

[428] L. D. Wittie. Debugging distributed C programs by real-time replay. In *Proc. of ACM Workshop on Parallel and Distributed Debugging,* Madison, WI, pp. 57–67, May 1988.

[429] L. D. Wittie. Computer networks and distributed systems. *IEEE Computer,* 24(9):67–76, September 1991.

[430] M. Wolfe and C.-W. Tseng. The power test for data dependence. *IEEE Trans. on Parallel and Distributed Systems,* 3(5):591–601, September 1992.

[431] J. Xu. Multiprocessor scheduling of processes with release times, deadlines, precedence, and exclusion relations. *IEEE Trans. on Software Engineering,* 19(2):139–154, February 1993.

[432] J. Xu and D. L. Parnas. On satisfying timing constraints in hard-real-time systems. *IEEE Trans. on Software Engineering,* 19(1):70–84, January 1993.

[433] J. C. Yan and S. F. Lundstrom. Axe: A simulation environment for actor-like computations on ensemble architectures. In *Proc. of Winter Simulation Conf.*, Washington, DC, pp. 424–429, 1986.

[434] C. Q. Yang and B. P. Miller. Critical path analysis for the execution of parallel and distributed programs. In *Proc. of 8th Int. 'l Conf. on Distributed Computing Systems*, San Jose, CA, pp. 366–373, June 1988.

[435] C.-Q. Yang and B. P. Miller. Performance measurement for parallel and distributed program: A structured and automatic approach. *IEEE Trans. on Software Engineering*, SE-15(12):1615–1629, December 1989.

[436] S. S. Yau and J. J.-P. Tsai. A survey of software design techniques. *IEEE Trans. on Software Engineering*, SE-12(6):713–721, June 1986.

[437] W. Yi. Real-time behavior of asynchronous agents. In J. C. M. Baeten and J. W. Klop, eds., *Theories of Concurrency: Unification and Extension Proc. of CONCUR'90, LNCS 458*, Amsterdam, pp. 502–520. Springer-Verlag, North-Holland, 1990.

[438] W. Yi. CCS + time = an interleaving model for real-time systems. In *Proc. of ICALP '91*, Madrid, July 1991.

[439] M. Young and R. N. Taylor. Combining static concurrence analysis with symbolic execution. In *Proc. of IEEE Workshop on Software Testing*, pp. 170–178, July 1986.

[440] P. Zave. The operational approach to requirements specification for embedded systems. *IEEE Trans. on Software Engineering*, 8(3):250–269, May 1982.

[441] P. Zave. An insider's evaluation of PAISLey. *IEEE Trans. on Software Engineering*, 17(3):212–225, March 1991.

[442] D. Zernik and L. Rudolph. Animating work and time for debugging parallel programs foundation and experience. In *Proc. of ACM Workshop on Parallel and Distributed Debugging*, Santa Cruz, CA, 1991.

[443] D. Zernik and L. Rudolph. Animating work and time for debugging parallel programs foundation and experience. In *Proc. of ACM/ONR Workshop on Parallel and Distributed Debugging*, Santa Cruz, CA, pp. 46–56, May 1991.

[444] H. Zhou, K. Schwan, and I. F. Akyildiz. Performance effects of information sharing in a distributed multiprocessor real-time scheduler. In *Proc. of IEEE 13th Real-Time Systems Symp.*, Phoenix, AZ, pp. 46–55, December 1992.

Index